Mountains of the Murgha Zerin

Mountains of the Murgha Zerin

Between the Hindu Khush and the Karakoram

ELIZABETH BALNEAVES

JOHN GIFFORD LTD : LONDON

Published by John Gifford Ltd.
125 Charing Cross Road,
London, W.C.2

SBN 70710213 8

PRINTED IN GREAT BRITAIN BY
BRISTOL TYPESETTING CO. LTD.
BARTON MANOR - ST. PHILIPS
BRISTOL

Contents

Acknowledgments

The Westburn Sugar Refineries Limited
Messrs. Vernon and Company Limited
Boots Pure Drug Company Limited
The Metal Box Company Limited
James Keiller and Son Limited
Glaxo Laboratories Limited
The Burmah Oil Company Limited
Bayer Products
Bovril Limited
The Nestle Company Limited
Imperial Chemical Industries Limited
Horlicks Limited
Messrs. Pollock Limited, Glasgow
Shell Petroleum Limited

INTRODUCTION

Mountains of the Murgha Zerin

This book, my third on Pakistan, contains the story of a journey of exploration among the peoples of the remote valleys of the Pakistan Hindu Khush and Karakoram, one of the most strategic areas in the sub-continent and a highway of invasion since Alexander, Tamerlane and Chinghis Khan. Its mountains include Tirich Mir, Rakaposhi, Haramosh and Nanga Parbat, its borders running with Afghanistan on the west, China on the north-east, with Russia a mere forty miles across the small strip of Afghan-held Wakhan on the north. Visitors are not encouraged and indeed, since my visit much of the Gilgit Agency has been declared forbidden territory.

I was accompanied by my second son, Stewart Johnston, newly-returned from a post as Tsetse Supervisor in the Gwembe Valley of what was then Northern Rhodesia. Our relationship provided a happy solution to the choice of a partner for my fifth visit to Pakistan. It had been obvious from the first that two pairs of hands would be needed to accomplish all the filming, photography and writing envisaged. As Stewart and I had still remained friends after several months in the bush, helping to rescue marooned animals on the islands of Kariba and tramping seventeen miles a day on tsetse control this seemed a good premise for a six month sojourn together.

We had worked on various projects in Africa with tolerable efficiency. Stewart was accustomed to living rough, had a natural aptitude for languages and proved to be a first class photographer. Above all, I knew with complete certainty that he would be immediately acceptable to all my Pakistani friends, which to me was the most important pre-requisite. I could have wished for no better companion, amusing, unruffled and uncomplaining. Neither of us will ever forget the friendships old and new that littered our path and made the hardest going seem like an unending adventure.

It took the best part of a year to organise the journey. Although I had been fortunate in having a unique and intimate knowledge of much of the western wing of Pakistan, having worked and lived in villages, hospitals and university, neither of us could claim the scientific qualifications necessary for us to qualify for grants or support from learned societies. Neither of us was an expert botanist, zoologist, scientist, or even mountaineer. We were interested in people, their customs and daily lives and in particular the historical background of the area we intended visiting.

It would be tedious to recount the months of preparation; the weeks spent in devising a brochure setting out our aims and hopes; sending it off with covering letters to societies, trusts, firms and individuals; in contacting Pakistan Government departments and friends both in Britain and Pakistan. Our files grew fat on replies varying from polite disinterest to curt dismissals.

At last, due in part to the previous work I had done in and on Pakistan and the ardour of a few staunch and enthusiastic supporters, a sudden telephone call announced the fact that Pakistan International Airlines were willing to fly us there and back as their guests and that the Pakistan Press Information Department, to which I had been for many years affiliated, would give us all the help they could.

So one day we found ourselves despatched in luxury a VIP might have envied, aboard a Boeing 707 bound for Karachi.

There we were welcomed by my old friends Iqi and Geti Shafi. Here we met Iqi Shahban, who with his wife Nishat, with typical Pakistani hospitality opened to us their house and their hearts and in whose home in Rawalpindi we eventually made our headquarters for the duration of the West Pakistan part of the journey.

Elizabeth Balneaves

1

The Roof of the World

Mountains interpos'd
Make enemies of nations, who had else
Like kindred drops, been mingled into one.
Cowper.

A steady flow of hot, dry air filtered through the fine mesh
screens of doors and shutters, as though sucked in from the sandy
wastes of Sind by some giant blower. Each year the desert is
pushed a little further back as Industrial Estates mushroom out
beyond Karachi's city limits and refugee colonies taper off in
a dreary perspective of row upon row of little flat-topped boxes.
From the shores that climb barely a few inches above the mud
of the Indus delta, the smell of rotting hulks mingled with a faint
odour of spices as the fisherfolk cooked their evening meal, curried fish of strange varieties, iron-scaled Karachi salmon and
delicious pomfret like thick, sweet sole.

In the shallows, men on lean, knotted legs clean their nets,
swinging the long, filmy parachute high above their heads in a
rhythmic arc to beat it upon the water. Behind them an outrigger
cuts across the slow swell, its ballooning sail balanced by the
three figures crouched on a plank like an arm thrust out over
the water. Country craft lean drunkenly in an evening stupor

against the sandbanks, masts angled to the sloping decks. Fishing boats ride at anchor, the single furled sail curved like a scimitar, the design almost unchanged since the Phoenician and Arab first came to trade there and Venetians from Ormus put in to the port of Diul-Sindi for a cargo of ' Turbith, Cloves and Cinnamon and Long Pepper and Musk, Pearls and Feathers . . .'

At Korangi yachts and sailing dinghies are being tied up after the day's racing, *tindals* stowing sails, swabbing decks and polishing gleaming brasswork and at Sandspit small grinning boys drag home the splay-footed camels, a few annas screwed up in the corner of a *lunghi*, the day's takings from rides urged on an occasional picnic party. The snake charmer with his basket of cobras and his fierce little mongoose curled up in a canvas bag, shuffles back to his battered hut behind the beach houses where the well-to-do escape from the heat of the city.

Along the now deserted beach moves a convoy of women, their *burqas* thrown back, billowing along like small white sails, carefully clutching their black leather town shoes, shepherded along by husbands or brothers so that the evening air can blow about their lovely faces in decent privacy. Made bolder by the emptiness that surrounds them, they giggle and shriek in mock terror at the cannibal crabs scuttling to and fro charting a lattice work of tiny furrows across the wet sand. The men chat and turn the other way as some of the daring ones, hitching their baggy trousers above silver anklets, splash their feet like children in the warm sea, tasting for a brief moment their small freedom.

From the garden outside the house came the nearer perfume of night-flowering plants and shrubs and the pungent smell of wet clay where the *malis* pattered up and down the dusty paths, the goatskins slung from their shoulders spouting seeds of water scattered by a brown hand, like a man sowing. Suddenly a blood orange sun plunged into the Arabian Sea and it was night. The lights in the bazaars flared into brightness, lighting up the cheap cottons and vivid silks, drowning the glow from charcoal fires where men cooked *chappattis*, *parathas* and sizzling *samosas*, the three-cornered envelope of pastry enclosing a hot, curried centre.

Pan sellers laid out the green glistening leaves and hovered over pots of spices, deftly concocting the paste to order and handing over the neat green bundles, the ground around them splashed red with betel nut, a Bengali custom much deplored by Pakistanis who have a habit of blaming the refugees for most of the unpleasant things that surround them.

The mountains seemed a long way off, and since our journey invisible ones have sprung up metaphorically, like dragon's teeth, sadly to divide not only nation from nation, but families, brother against brother and Muslim against Muslim. But on that enchanted evening the cloud was a thousand miles away, everyone was happy and thankfully, we could not see into the future. The room behind me was full of friends and our welcome had been touchingly sincere. The babble of conversation, drowned by the music, rose again as the record player throbbed to a finish and the girls all shrieked : ' Let us have it again Fazi, please . . . uncle you were quite fabulous !' and Iqi Shafi patted his brow with a silk square, the dome of his bald head with its nimbus of white hair glistening with sweat. ' Stewart . . . come along ! You dance so nicely,' and Stewart was borne away again in a circlet of shining pony tails and tight, bell-bottomed jeans.

Bearers in immaculate white with purple cummerbunds sidled in smooth bare feet between the guests, filling up any glass that appeared to be even half empty as though by some sleight of hand, so that it was almost impossible to catch them at it. The mothers, aunts and elder sisters, bunched together in fluttering groups like jewelled moths, sipped *nimbu-pani* from long glasses tinkling with ice – the women rarely drank alcohol – gold bracelets clinking, gesticulating with hands and wrists flexible as a dancer's, discussing the servant problem, their respective dressmakers and women's rights. On the first two I was abysmally ignorant and only to the latter could I make a tentative contribution.

An unknown gentleman breathed heavily down my neck, a pudgy hand flashing a gold cigarette case filled with Balkan Sobranies : ' But Miss Balneaves, why do you wish to bury yourself in these distant parts? They are wild people, so primitive. My car is at your disposal, why do you not stay with us here in Karachi? And the young man too,' he frowned disbelievingly, 'he is your son, isn't it?' I flung a despairing glance at Stewart who deliberately ignored my distress signals and waved his glass of whisky at me gaily. It was very hot and lack of sleep was catching up on me with alarming results.

Twenty-four hours ago, or was it years, we had waved good-bye at London Airport. Too much had happened too quickly, one of the less agreeable aspects of air travel being paradoxically the speed with which one may be transported to all corners of the globe. There is much to be said for the kind of travel that does not have to depend on the use of a machine as a means of propulsion, where the changing scenes are imperceptibly imposed one on the other along the road, the first palm tree, a minaret like a pencil stroke on the skyline and the first tang of the acrid smell of camel dung.

Walking or riding is a natural means of getting from one place to another which can be understood by anyone. The humblest villagers along the way will know that you are hot, tired and thirsty and will immediately press you to the food and drink they have to offer. Once there was time to rest thus upon the way to stop and look and even to wander off the chosen path if one so wished and at night to halt with couched camels and tents within the walls of one of the old *serais* built for the Moghals, strung out along the old Trunk Road between Delhi and Peshawar, where travellers could take their ease, eat and drink and exchange news of the road with those who had come the other way.

The Eden sisters, travelling in the wake of their brother Lord Auckland, then Governor General of India, were borne pleasantly in palanquins at the rate of five miles an hour which Emily remarked upon as being fast for *dak* travel. Although they were very grand indeed, moving with an entourage of as many as 260 souls, ' After dinner we send on our dining tent and two of our sleeping tents and our cooks, baker and half the servants so we find breakfast ready and tents pitched when we arrive next morning at the new camping ground' they were alive to peoples, places and things, surely the most important part of a journey, with a sympathy and understanding far in advance of their time.

While no one would wish for quite such an opulent slowness of progression, to be catapulted into space, hermetically sealed into a capsule probing a cloud cover that might hang like nebuli impersonal above any country in the world, is unnerving to say the least of it. But if one must travel by air then choose if possible an airline belonging to the country of one's destination. Swept up, escorted with care, my son and I had boarded our Boeing 707 of Pakistan International Airlines on Wednesday 26th September, a drizzle of English rain curtaining the runway, disposed of our vast amount of hand luggage – extra allowance – fastened our seat belts and, sceptical as the original earthbound man, miraculously took off in one heart-stopping shudder of flight.

We might have been forgiven if we mistook the exquisitively beautiful air hostesses in elegant *shalwar qamiz* for houris of Paradise, proferring champagne, gifts and hors d'oeuvres in place of a jug of wine and bread. We ate delectable food. We slept a little. We lay back, sterile earphones glued to our ears and watched, with a fascination the epic ill-deserved, the hordes of Chinghis Khan pillage, plunder and posture across the narrow screen, borne through the night towards the country of their bloody forays with a ruthless speed of which they certainly would have approved. Our fellow passengers may have been bored. To us it was like an omen.

By the end of the evening we had been besieged with invitations. Iqi Shahban had invited us to stop over at his house in Rawalpindi on our way north and two days later at four o'clock in the afternoon, Government interviews over, Press Cards in our hands, we sank exhausted into an air conditioned compartment roaring up through Sind on our way at last to what we had grandly described in our Press hand-outs as an Expedition into the Hindu Khush and the Karakoram. It is always so easy

B

to *talk* of such an undertaking, to imagine oneself there in a vicarious thrill of adventure but the actual mechanics of the journey had become so complex that defeat lurked round every corner and we felt rather like the inventors of some early flying machine, who having dreamed up the design and overcome all possible engineering problems, failed dismally to get it off the ground.

No small scale maps of the area were obtainable. In fact we were assured that one part of our proposed journey had not yet been charted. The overall picture presented by a standard atlas looked like a climber's paradise. Poised as they are at the epicentre of Central Asia, the great barrier ranges of the Hindu Khush and the Karakoram sprawl across the map in a vast, jagged crescent of palest grey, splashed with the white of countless untried peaks: scrawled over with the blue outlines of ancient glaciers, looping, receding and advancing in a complex pattern of delicate whorls like thumbprints. Springing from a central axis in the Pamir, they curve off east and west, between them forming and enclosing the greatest concentration of lofty mountains to be found anywhere in the world.

Amid such a turmoil of icefield, rock and pinnacle, it seemed scarcely possible that man could live. But there are place names scattered like pinpricks throughout this tortured landscape, tripping off the tongue like an incantation: Chitral, Mastuj, Yasin, Astor, Chilas, where small outcrops of forgotten tribes became stranded in the wake of countless historical tides, landlocked, inaccessible for six to eight months of the year and isolated as islands.

Between the twin points of the two ranges, under the very shadow of Tirich Mir, Rakaposhi, Haramosh and Nanga Parbat, the entire region is interspersed with valleys. Valleys gouged like giant slit trenches out of the sheer rampart of the mountain: valleys like gaunt funnels tumbled with immense boulders and rushing torrents, and other valleys rich with walnut, apricot, peach and mulberry, nurturing tiny villages festooned with grape vines, surrounded by pocket-handkerchief fields of yellow maize, painstakingly terraced half-way up the scree-covered rock.

On the fringe of West Pakistan's northern frontiers and mark-ing her boundaries with Afghanistan and Chinese Sinkiang, these remote States and Agencies to which we had committed ourselves – Chitral and its pagan valleys of Kafiristan, Swat, Gilgit, Hunza and Nagar, lie at the cross-roads of the early trans-Asian trade routes, a cocoon of silk the first tenuous thread linking China, India and the Roman Empire. At the same time and stretching out over the centuries into the nineteen hundreds, long after the silk road had served its function, an old trade route from Kashgar and Yarkand ran over the 15,400 foot Min-taka, the 'Pass of the Thousand Ibex', through Gilgit, below the heights of Rakaposhi and Nanga Parbat, bringing silk, tea and porcelain for exchange in the bazaars of northern India.

From Swat and Buner I had gazed longingly at the fold upon fold of distant hills and once glimpsed from the Salt Range in the Punjab the jagged blue outline of the eternal snows. For years they hung in my imagination, half real, half faery, almost wholly unknown and therefore infinitely desirable. When the chance came to return, largely made possible through the kind-ness and courtesy of the Pakistan Government Press Informa-tion Department and the Pakistan International Airlines, there was no doubt in my mind as to where I should go.

No one in Karachi could offer us much advice. Information had to be garnered almost piecemeal like a jigsaw puzzle from dusty records of early pilgrims, cartographers, travellers and con-querors, whose tales were spiced with startling accounts of murder and intrigue and the truth was hard to come by. Passages cropped up from time to time out of the past, enough only to whet the appetite for more. Place names varied over the years, peoples ebbed and flowed and tended to retreat or disappear un-accountably.

In the nineteenth century, classification of the different tribes was frequently an arbitrary one, their character, antecedents and behaviour judged more often than not against a rigid background of British Imperialism. The very ruggedness of the interior and the strategic importance of its borders served to deter the casual visitor, constantly frustrated by fluctuating policies and politics. Opened up to a certain extent after the Partition of Pakistan and India, since our own visit, the authorities have once again seen fit to label it in part, forbidden territory.

Descriptions of the area even by the intrepid travellers of the late eighteenth century were daunting enough. A Major Biddulph, Political Officer in Gilgit in that era and author of *The Tribes of the Hindoo Koosh*, found its apparent neglect due to the almost impenetrable nature of the country. ' This immense mass of mountain,' he wrote, ' is intersected by numerous deep valleys and these, owing to some peculiar geological formation which I have not remarked in other parts of the Himalayas, are generally narrower at their mouths than higher up. It is not unusual to see among them valleys of from ten to thirty miles in length . . . with an embouchure so narrow that it is difficult to find a pathway beside the torrent which issues between overhanging rocks.'

If I felt extremely doubtful of my own ability to negotiate such perilous terrain, I kept it to myself. I was also careful to stress the point that on this occasion I would not be, as on previous journeys, alone.

In spite of the perils of the way, by 545 B.C. at the beginning of the historic period, Darius the Persian, second in the Iranian dynasty, had annexed the gold-bearing lands of Kafiristan, Kashmir and part of the Gilgit Agency, to become the first in that glittering pageant of conqueror and invader, plunging roughshod through the centuries in the beauty and cruelty of their manhood and whose brilliant shades still haunt the rocks and rivers that have seen their passing.

Two hundred years after Darius came Alexander of Macedon whose pathway flared like some bright comet from the Aegean to the Oxus. Leading his great army by way of Sogdiana and Bactria, today's Uzbekistan, he crossed the Hindu Khush by the 14,300 foot Kaoshan Pass, to fight his way southward along the rocky gorges of the Kunar River that rises amid the glaciers of the Baroghil Pass, its upper reaches in Chitral. Four years later, he lay spent and dead in Babylon, but his fame is legendary and his name perhaps the most familiar one on the tongue of Pathan and Kafir, the Greek profile, the red-gold hair and blue eyes that startle in their intensity, quite naturally and simply attributed by their owners to the great Iskander.

We are so accustomed to regard history almost in the nature of a dead language that to travel in a country where it has been kept fresh and vivid in the minds of the inhabitants makes one feel ashamed of one's own meagre knowledge. This kinship with the past embraces a most diverse assortment of the famous and infamous, conqueror and hero, in a galaxy of races from Persian and Greek, Turk, Mongol, Afghan, Rajput and not least our- selves, who, in addition to the British Raj, left some quality of integrity, still talked about by the old in a wistful kind of way. The restless ghosts of Mahmud of Ghazni, Chinghis Khan and Tamerlane have left something of their lives behind them; Moghal paintings and miniatures are reproduced with meticulous care and artistry by old men who sell them for less than half their worth; the poetry of the Emperors and their gifted consorts has been passed on by word of mouth like that of Khushhal Khan Khatak, greatest of Pakhtu poets who lived through twenty years of Moghal rule, his songs still sung in the *hujras,* the men's common rooms of the North West Frontier. And if the past is sometimes too much with them, these tangible memories light up one's journey like lamps upon the way, the seeds of their cultures having persisted in sporadic flowerings here and there, to be recognised with astonishment as an influence still visible from Kafiristan to the Gilgit Agency and which one can no more ignore than the monuments they left behind them.

The pattern changed from Persian to Greek and Greek to Indian and the foundations of Buddhism were laid in the fourth century B.C. Three centuries later from the vale of Peshawar, a focal point in the commerce of the day, with its outlet by way of the Indus Valley to the sea at what is now Karachi and its virtual command of the passes of the Hindu Khush and the

Karakoram, the Buddhist influence ranged far and wide, leaving behind it expressions of its faith from Bamian to the great carved Buddha we found chiselled into the rock face high above us in Gilgit's Kaghah Nullah.

But nothing remained static for long in these seemingly pathless heights and in A.D. 978, Sabuktagin, Governor of Khorasan, garrisoned Peshawar with 10,000 horses, and, the first of the Ghaznavides, began that great migration of wild, barbaric tribes from the heart of Asia and the first Muslim rule in Gandhara. Fast on his heels came his son, Mahmud of Ghazni, who, before the days of the Norman conquest had ten times descended and laid waste vast areas of the country. Followed by Tajik and Seljuk Turks, they were in their turn to be swept away by the terrible Chinghis Khan from Karakoram.

No one was safe from the Mongol hordes and repercussions of their wave of terror even reached the shores of England where Matthew Paris, writing at St. Alban's, records that in 1238 there was a glut of herring at Yarmouth because the Scandinavian merchants who normally marketed their catch in the Baltic ' were deterred from the venture that year for fear of the Mongols.'

Economic pressures were bad enough but before the century was out, England was to hold the Tartar horsemen of the Steppes to account for the annihilation of half the country. In a small Genoese grainport in the Crimea, a band of silk traders, operating at the end of the great caravan routes from China, had taken refuge from the Mongols. Suddenly the besiegers had been struck down by a pestilence which, spreading throughout Tartary, became known as ' the death ' and had begun, it was believed, in the putrefaction of unburied multitudes killed by earthquakes in China. Before they raised the siege the Tartars are said to have catapulted some infected corpses into the town. The disease was bubonic plague and ships, infested with rats and trading with the Black Sea, carried ' the death ' to Europe.

Fifty years later the plague was forgotten in the new terror that swept northern India in the person of Timur the Lame. From his capital at Samarkand he marched on the sub-continent, capturing Herat, Sistan and Kandahar and after subduing Chitral, descended on the Punjab, penetrated India as far as the Ganges at Hardwar and placed a viceroy on the throne of Delhi. The sack was so complete that after his departure ' not a bird moved a wing in the city for two whole months.'

From this stock was to emerge the first of the Moghal Emperors, Zahir-ud-din Muhammad Babur. The blood of Tamerlane and Chinghis Khan flowed in his veins in a mingling of Mongol, Turk and Persian stock, the roots of his greatness laid down for him like saplings long years before his conception. His father was ruler of Ferghana, his mother a scholar's daughter, but it was his grandmother, Aisan-daulat, ' nomad born and sternly bred, brave to her opinion of right ' who gave to him her harsh courage and staunch counsels in his youthful struggle to hold Ferghana.

A poet and diarist of outstanding brilliance, the *Babur-nama* or Memoirs of Babur has been ranked with the Confessions of St. Augustine and Rousseau or the memoirs of Gibbon and Newton. He seems to have combined, like the knights of chivalry, a magnificent lustiness of body, an almost holy dedication to the arts of war, with a sensitivity unusual in his day and age.

To the accuracy of his geographical observations we owe the first clear picture of the lands between the Oxus and the Indus, the opening lines of his recollections eloquent and concise : ' In the month of *Ramzan* of the year 899 (June 1494) and in the 12th year of my age I became ruler in the country of Ferghana. Ferghana is situated in the fifth climate and at the limit of settled habitation. On the east it has Kashgar : on the west Samarquand : on the south the mountains of the Badakshan border; on the north though in former times there have been towns, at the present all is desolate.[1]

From Babur the historic line descended through Humayun to Muhammad Akbar called Jalal-ud-din, Glory of the Faith; Jahangir and his Persian wife Nur Jehan, to Shah Jehan and his Mumtaz Mahal, Ornament of the Palace to whose immortal

[1] *Babur-Nama* : Tr. by Mrs. E. Beveridge.

memory the Taj Mahal stands today, until Aurangzeb, the last of the Moghals.

From Delhi to Peshawar, along the Serak-i-Azam, the Grand Trunk Road, the glittering retinue of Moghal Emperors passed and re-passed in war and peace, leaving behind them wherever they journeyed a string of monuments, forts and mosques and walled *serais* laced with flowering shrubs and tumbling water-falls where the ladies of the court might take their ease and dream again in that hot, dry climate of the cool beauty of those distant Asian gardens.

With the passing of the Moghals, some of the colour is drained forever from the scene and between 1747 and 1846 apart from a brief period of Sikh rule, an Afghan dynasty held sway from Kabul. The entire area between the Hindu Khush and the Karakoram, buffeted over the centuries by Persian, Greek, Mongol and Turk, withdrew into a kind of historical backwater, disturbed only with monotonous regularity by internecine strife. In the 1840's its isolation was interrupted by a Sikh invasion of Gilgit, but the Dogras of Kashmir who succeeded them, re-mained the suzerain rulers of much of that area until 1947, the Partition of the sub-continent and the bitter and still unresolved struggle for Kashmir.

The picture emerged slowly like prints from old negatives, the developing fluid not quite strong enough; faces, peoples and background began to take shape, the image often blurred, scratched by the passing years, occasionally startling in its sharp-ness and sometimes so faint as to be barely visible and I could only hope that closer inspection might reveal the original.

2

Chitral

In the list of the Turk dynasty of Cabul kings who preceded the
Ghuznavides, the last is called Katoran, King of the Kators.

Tarikh-i-Binakiti

And Kank returned to his country and he was the last of the
Kataurman kings.

Jamir-i-Tawarikh

Our journey in these famous footsteps began in Chitral, at the
beginning of the *Chunchoori,* ' the leaf falling ', and the 10,000
foot Lowarai Pass giving access to Chitral by way of Malakand,
Swat and Dir was closed for the winter. The Chitralis call it the
Rowalai and dread it more than the higher Shandur Pass because of its tendency to avalanches, and so for six months of the
year the Pakistan Airlines' twice weekly flight from Peshawar
is Chitral's only link with the outside world.

We had been seen off from Rawalpindi earlier in the day
with the blithe assurance – surely that ought to have forewarned
us – that someone would meet us at Peshawar and if not exactly
accompany us to Chitral would at least provide all the necessary
introductions and advice. Everyone meant well and having thus
wishfully sent us on our way, much as one consigns a letter to

25

the postbox, took for granted that our ultimate reception would somehow come to pass. I know of few countries in the world where this haphazardly delightful state of affairs would actually work, but such is the helpfulness, natural trust and kindness with which even the most humble Pakistani is endowed that one can safely leave matters to resolve themselves perfectly in the end.

After a few tentative and unrewarding enquiries at Peshawar Airport, in which the entire staff took part, pressing on us cups of tea and condolences with equal vigour, we gave up the search and settling ourselves on the veranda passed the time by observing our fellow passengers. Everything was very orderly and subdued, with nothing of the hubbub and near panic which surrounds a similar departure by rail. Would-be travellers are not encouraged to camp-out on the tarmac sustained by relatives, cooking pots, tin trunks and mysterious cloth-tied bundles. No flocks of red-turbanned porters hover like vultures ready to pounce on a pile of luggage to seize with triumph one morsel apiece. No shrill cries of : ' Lemon *bu . . . rif*!' ' Soda *bu . . . rif*!' from small boys, bearing on their skinny shoulders wire cages of violently hued bottles, disturb the morning peace. Aeroplanes have obviously come to be regarded with the respect which they deserve and we marvel at how all this has been accomplished.

Small, colourful groups stroll quietly to and fro or squat on the grass verges, lost in contemplation and the infinite patience of the East. Two ladies in *burqa* stand modestly apart from the rest of us, one draped in the heavy white *chador* of the village, the tent-like garment with the small crocheted insets for the eyes, her feet solidly shod in thick black shoes like a schoolboy's, a baby clinging to her shoulders, another just walking, clutching the tucked and fluted hem, and I think how puzzling it must be to have mother's face so often disappearing behind a mask.

It is immediately apparent that the other *purdah* lady wears hers under protest, in unwilling deference to her husband or perhaps his family. A mere token of a *burqa* made of thin black silk, it serves simply to enhance her graceful carriage. Every so often a slender wrist, on which gold bracelets tinkle and shine, lifts the small square of material veiling her features, giving us a fleeting glimpse of an oval face lovely as a Moghal painting, out of which great velvet eyes ringed with *sur'ma* glance obliquely in our direction. I am only too well aware that Stewart is the willing victim of her reckless immodesty, and hope fervently that her lord and master is fully occupied at the baggage counter.

Little wonder that the Prophet considered that the most perilous contact with the opposite sex lay in the meeting of two pairs of eyes, or that the Pushtu *Ghazal* is strung with symbolic allusions to the powers with which these primarily functional organs are endowed. ' Do you see those arrows of eyelashes in that highly strung bow of the eyebrow? God knows whose heart they are going to pierce ': or again : ' Look at these dark eyes. Antimony has made them still darker as if alone they were not sufficiently able to kill.'

It seems a pity to start off exposed to such lethal risks so I succeed eventually in drawing Stewart's attention to a less dangerous subject, wondering privately at the same time just which of us is supposed to be looking after the other. A couple of stout gentlemen buttoned up to the neck in grey *atchghans,* bulging leather folders under their arms from which flutter like streamers tell-tale loops of bright red tape, drift sedately to and fro. As they walk they carry on an animated conversation in Urdu, peppered liberally with the English words and phrases so beloved of Government servants. Each time they pass, some sentence is left hanging tantalisingly on the air :

> ' *Char yeh* feasible *be hai,* practical *be hai* !"
> ' *Apko* sanction *dediyeh* ?'

We hope it is possible for greybeard to give his companion permission for this mysterious project whose feasibility hangs in the balance, knowing only too well that sanction in any form is as difficult of attainment in Pakistan as a passport to Paradise.

There is also, standing slightly aloof, a tall, red-bearded Pathan, impressive in immaculate white *shalwar,* the baggy

27

cotton trousers, his long shirt worn outside and surmounted oddly by a loose tweed jacket under which I can just see a brown cartridge belt. There are deep creases at the corners of his eyes from looking out into long distances of lion-coloured rock and sun-baked scrub. Above them rises the *khulla* of gold thread round which his turban or *lunghi* is bound tightly, one end starched stiff like a fan standing up in the air, while the other hangs behind his shoulder.

'He looks like an Afridi,' I whisper, 'his beard is dyed with henna, he's probably made the *Haj*, the pilgrimage to Mecca.' And I am suddenly carried back in time to a *zenana* on the Frontier, and I see again the small palms and feet of the women being decorated with henna for the '*Id* celebrations and hear the giggling and the heavy breathing as the paste is carefully applied, for, on the advice of the Prophet Muhammad who held ideas on cleanliness and hygiene far in advance of his time; 'to bind henna, to clean the teeth, to take wife and to use perfume are four things every believer should do.' The benefits that accrue from its use are so diverse that one is surprised that the West is yet ignorant of its properties.

'It drives out shifting pains through the ears, restores sight when weakened, keeps nose membranes soft, imparts sweet odour to the mouth and strength to the roots of the teeth; removes body odours as well as temptation from Satan (though this last must remain open to question), gladdens angels, rejoices believers, enrages infidels, is an ornament to the user and diminishes trials in the grave.'[1]

At last we are allowed to file out on to the runway, white *burqa*, tagging along deferentially some paces behind her husband who carried the older child, was left to struggle awkwardly up the narrow gangway, the cotton folds billowing around her like an inverted tulip. There are no air hostesses on this flight and no man dare offer a helping hand. Once on the plane, her small window on the world left her totally incapable of fastening

[1] Donaldson: *The Wild Rue.*

28

her seat belt, and advice to her husband, fumbling awkwardly with the straps, was proffered politely from a suitable distance. One of the most infuriating things about wearing a *burqa* is the loss of one's identity. Like a piece of luggage one becomes an 'object', inanimate, occasionally talked 'at' but not 'to' and more usually completely ignored. Across the passage one of the Government gentlemen, patently aware of flying conditions and his own weakness, immediately whipped the paper bag out of the seat-pocket in front of him and clutching it to him like a life-jacket, huddled miserably in his corner.

With a disarming burst of music over the inter-com, the white and green D.C. 3 lifted off the runway, tilting against the Khyber hills, camels seen suddenly from above like strange, prehistoric creatures, their elongated necks straining out in front. The narrow bazaars were dark slashes in the dun-coloured streets, the flat-roofed houses falling away in chequered squares, and here and there in smaller inner courtyards there appeared a bright flowering of women, like hothouse plants, ostensibly hidden from all eyes but those of their husbands. Stewart had seen them too and together we wondered whether these orthodox gentlemen ever gave a thought to the fact that although invisible to all around them, roving eyes like hawks might gaze for one brief moment on their secret beauty at least four times a day.

The last time I had flown over Peshawar had been in a two-seater Harvard from the Royal Pakistan Air Force Fighter Squadron, piloted by 'Lucky' Hayat Khan, a red-haired Pathan and son of one of the leading families from Wah. We made a small if irregular contribution to the annals of that splendid force as we looped the loop over the Frontier hills, executed a couple of barrel rolls above the Kabul and flew brazenly upside down with appropriate unreality over the Street of the Storytellers, in a heady, bird-like flight, and I suddenly understood the limitations imposed by a wholly earth-bound existence.

Although ten years have left their mark on the city of Kanishka and Sabktagin, Peshawar still retains, like an ageing *femme fatale*, an irresistible aura of mystery and intrigue. The Powindahs or Ghilzais who used to filter through the passes from Afghanistan to winter in Pakistan, bringing their flocks, their camels and their tents, unveiled proud women, and fierce mounted men, have gone for ever, their entry now prohibited. Some of the wildness has been temporarily tamed – although we did crouch in a doorway one day while a couple of Pathans tore through the bazaar, knives flashing in the muted sunlight – and if in the place of the *kaisora* of tobacco or the cage of *battera*[1] dangling from his wrist the Pathan *jawan* carries a bundle of books to the University or the Technical High School, and instead of a starched turban, a rose behind his ear and baggy *shalwar*, he squeezes himself into a western lounge suit which sits ill on his loose-limbed tribesman's body, this is the price of progress.

The rich give parties and buffet suppers and whisky flows with a lavishness rare even in the land of its origin, to a background of Sandhurst and a P. G. Wodehouse English which is at once nostalgic and touching. The Begums are dazzling entrancing creatures, fluttering like butterflies fresh from the chrysalis, bursting forth upon their new world in elegant saris and glittering jewels. Generations of *purdah* have left their mark, for which we must be thankful, and they still tend to congregate together in a shy diffidence which is very becoming, but now ride uncurtained in smart cars to the hairdresser, dine at the Club and run A.P.W.A. shops, cottage industries, schools and occasionally hospitals like our dear friend Dr. Begum Shafkat Munir, Medical Superintendent, Peshawar Hospital, with equal ease.

In the bazaar an overt air of commercialism pervades the small shops. With the advent of the American and the virtual disappearance of the British, an easy market has almost put an end to the interminable cups of *sabaz chae,* the green tea over which we used to linger and exchange family gossip, bargain a little happily, or never buy at all. No doubt it is all for the best

[1] Fighting Quail.

but the effect of western civilisation, so called, seems to have a kind of tarnishing effect wherever it touches, like cheap and ill-becoming foreign clothes.

In spite of, or rather because of the century of conflict between the British and the tribesmen, there are battles both remember with honour, and men whose names are indelible in Frontier history, still spoken of with respect and not a few with love, and so far no one has been able to take their place. Like the Highland Scots the feuds are being resolved, the national dress less worn and therefore more conspicuous, and the axe, like the claymore, becoming a curiosity. With new opportunities, Pathans have proved their capabilities in other fields than war, but no man has yet contained them.

Out in what was tribal territory, something of the old order still remains. Beneath the veneer lies the ruthlessness, the insouciance, the friendship unto death, a whole philosophy of living which nothing can wholly destroy and which is still liable to erupt into violence on the most slender provocation, and I am reminded of Higden's description of the Scot: 'Scots be light of heart, strong and wild enough. . . . They be cruel upon their enemies and hate bondage most of anything, and they hold it a foul sloth if any man dieth in his bed and great worship if he die in the field. . . .'

The aeroplane was well on its way, probing the mountains with small dips and eddies between and around the jagged heights pointing black out of a snow collar, and beyond, like a backdrop, hung an endless vista of sugar-loaf peaks. Banking steeply, a small shadow on the land's great turbulence, it lurched and lifted, skimming the ridges, abutments and precipices streaked down to the tree-line with long fingers of snow. A glacier-fed stream wound far below, its ripples stilled and meaningless. Our wing tips seemed almost to brush the crests of the pines in the narrow valleys, or grazing the scree slopes we watched the rocks set on edge like teeth, opening a black wound in the white snow.

Flying over these historic ranges where here and there the

mountains have yielded a grudging passage through the centuries to countless armies, traders and travellers, has a humbling effect. Out from Peshawar in Babur's time ' trading caravans came to Kabul from Hindustan, ten, fifteen or twenty heads of houses, bringing slaves, white cloth, sugar candy, refined and common sugars and aromatic roots.' Below us here in Bajaur, Babur himself rode out to visit the Fort and enjoyed one of his frequent drinking parties ' in Khwaja Kalan's house, several goatskins of wine having been brought down by Kafirs neighbouring on Bajaur.' The Hindushahi kings must have braved these wild passes when Jaipal, who ruled for a time in Swat, fought Sabaktagin and Mahmoud of Ghazni.

Far out on our right amid the tumbled confusion of valleys and heights lies the Katgala Pass where Alexander came to fight the battle of Massaga. Defeating the Aspasii and crossing the Kunar-Panjkora watershed where these threads of silver tangle in the gorges, he went on to take Massaga by storm. There, according to Arrian and Curtius, he was wounded in the leg by an arrow. The barb was extracted and calling for his horse, Alexander saw the day out without further treatment.

Somewhere below our shadow he must have lain that night, the Iliad and his dagger together beneath his pillow.

Our first sight of Chitral was a great shoulder of hillside heeling away on our left, the sudden opening of a folded slope shelving giddily down to the floor of the valley, an airstrip running almost its whole length and a sea of flat, Chitrali hats. Clambering out into the blinding sunlight reflected hotly off the white dust, we came face to face with a twinkling, handsomely bearded countenance, whose owner might with ease have posed for a portrait of Henry VIII as a young man. The hat needed only a jewelled plume to sweep down from the side of the full, clipped brown beard. His square, sturdy figure was set off by a homespun hacking jacket and neat jodhpurs, and bowing with charming, old-fashioned courtesy he greeted us as though we had been long lost friends.

Cautious enquiry elicited the information that this was no

less a person than Prince (Shahzada) Burnhanuddin, uncle of the *Mehtar* or Ruler of Chitral, and who was to prove throughout our stay, counsellor, friend and inimitable host. Somehow the aeroplane, the airstrip and all the trappings of modern travel seemed suddenly out of context against Burhanuddin's mediaeval bearing and I sighed for some time machine to re-capture another meeting a few miles from where we stood, when the Prince's ancestor, Aman-ul-Mulk, thirteenth in the royal line, received Sir Algernon Durand on his visit to Chitral.

' The scene was one of the most brilliant and striking it is possible to imagine . . . the *Mehtar* dressed in green silk . . . riding a big horse covered with brilliant silver trappings, moved off with me on his right hand, the centre of a crowd of hundreds of horsemen and footmen in the brightest array. Cloth of gold, the rich silks of Central Asia, the most superb velvet coats, the colour almost hidden by the gold embroidery, the brightest English and Chinese silks in all colours, scarlets and blues, crimsons and purple, plain and brocaded, *choghas* of plain whole-coloured velvets or of English broadcloths, flaring cottons and the dull brown haircloth of the country were all mingled without the semblance of order in inextricable confusion . . .'

The Kator family, rulers of Chitral, and the Kushwaqt of Yasin, claim descent from a common ancestor, one Kator, said to be a Kafir of the Hindu Khush who ruled from Jelalabad to Gilgit. When the present dynasty in Chitral came into power in the seventeenth century, the founder of it, Motaram Shah, was given the name Kator by his people, and the senior or Kator branch has been on the throne of Chitral ever since.

' People will not look forward to posterity, who never look backward to their ancestors,' and Prince Burhanuddin was the last person to deny his family's past. There are few of us who do not keep a skeleton or two in our ancestral cupboards and the early rulers of Chitral, in common with their counterparts from Afghanistan to Hunza, seem to have indulged in a most formidable array of criminal activities.

Aman-ul-Mulk, who so graciously rode out to meet Durand,

C

was subsequently described by him as ' a very remarkable man ', the understatement of all time when one reads the following pages : ' Steeped to the lips in treachery; his hands crimson with the blood of his nearest relations; two out of his three brothers he had murdered . . .' His people continually subject to forced labour or being sold into slavery, he was at the same time ' a kind and indulgent father and devoted to his small sons.' He had seventeen legitimate ones, but making full use of his *droit du seigneur,* had scattered his image throughout the land to the grand total of eighty offspring. ' But in a country where un-natural vices were rampant he was unstained and . . . attributed his success over the Kushwakt chiefs to their depravity against which God's wrath had been kindled . . . his bearing was royal, his courtesy simple and perfect, he had naturally ' the courtly Spanish grace ' of the great hereditary noble, the dignity and ease of manner which is the birthright of every gentleman in the East.'[1]

The unnatural vices to which Durand obliquely refers perhaps require some elucidation in the light of Central Asian society. In spite of God's warnings, revealed through His Prophet Muhammad, the Kushwakt chiefs were at one with the Pathan proverb which, among other sources of masculine pleasure, accepts the need for a boy's company on a journey, women being relegated to the category of a diversion mainly concerned with the be-getting of sons.

This last, which in the days of the early Islamic wars allowed a Muslim to take four wives (now frowned upon as retrogressive and economically impractical) provided he could keep them in equal status and comfort, was enjoined primarily to take care of the countless women deprived of their male relatives through battle, and did not, as is so frequently believed, stem merely from an intrinsic sexuality. The women, however, until most recent times were largely illiterate and wholly incapable of the mutual companionship implicit in Western marriage.

Like David and Jonathan, the love engendered between two

[1] Sir Algernon Durand : *The Making of a Frontier.*

young men supplied that missing affinity and was not always a degrading one. To see a couple of Pathans hand in hand rarely carries the implications associated with a similar sight in other countries. Babur himself suffered his greatest agonies of heart over a boy, Baburi, for whom he frankly reveals his love in these words: ' I used to stroll bareheaded and bare-foot, through lane and street, garden and orchard, neglecting the attentions due to friend and stranger. Sometimes like a man distraught I roamed alone over mountain and desert; sometimes I wandered from street to street in the city, in search of a mansion or a garden where I might abide. I could neither sit nor go, I could neither stand nor walk.'

The present *Mehtar,* nephew of Burhanuddin, came to the throne, like so many of his ancestors, at an early age after the tragic death of his father, Captain Nasr-ul-Mulk in an air crash on the route which we had just travelled. Nasr-ul-Mulk was, like Burhanuddin, a man of education. He had served in a fine Frontier Force Regiment and was trained in civil administration in the North West Frontier Province. The young ruler was away at school during our visit, but one had little doubt from his uncle's remarks that he would prove one day to be a fit and able successor to the throne.

Meanwhile Prince Burhanuddin lived simply and being truly great was also extremely democratic and acted as official or un-official – we never really discovered which – representative of the Pakistan airline in Chitral. He met and saw the departure of both weekly planes and greeted foreign visitors of distinction or ordinary travellers like ourselves with the same welcoming smile. Somehow he organised our transportation to the Government Rest House, arranged with Mr. Idris, Pakistan's able Political Agent, that we should be accommodated there for two or three nights, eventually insisting that we make his own home our headquarters.

3

The Fairy Mountain

The grace of God is upon the high mountain,
Upon his head a mantle of snow,
And at his foot a flower carpet.
        Tr. from the Pushtu by Sir Olaf Caroe.

Our arrival in Chitral quite unheralded could have posed a
serious problem, for permission must be obtained in advance to
stay at any Government Rest House. Apart from these official
residences, there were no hotels. Thus sponsored, welcomed by
Mr. Idris and escorted by Prince Burhanuddin, we created a
small ripple of curiosity among the other guests, each one of
whom came in turn to call on us. There is no false reticence
about Pakistanis; the Englishman's traditional scandalised with-
drawal as soon as a stranger talks to him in a train would puzzle
and upset them. We had a mean advantage in this respect, being
Scots, who for some reason are looked upon with greater tolerance, perhaps being inseparable in most minds from the pipes,
still played by many regimental bands, the tunes rigidly Scottish.
    The discovery that I had travelled and lived in their country,
often in places they themselves had never seen, which is hardly
surprising considering its great extent, never failed to delight,
and when I essayed my way stumbling a little over the words

and phrases I had known so well but mislaid temporarily over the years, their pleasure knew no bounds. When I explained too that I had wished at least one of my family to see and enjoy at first hand the country and the people who had given me so much pleasure and hospitality, they nodded wisely and welcomed Stewart with unequivocal joy. In such innocent and warm-hearted acceptance the painful comparison was forced upon us as to what *their* reception would have been had our positions been reversed.

One of our most frequent visitors was a young man from the Tax Office in Peshawar, who at once invited us to stay at his house on our return journey, which in effect we did. Abdul Malik was round and pleasant of face and due to be married shortly to a girl chosen – in strict accordance with tradition – by his parents, and whom he would not see until his wedding day. This is a state of affairs which the western world can rarely understand, that in spite of the relative emancipation of the young, and although in many cases they do meet before marriage, they still bow to the wishes of the real head of the household – the mother.

She it is who holds the family purse strings and our old music hall jokes about the subterfuges employed by wives to wheedle money out of their husbands are quite incomprehensible to them. In this connection I remember the story told me by an old friend, then in the Indian Civil Service. A very senior Muslim official came to him one day in great distress: ' You know sir,' he moaned, ' it is really getting very trying. My wife is only allowing me ten rupees a month !'

In most Pakistani homes, even today, men do not merely respect and obey their mothers; their word is law, their slightest wish a command. Daughters have always been regarded even more tenderly and given greater care and attention than the sons. They are often referred to as ' another's trust ', ' a lent treasure ', or as ' *sawan-ki-chirlan* ' – the summer swallows which come to delight us for a short while before they fly away.

We discussed the matter at length with one of our close

friends, a young Captain in the Signals, who, not yet betrothed, was quite aghast that Stewart should insist on choosing his own wife. In fact I think it was the only thing on which they never really saw eye to eye. I knew that I had fallen in Riaz' estimation because I had failed in my duty of finding Stewart a suitable wife. 'But,' he kept insisting, 'your mother who has known you all of your life, who knows all your weak points and all your good ones, should surely know better than you what kind of girl would be right for you!'

Poor Malik, however, while bowing to the inevitable, was obsessed with doubts and went through recurring bouts of brooding melancholy. 'But why?' 'What's worrying you?' we asked. 'Supposing I don't like her?' he groaned. Driven one day to the point of exasperation by the sheer arrogance of his male outlook, I snapped back; 'Has it never occurred to you Abdul, that *she* might not like *you*?' This was something which had obviously never entered his head. "But how could that be?" he protested, his brown eyes widening in horror at such sacrilege.

We had barely time on that first day however, to wash the dust from the journey off our hands when a knock came to our door. There stood the lean red-bearded Pathan I had pointed out at the airport, beaming down at me. 'Good morning,' he said, 'My name is Afzal and I am Chief Secretary. Welcome to Chitral!' Unable to resist the sight of that familiar gold *khulla* and stiffly starched headdress, I threw caution to the winds and murmured the Pushtu greeting:

' *Stare mah sheh!*' His eyes lit up:

' *Khwar mah sheh!*' he smiled taking my hands in both of his, all formality gone: ' *Jor yeh? Khush-hal yeh?*' I tried to indicate that I was indeed well and happy and not in the least tired, although I might have added that I was both hot and hungry, but floundered about trying to keep up with the flood of Pushtu I had released, while Stewart, uncertain as to whether I was about to be abducted under his very eyes, or was becoming involved in some desperate argument, dashed out to the rescue.

The result was a foregone conclusion. We were both immediately swept off to lunch at a nearby house where Afzal Khan's friends were awaiting him. Down the steep and rocky path we strode, Afzal talking and gesticulating all the way. A doorway opened up and suddenly we were produced like rabbits out of a conjuror's hat to a chorus of admiring ' *Wah! Wah!*'s ' and countless ' *Stare mah Sheh*'s '. Our hands were wrung, extra chairs were found and we were somehow wedged in around an already crowded table. There is invariably more than enough if it is a Pathan meal and after the copper basin and ewer had been brought round so that we could wash, great dishes of *pilau, kebab, dhal* and thick Frontier *nan* with which to mop it all up were pressed upon us.

' *Da wakhlah!*' ' Take it !' insisted Afzal.

My eyes swimming at the remembrance of so many other Frontier feasts, it was as though I had come home again. Afzal Khan waved his arms and embracing the entire company with his smile, announced ' She is my sister . . .!' and, I added, ' A Scottish *Puhktun* !' In the general merriment and approval that followed, I felt like a visitor to a strange country who has rather selfishly preferred to spend the first day with his own people and a slight feeling of guilt came over me. We were to get to know Chitral and Chitralis well in the coming weeks, but our lunch with Afzal the Pathan gave to our visit a kind of blessing, an auspicious beginning to all our travels, and we could not have wished for more.

Our host took a mischievous delight in telling all kinds of stories about Chitral and especially its folklore. The Chitralis, it is said, are great believers in fairies and in the Ziwar Gol valley, the river that joins the Turikho, there is a juniper tree on which people tie pieces of cloth from their garments, as they do in various parts of Pakistan near the tomb of a *Pir* or holy man. Here they lay small offerings of apricots or *brat*, a thick, unleavened bread, in order to appease the creatures. Failure to comply with these observances is almost certain to result in some disaster befalling the unwary traveller, already haunted among the glens and mountains by the *Pari*. When there is mourning in Chitral their voices can be heard weeping for the dead, up and down the country, but Tirich Mir is the epicentre of fairy-land.

The whole of the main Chitral valley is dominated by the cloud-hung cupola of Tirich Mir, at 25,260 feet, the highest peak in the Hindu Khush. Here dwells Kol-i-mukhi, the fairy Queen. Innumerable legends surround the mountain, hiding her face as the Chitralis say, like a beautiful woman veiling herself modestly behind her *dophatta*. When the veil is cast aside, danger threatens. This was proved beyond all doubt, at least in the minds of the inhabitants, when a major earthquake rocked the State two or three years before our visit.

As we gazed entranced from the Rest House veranda on that first afternoon through spikes of pale green acacia, across the squares of orange maize drying on the rooftops below, we realised uncomfortably that Tirich Mir had most immodestly dropped her veil and was revealing herself to us in all her white and naked glory. It was scarcely surprising, therefore, to be wakened just after midnight by a noise like thunder and the unpleasant impression that the entire Rest House was rocking on its foundations.

A tremendous scuffle ensued. Doors were flung open to disgorge dishevelled figures in every state of undress, blankets clutched like shrouds over striped pyjamas, as, half-asleep, the occupants poured out into the moonlight. Most of us, in passing, snatched up his or her most valued possessions, in our case the cameras, but from our government friends, who had abandoned their precious papers in the flurry of departure, came cries of 'Toba! Toba!' which can signify anything from 'God forgive us!' to 'All is finished!' and could equally well be construed in the circumstances as relating to the end of the world or their hard-won offices.

Having twice experienced such unpleasant upheavals beneath my feet in varying degrees of intensity, once on the banks of the Kabul and again in Lahore, I was beginning to feel slightly earthquake prone. Throughout the Hindu Khush, however, there has been for a very long period of time some subterranean faulting or sudden contraction below the earth's crust, often found in steeply mountainous regions. Certainly the Himalaya come into this category. Babur himself reported and timed an earthquake not so very far away, on the western flank of the Hindu Khush which he said lasted nearly half an astronomical hour.

Fortunately our slight disturbance was of shorter duration and with many ' Bishmillahs ' the shaken occupants were persuaded to return to the Rest House, converging unaccountably on our quarters where we ministered to them with a dram all round. In accepting it, they carefully pointed out that although wine was forbidden them, alcohol medicinally administered could scarcely be considered a sin, for it had not been invented in the early days when the Prophet (' Whose Name be praised !') set out his rules of conduct. We felt that, ethically speaking they might be on very thin ground, but refrained from spoiling their quite innocent enjoyment.

Naturally they all settled down for a chat. Accustomed from childhood to odd siestas during the day, when he drops off to sleep like a cat, the Pakistani is prepared on the slightest provocation to sit the night through. With all the many-hued pyjamas now scattered cross-legged and wrapped in blankets on our beds and floor, the scene needed only attendant *houris* to resemble A Thousand and One Nights. Unfortunately I was a trifle miscast in the role of Scheherezade, being neither beautiful nor a princess, besides being clad prosaically in faded blue jeans. But something of that Arabian Nights atmosphere hung over our gathering and Malik dragged us both outside again about two o'clock in the morning to point out the constellation of the Great Bear, which he assured us was called in Chitrali ' The Maiden's Corpse ', the four corners being supposed to represent the bier.

We stared up into the sky and tried to imagine our well-known Bear as a lovely maiden, hastily affirming that we did indeed notice a small star above the middle star of the erstwhile tail, called 'The Star of Life' for Chitralis believe it to be invisible to anyone forty days before his death, and we shuddered to think of the psychological effects of a series of cloudy nights. Finally, all assured that the danger had passed, with dawn a pale portent in the lightening sky, we tried to compose ourselves to sleep, vowing henceforward to keep a firm weather eye on the fairy mountain.

Unlike our visitors of the previous night, Chitralis are in the main *Ismailis*, followers of the Agha Khan, and as such are not forbidden alcohol as are the *Sunni* or other *Shia* sects of Islam. The great majority of Muslims are *Sunnis*, the people of the *Sonna* or tradition, their *Kalama* or profession of faith; 'There is no God but God, and Mohammad is the Apostle of God.' To this the *Shias* add: 'And Ali, the companion of Mohammad, is the Vicar of God.'

The etymological meaning of *Shia* is either 'a stream' or 'a section' and the *Shias* believe that as the Prophet died without appointing a *Caliph* or successor, Divine guidance and leadership, both temporal and spiritual, passed on to Hazrat Ali, the Prophet's cousin and son-in-law, husband of his only surviving child Fatima, as the first *Imam* or spiritual chief of the devout. The *Sunnis* consider Ali the fourth in the succession of *Caliphs* to purely temporal power, while the *Shias* hold that this authority is all-pervading and is concerned with spiritual matters also, that it is transferred by inherited right to the Prophet's successors of his blood.

Of the *Shias* there are many sub-divisions; some of them believe that this spiritual headship, this *Imamat* which was Hazrat Ali's, descended through him in the sixth generation to Ismail from whom the Agha Khan claims his descent and *Imamat*. The *Ismailis* themselves are divided into two parties, a division which stems from the period when the Agha Khan's ancestors moved first to the highlands of Syria and the Lebanon, then east to the Iranian mountains where they established a stronghold on the craggy peak of Alamut, where the Hereditary Grand Masters of the Assassins held sway for nearly two hundred years.

The world of Islam is still virtually a closed book to much of the Western world and there are many misconceptions surrounding its tenets, but, broadly speaking, all Muslims believe as do Christians in one God, and as the Christian faith is divided within itself into Catholic and Protestant, each with its own subsections, so it is with Islam. It would require an Ibn-Rushd, the great Muslim philosopher known to Europe as Averroes, a Roumi or a Hafiz, to expound on the direct experience of living, moving and having one's being in God as expressed by the Quran and I am ill-equipped to enter into a theological debate as to the merits or demerits of any religious dogma. If, metaphorically speaking, as we are led to believe, there are many gates to the kingdom of heaven, then it seems to me that having chosen one's mode of entry it becomes illogical in the extreme to indulge in a pitched battle outside over the relative merits of individual procedure.

Sir Francis Younghusband, whose name must of necessity crop up from time to time throughout these pages, who captured the imagination of his countrymen by his intrepid explorations of Central Asia, himself a convinced Christian though of no orthodox persuasion, deeply sympathised with the convictions of those who were not. In later life he became the founder of the World Congress of Faiths and had much to say on the principles and practice of the peoples among whom he lived for so long.

Apart from being, like all my Muslim friends, sincere, honest and God-fearing folk, Ismailis have impressed me as being in addition broad-minded, great humanitarians and yet a lighthearted and essentially happy people. Wherever they find themselves they utilise the juice of the grape, as doubtless the good God intended they should, and before our journey's end we had been treated to an infinite variety of its distillations, from *Hunza Pani* to *Punyal Water*, poor names for the deceptively mild-looking amber fluid. Hitherto accustomed to the orthodox Muslim's horror of *sherab* except in cases of dire emergency such as our earthquake, it came as a pleasant if bewildering surprise

43

next evening when Prince Burhanuddin came chugging up the hill to the Rest House in a rackety jeep, to invite us to supper and to taste his wine.

There were, I believe eight of us crouched in this ancient vehicle, cheek by jowl in the semi-darkness. The road was invisible to all but the driver, at least we assumed by his confident acceleration that he could see where we could not. Speeding across the airfield, we bumped, slithered and scraped with spinning wheels over what can only have been a dried-up river bed, then skidding abruptly in a ' U ' turn, proceeded to climb, wheezing and steaming in a continuous spiral of giddy loops and bends, the mountainside leaning darkly over and above us on our left, while on the right, the edge of the road, innocent of parapet, crumbled vertically down to the valley below.

Clutching each other and the sides of the jeep, our faces must have betrayed us, for the Prince roared with laughter. ' It will be all right going back!' he smiled, his eyes twinkling. ' By then you will have drunk my wine and it will give you courage so that you will not care about the road, you will never see it!' Privately, I hoped that our driver would not be so lavishly entertained, but whether or not the wine gave us courage or merely fostered an alcoholic spirit of bravado, we were only mildly aware of the perils of the return journey and later in our travels came to look back with longing on the comparative safety of the Chitral roads.

The jeep came to a shuddering halt and we stepped out on to a crackling carpet of dry leaves, the branches of the trees low over our heads. ' My orchard!' announced Burhanuddin proudly, waving his arms in a wide, sweeping arc that seemed to embrace the moonlit ghosts of a veritable forest. ' But come, you shall see it tomorrow.' The outside air was cold with the smell of snow but inside the living room a couple of oil lamps were coaxed into unwilling life in small pools of warmth and light. As he bent over the purple flame, our host mentioned casually that the other day, having run out of methylated spirit with which to start the Tilley lamp, he had in a moment of inspiration substituted home-made brandy. He chuckled : ' It went very well . . . like a bomb !'

Excusing himself, he disappeared into the night in order to fetch this potent brew and an ancient bearer shuffled in, straightened the well-worn tablecloth and laid before us brimming dishes of dried apricots, walnuts and sweet red apples, while an engaging urchin of about 13, gave a perfunctory polish to a line of wine glasses, drawn up like troops in battle array on a long side table.

A few seconds later the door flew open to admit a blast of cold air together with Burhanuddin, a bottle in each hand and bulging visibly in unexpected places. Reverently he placed the tall wine bottles on the table, removed a couple from under each arm and then, with the air of a leading member of the Magic Circle, one from each pocket of his hacking jacket, both inside and out – and he was determined that we sample the lot. Carefully he filled the glasses with white wine, pale and clear like Moselle; red, smooth as Château Neuf du Pape, an extremely potent gin and his fiery if colourless brandy.

Dear, kind Burhanuddin, most generous of hosts, prince of storytellers and most sympathetic of listeners, who spared no effort that we should see everything we desired. Our visit coincided happily with the end of the polo season and scarcely had we time to draw breath or recover from the wine-tasting session than we were bidden to the final match between Owir and Mastuj.

4

The Spinning Ball

Swirling and spinning like a ball
Before the polo-stick of Fate,
Run right or left, yet run thou straight
And never speak a word at all :

Remembering that He who throws
Into the field of mortal play
Thy ball and mine to spin today,
He knows the game, He knows, He knows !
Omar Khayyam : Tr. by Arthur J. Arberry

Islamic literature is full of references to the game of polo, allusions being found to it in the great Firdausi's *Shahnama*, the Persian poetry of Nizami, Jami and Omar Khayyam. In fact, the earliest records referring to this sport are Persian. From Persia it spread to Constantinople, eastwards through Turkestan to Tibet, Gilgit, Chitral, Mauripur, China and Japan. Hockey, the Irish national game of hurling, and possibly golf and cricket are all said to be derived from this ancient Muslim game.

The origins of the name ' polo ' are accepted as stemming from the Tibetan ' *pulu* ' or the Balti ' *polo* ' meaning a ball. Both of these countries lie far from the land of its birth, but perhaps the word is indicative merely of the strange influences of international commerce, although is is fascinating to speculate on where the first ball was invented. The horse was undoubtedly the pre-requisite, having become a source of pleasure as well as of convenience and it is exciting to learn that its domestication, probably before 2000 B.C., was not only responsible for the birth of this unique game, but for the expansion of the Indo-European languages, the most widely used in India and Pakistan. The arrival of the Indo-European speakers coincides with the use of the horse for drawing light war chariots.

Once having seen the game as it is played in the wild, mountainous regions between Chitral and Gilgit, each of which obstinately claims credit for its innovation, we were not surprised that Qutubuddin Aibak, who founded the Slave Dynasty in Delhi, was killed when he fell from his horse while playing polo in A.D. 1210. Prowling round the back streets of Lahore, I had seen his sarcophagus where it lies south of the Lahori Gate, one of the few surviving ancient monuments prior to the Moghals and thought in my ignorance how careless he must have been to come to such an end.

We were to see perhaps more exciting polo later on in Gilgit, but nothing could have bettered that first thrilling introduction to 'The Game of Kings'. Polo in these districts bears little resemblance to its counterpart played at Hurlingham or Rawalpindi. Like hurling and shinty it is a wild game for wild people. There are few hard and fast rules. The only one which is rigorously enforced, we were told, was that a man may not use his teeth. But put one of these northern horsemen in the saddle and he becomes a demon, a very centaur. It is as though the smell of leather and sweat and the rhythm of the thudding hooves evokes from deep within him some dark, ancestral memory, a throwback to the merciless riders of the Steppes and the blood that beats and sings in his ears, the blood of Chinghis Khan and Tamerlane.

By mid-morning every shop in the bazaar had firmly closed its wooden shutters and by early afternoon every male in Chitral old enough or fit enough to walk on his own two feet was hurrying down the steep hillside. Men and boys in grey *mahzri shal-war*, shirts flapping, mingled with the horses and riders, bright, moving, staccato notes of colour, each one followed by a small boy, a bundle of spare sticks bristling under his arm like porcupine quills. These are locally made, the shafts of willow and the head of chinar or fig, and so fierce is the play that at least a dozen extra sticks are always taken along. No district is complete without its polo ground; long and narrow, it is often the sole flat area of any size. The ground at Chitral had an almost pastoral setting, slopes of chinar and walnut rising on one side, the others fringed with stately trees and beyond and around a backcloth of mountain.

In a small pavilion, rather like a square grandstand with sharply-tented roof supported by wooden pillars, the foundations neatly painted white, the local notables assembled. Prince Burhanuddin; Mr. Idris, the Political Agent who would present the prizes; officers from the Chitral Scouts at Drosh; Jan Badshah, Superintendent of Police and a crowd of fine-looking *Khans* from outlying districts. It was all oddly reminiscent of a cricket match and one half expected to see the opening batsmen walk sedately forth in white flannels, bats under their arms.

Horses and riders gathered at the pavilion end of the field that stretched like a long green wake, the red and white striped goalposts like barbers' poles, miniscule in the distance. Small groups eddied and surged around the players, their horses restive, pawing the ground, ears pricked and manes tossing. Boys fought for the privilege of holding a horse's head while its owner checked bridle, girths and leathers. Every kind of saddle topped the vivid blues and scarlets of embroidered *numnahs*, from mere pads of grey homespun blanket to high elaborately-decorated Chitrali ones and the whole scene vibrated with movement and light, the teams decked out in a startling variety of garments. There were at least three identical shirts of almond green; one in cerise worn with apricot trousers in corded velvet tucked into black socks; there were johdpurs, tweed jackets, soft boots of

48

Polo ground Gilgit wiho Markhor.

In Gilgit's bazaar

Chitral main valley.

Bazaar in Gilgit.

A gaudy heap of orange cobs
beaten with wooden implements
like hockey sticks.

markhor skin and hefty Pathan *chappals*. Bits jingled and leather creaked.

Each side of the ground was banked with row upon row of spectators, a densely-packed multitude in round, flat Chitrali hats, knees tucked up to the chin, settled in, but ready to break ranks if the game flowed its way. Near the pavilion on the grassy slope of the hillside squatted an elderly *khan,* quietly enjoying the sunshine, on his gloved right hand a goshawk, the leather jesses looped round its owner's neck. Above a clipped white beard, the old man's face held such an expression of peace and kindliness, lean and lined, with the long, finely-chiselled nose so typical of this northern race, his eyes bright, the skin around them crinkled like an apple, that we stopped to ask if we might take his picture.

Meanwhile the master of ceremonies, very dashing in white *shalwar* and Chitrali hat with its tuft of *chikor* (partridge) feathers setting off his ruddy complexion and handsome moustache, strode round checking in the players as they arrived, then, mounting his own horse, a beautiful bay with white stockings and smartly knotted tail, left the field. The musicians, who play continuously throughout the game, had grouped themselves half-way down one of the sides with a large drum, kettledrum and *surnai,* an instrument rather like the pipes without the drone. A scoreboard was already in place with OWIR and MASTUJ, the opposing teams, marked in large letters with white chalk. At a given signal the Police Pipe Band marched on to the ground, bright scarlet ribbons flying gaily from each set of pipes and playing a tune which sounded strangely familiar. It was some time before we recognised the old Scottish air ' I lo'e nae a laddie but ane, He lo's nae a lassie but me . . .' played in double slow time. Although it seemed singularly inappropriate to our present polygamous society, it almost brought a lump to our throats.

With the players all lined up along the goal post at one end of the field, the captain of one of the teams, usually the most important man present, picks up the ball and takes off at a flat out gallop followed by the entire field. Without checking his

D

speed for a second, the holder of the ball throws it into the air and hits it mightily towards the goal before it reaches the ground. The hit is supposed to be made from the centre of the field and occasionally an exceptionally good player will hit a goal. It was a perilous business trying to film the game as the ball seemed to be 'in play' both on the field and off it and one or other of us was continually being forced to make a frenzied dash for safety as the foam-flecked horses, eyes rolling and nostrils flaring, swept down on us. Like a child on the sea shore I panted back and forth from the pounding waves, panic lending me an agility I had not known I possessed.

There are no *chukkas* in this kind of polo, the play going on for 30 minutes, take or leave a few, each way, and always on the same horse. It was all breathlessly exciting, the puffs of dust from the horses' hooves spurting up like smoke in the distance, the flying knotted tails, the flash of a bright saddlecloth, the gleam of a silver bridle. Small boys dashed heroically in between the flying feet to hand the riders fresh sticks and retrieve the broken ones and above everything was the wild, insistent music that throbs and shrieks, taking up each move, each triumph in the game, urging horse and rider to greater effort.

But more was still to come and we were totally unprepared for the end of the match and the sight of the players all obviously girding themselves for some new event, replacing the polo sticks with short leather quirts, assiduously tightening girths and checking reins, bits and leathers. I had taken refuge in the pavilion in order to change a film and was immediately aware of a ripple of excitement running through the crowds like wind through corn.

'*Buzkashi!*' nodded Jan Badshah. 'Goat snatching!' 'Oh God . . .!' I moaned, all my tiredness forgotten, as with shaking hands I completed the operation and closed the camera. Stewart hadn't heard him and could not understand what had made me suddenly leap to my feet. '*Buzkashi?*' I hissed: 'you know, they play it in Afghanistan – you've seen it on film – it's fantastic – they have a dead goat and everybody tries to get hold of it . . .' Desperately I sought some vantage point from which to film this wild and most barbaric of games. I am only now vaguely conscious that someone must have hoisted me on to a flat roof at the back of the pavilion. At any rate, I just succeeded in getting high enough to see over the heads of the spectators and record the highlights of the game.

This is the game the Mongol horsemen of Chinghis Khan loved above all others; this is the game that only the strongest and bravest among a thousand men and horses were elected to play, and ' when fame had made him known through the three provinces, the oldest and most rigorous of the *chopendoz* (riders in the *buzkashi*) come together. Before them he goes through the trial. If they are satisfied, and only then he has the right to the glorious name and the fox or wolf skin hat. He no longer has any other calling than playing *buzhkashi*. And at it he earns close on a hundred thousand *afghanis* a year. . . .'

' They choose a he-goat from the flock. His throat is slit. His head is cut off. To make his body heavier they stuff it with sand, fill it with water. They put it in a hole just so deep that the hair is on a level with the ground. Not far from the hole they draw a little circle with quicklime. And this is call *hallal,* which in Turcoman means circle of justice. And to the right of the *hallal* they set up a pole in the steppe, and to the left, another. At an equal distance. As for the length of this distance, there is no rule. It may call for an hour of galloping or perhaps three or perhaps five. . . . When the judge gives the signal all of them fling themselves upon the headless body. One grasps it and gets away. And pursued by the others he races towards the pole on the right. For the remains of the goat must go around it, and then pass behind the pole on the left and finally it must come to the *hallal.* And he is the winner whose arm throws the headless goat into the middle of the white circle. . . .'

Joseph Kessel's description could not be bettered. In 1956 he went to Afghanistan to film a documentary with particular emphasis on the expert horsemen who are descendants of Chinghis Khan. He must have seen the game at its best and fiercest, but although to him the Chitrali *Buzkashi* might seem a poor imitation of the game as played in the land of its origin, to us it was one of the most powerfully stirring incidents in a long journey that was not uneventful.

In front of me the black he-goat, headless, with long shaggy hair, was dragged into the middle of the field and thrown into the centre of a rough circle marked out on the ground. Suddenly, all the horsemen who had just finished an afternoon of the most arduous polo erupted from one end of the field and with wild, throaty cries, taken up and repeated by some hundreds of voices, reins knotted in one hand, threw themselves and their horses into the circle. Swooping down, one hand and foot somehow keeping horse and rider together, they bend at a gallop, sweeping the ground. Presently, one stronger than the rest, his head almost brushing the grass, grabs the goat and in one flowing movement, swings the carcase in front of him and himself back into the saddle.

His horse needs no urging and neck stretched out, takes off like a rocket. The whole field thunders alongside and behind in hot pursuit. Both horse and rider must be incredibly powerful, capable of withstanding the attack of teeth, hooves and quirt, able to stick together through the frantic mêlée that ensues. There are no holds barred. Breathlessly I follow the mad confusion of man and beast, my eye glued to the viewfinder, so that the whole, wild, fantastic sequence is like some dream vision passing across the lens. A horse and rider come down in front of me. The man lies where he fell, unconscious, while the horse scrambles to his feet and the rest of the field sway and struggle around and past, the smell of sweat and hide almost choking in its intensity. A couple of onlookers roused to action by the motionless body, dash in hastily and haul him to safety.

Wheeling almost on its own axis, the entire field turns and like a wild, foam-flecked tide surges now up the almost vertical hillside, crashing against the trunks of trees, scrabbling for a foothold on the steep slopes, scattering spectators in all directions. Up goes the wave of panting, yelling horsemen, disappears into the distance, turns and pours like a bursting dam down towards the field again. By some brilliant manoeuvre a young man has managed to keep possession of the goat. With a final, splendid burst of speed he outdistances his pursuers and flat to his stallion's neck he crosses the white arc of the circle, throwing the headless body into its centre to a great roar from the crowd.

The prizegiving afterwards seemed like a school speech day and even the dancing by the defeated team an anti-climax. Unusually, neither of us had much to say that night. I for one felt limp and drained after the emotional and physical turmoil of the day, the effects of the re-creation of history played out in front of one's eyes, impossible to dispel.

5

Garam Chashma

If thy heart fails thee, climb not at all . . .
Queen Elizabeth after Sir Walter Raleigh's
'Lines Written on a Window Pane

We were never quite sure who first suggested a visit to Garam Chasma, but it seemed generally agreed that to leave Chitral without having seen the Hot Springs, known in Khowar as Utz, the Spring, would be something akin to visiting Agra and turning a blind eye on the Taj Mahal. I think there seems to be a peculiar attitude of mind when travelling which allows things to happen to one, and very often the results of masterly inactivity are infinitely more rewarding than a frantic effort to cover as much ground as possible in the shortest time. Like a squirrel on a treadmill one works very hard at getting nowhere.

It was again kind Burhan who arranged with his friend Jan Badshah, whom we had already met at the polo ground, to find horses to convey us the thirty miles from Chitral town. Up at daybreak to see us safely despatched on our journey, he fussed over the tying up of our modest baggage, the saddling of our ponies. Agreed, I had begged for some quiet, docile beast, but when the men arrived with our mounts, I wondered whether I had not perhaps been taken too literally. '*Bohut gherib!*' com-

miserated the servants, which can be translated as 'very poor'
or 'very weak'. However they were both stallions. In this part
of the world it is considered beneath a man's dignity to ride a
mare, and if we were at first inclined to regard them with a
certain degree of levity, before the journey was over we thought
them the most sure-footed, obedient and courageous of quadru-
peds.

In addition to a couple of porters, our small cavalcade was
augmented by the owners of the two ponies. Whether their presence was due to lack of faith in our ability to look after the
animals, the suspicion that we might spirit them away across the
Afghan border, or a simple hope that by making noises like
grooms they might earn a little extra, they stuck to us like
shadows for the rest of the week. One was young, brash and
regarded any form of physical labour as something to be avoided
at all costs; the other, a spare, decrepit old man who looked as
though the first breeze would dissipate his withered bones, painfully obvious through his thin grey shirt and *shalwar,* trotted
gaily at our heels without so much as a deep breath for the full
30 miles. We frequently felt guilty about this, feeling so much
younger and stronger than he, but he was so patently enjoying
himself, and even when we walked experimentally he would not
ride, so we eventually ceased to worry about him.

No one in the party spoke *Urdu*; only *Khowar*, the language
of the *Kho*, the inhabitants of Chitral, who are believed to
represent the earliest waves of invasion which swept down from
the north over the passes of the Hindu Khush. However, by dint
of much sign language and perseverance, we learned a few
simple phrases calculated to be of use on the road, such as ' *Ma
ishtor*' 'my horse'; '*taroo ishtor*', 'fast horses', which ours
were not, and '*Bo jam!*' 'very good!' the repetition of which
never failed to throw the men into paroxysms of mirth, but made
at least for a general feeling of enjoyment and camaraderie. A
few *Urdu* words have crept into *Khowar* such as ' *mushkil*',
meaning difficult'; '*dost*', 'friend'; '*mewa*' – 'fruit', and
the word for name which is '*nam*' in both *Khowar* and *Urdu*

55

and turns to ' *num* ' in *Pushtu*. This was all both helpful and interesting.

Neither Stewart nor I had ridden for about eight years so we felt an understandable trepidation about what might be expected of us, but had we been given the barest inkling of the nature of the tracks we were about to tackle, I believe that even our reasonably stout hearts would have quailed. One of my stirrup leathers was shorter than the other and no amount of ingenuity could reconcile the two, which could certainly never have been a pair. Stewart was hampered by a hard wooden native saddle and the addition of panniers behind him holding the smaller of our possessions. Inadequately secured, they continued to slip and shift at the most inopportune moments.

In spite of these minor discomforts, or so they appeared at the beginning of the day, we jog-trotted along by the side of a foaming torrent of green silk, learning gradually not to post but to sit down in our saddles, long-legged like the colourful horsemen we met along the way. Now and again I stopped to photograph and on one occasion found myself rather far behind. Hurrying to catch up, I rounded a corner to see in front of me a figure on horseback whom I took for granted was Stewart and rising in my stirrups yelled out something like : ' Hi! Wait for your poor old mother!' An elderly stranger with a fine white beard turned round in astonishment and was even more taken aback when in the utter confusion of the moment I stammered out in Urdu: ' Oh, I'm so sorry, I thought you were my son!'

It must have been disconcerting enough to be thus confronted by a strange woman riding astride and clad in western clothes, but even taking into account my undeniable middle age, not by the wildest stretch of imagination could I possibly have been mistaken for his mother. Trotting up to him I plunged desperately into involved explanations and only the happy appearance of Stewart round the next corner saved me from being taken for a complete lunatic. After this slight contretemps we all became ' acquainted ' as the Americans say, and for the next half-hour enjoyed his presence, exchanging family histories and learning something of the country round us.

It has become the custom, he told us, for many of the young men to leave Chitral in the winter to find work on some of the construction schemes in the North West Frontier Province and even as far away as the Punjab. He obviously regarded this defection with alarm and possibly foresaw the beginning of what we call in the Scottish Highlands and Islands depopulation. But for the moment at any rate, the men come back in the spring to help with the crops, and the air link between Peshawar and Chitral has meant a saving of weeks on the journey. In the bazaars of Chitral now are goods their fathers never knew, and extra money must somehow be earned to buy the coveted cigarettes, biscuits, cotton cloth and sugar.

While far from being affluent, Chitralis are well nourished, happy people and usually extremely good-looking. Durand, who was inclined to regard most of the tribesmen with the severity of a Victorian schoolmaster, found them ' bright, cheery, impervious to fatigue, splendid mountaineers, fond of laughter and song, devoted to polo and dancing.' The women work in the fields unveiled and are not too shy to stop and chat or have their photographs taken. They look you straight in the eye with a simple directness, although a young girl might instinctively cover her mouth with her *dophatta*.

Our horses' hooves clip-clopped quietly, muffled by the white dust rising from the road in a luminous haze of light and I imagined the ancient track like a kind of crematorium, always a little left from the year before, so that the tiny particles had mingled like chromosomes, holding in their floating, almost invisible, world all the inherited imprints of generations. With the water chattering over the stones beside us, a gentle tinkle from the old man's silver-plated harness, we could feel a kinship with the past, knowing that men had travelled thus with Alexander and with Babur. On this same route a rough *qafila* or caravan road has, over the centuries, linked Badakshan through Chitral, Dir and Swat, with the Indian sub-continent.

57

These dreamy, sun-drenched valleys had lulled us into an entirely false sense of security for we suddenly began to climb what appeared to be an unscalable mountain ridge or *parri*. A mere one and a half foot shelf of rock, chiselled out of the face of a vertical cliff, much of it was so steep that it had been hewn into actual steps. Even Durand was suitably impressed by Chitrali roads :

' In fact yesterday and today,' he writes, ' we have been riding gaily over places I should be afraid to lead an English horse over, but my Badakshani . . . with his unshod feet goes over them as smoothly as a cat. . . . Still, however bad the track, so long as a man stuck to the riding road he stuck to his horse; nowhere in the world I should think do men habitually ride over such awful ground and yet the Chitrali is no horseman ' (he had obviously never seen them play *Buzkashi*) ' but then he has no nerves. I used to get off the first few days after leaving Gilgit at particularly vile places, but when I found that this entailed everyone else doing the same and that the men of the country would not have thought of dismounting I saw that this would never do and I put a horseman in front to show me the way and followed till he got off. It was a liberal education and my heart used to be in my mouth when my inner leg would be brushing the cliff and the outer hanging over eternity.'

It was at least comforting to know that others had felt as we did and also that we had official confirmation of our hair-raising stories. It is so easy to exaggerate in retrospect. The road began across a shingle slope, one of the two most marked features of the roads throughout the Hindu Khush being shingle slopes and the other, *parris*. Climbing over these great spurs of rock, the angle was so steep that we found ourselves clinging to the pommel of the saddle going up and lying flat out on the horse's back going down, and we would emerge every so often at the top of one of these Jacob's ladders, our pony's head and withers projecting eerily into space while the animal cleverly manoeuvred round an acute-angled bend in order to descend an equally alarming stone stairway on the other side of the ridge.

The view, if one could bear to look down, was magnificent, the river now a trickle of green streaked with white, from this altitude the foaming currents arrested in flight, like little flags of bog cotton, while sheer from its gravelly bed rose on the opposite bank a solid slab of blue mountain. I had just enough sense to leave my horse to pick its own way, controlling my beating heart by talking to it continually, soothing my fears by proxy as it were. Never had a four-footed creature been so praised. I had exhausted my entire stock of *Urdu* reassurances before I stopped to reflect rather ridiculously that the animal probably only understood *Khowar*.

Looking back it all seems like some impossible nightmare but at the time a curious elation occasionally got the upper hand and I overcame my fears sufficiently to raise the camera shakily to eye level and press the trigger, while Stewart, whose horse was in the lead, looked round anxiously to check that I was still with him, his grin conveying a kind of ' This is hell . . . are you still all right?' message, to which I would respond with what I hoped was a nonchalant smile.

On the return journey, occasionally stung into speech by the terrors of the path, I would suggest mildly that we might dismount, but Jan Badshah, then in charge of the operation, dismissed my tentative plea, offhandedly munching an apple and sticking to his horse like a limpet on a rock, he pointed out: ' After all, Allah has given the horse four legs, so that if two should slip, he still has two with which to grip.' He spat a pip out into space and added as an afterthought . . . ' But you have only two.' In the face of such irrefutable logic I was silent, but thereafter was haunted by a vision of one or other of the ponies, two legs over the precipice, scrambling wildly for a foothold and disappearing for ever into the abyss together with his rider, in spite of all the legs provided by a beneficent Allah.

We had stopped to stretch our legs and rest the horses perhaps ten miles or so on our way, by the side of one of the locally-built wooden bridges, cantilevered across the rushing torrent of the Lotkhuh River. Stewart and I made Bovril with the ice-cold water and hoped that it would sustain us for the rest of the journey. Above us, suddenly appearing head and shoulders over the rocks, a man on horseback reined in with a flourish and gazed down upon us. With his full moustaches and shaven head, he might have been Chinghis Khan in person. It was difficult to know which of us was most startled.

' *Assalaam Aleikum!*' we called up.

' *Waleikum Salaam!*' he nodded gravely, and swinging himself out of the saddle, strode down to where we sat. We told him we were on our way to Lotkhuh Tana and, with vivid memories of Babur ' Whether on the mountains or on the valley bottoms, Kafir highwaymen are not few . . .' we mentioned that we expected Jan Badshah to catch us up at any moment. Our entourage had gathered themselves together some little distance away and were sitting on the grass, passing round a cigarette in cupped hands. They took no notice of our visitor, why we never discovered but thought a little odd at the time. However he assured us that he was delighted to know that we were going to visit Garam Chashma, stayed to smoke a cigarette with us and departed as abruptly as he had come. It was useless questioning our escort. They simply scowled in his direction, shrugged their shoulders and muttered something in *Khowar* which sounded anything but complimentary.

Jan Badshah descended upon us about Shoghot with a pounding of hooves, stones flying in all directions, which had the effect of totally demoralising our hitherto placid mounts, with the result that Stewart lost most of the baggage and we had a great business tying it on again. These panniers and the inept way in which they were continually being re-tied, were to cause us even greater trouble on the way back when an extra pony was acquired to carry them.

Shoghot is the point at which all the roads leading from Afghanistan over the Dorah, Agram, Muksan and Katinza Passes, converge. It was a bleak, wilderness of a place, but Jan Badshah told us that the Sasha Gorge through which we were riding had once been a fertile valley, full of chinar trees and orchards. A flood in the time of Aman-ul-Mulk had devastated it, sweeping everything before it, including what was reputed to be the largest walnut tree in the country. Above us loomed the ruined towers of Shoghot Fort where the fairies are heard to sing and wail ten or twelve days before the death of one of the ruling family. According to legend, Motaram Shah, the founder of the Kator rulers of Chitral, married a fairy. The king and his fairy bride lived on for years as husband and wife without anyone guessing the truth of this Gilbertian relationship, for he used to slip away and meet her at Gairat, a village seven miles below Chitral where the fairies from Tirich Mir are supposed to gather every Friday night.

There are in reality the remains of two forts on the left bank of the Lotkhuh River at Shoghot, one of which belongs to one Khan Bahadur, who ruled there about 1820 when Motaram Shah II was *Mehtar* of Chitral. Like many another ruler before and since, Motaram Shah coveted his neighbour's castle and came with his army to seize the place. The Khan who owned it fled across the Dorah into Afghanistan to seek help, leaving the Fort in charge of his wife. Unfortunately his mission was ill-timed, for just after he left Shoghot the first snows of winter fell, the passes were closed and it was impossible to send back aid. Meanwhile his wife defended the Fort with great gallantry for six long months, when she was forced to capitulate. Legend has it that she marched out with all the honours of war and her fame, if not her name, is still remembered.

One of Motaram Shah's descendants, Sangin Ali II, became very fond of the Fort at Shoghot and made himself notorious, though perhaps unloved, by building a long gallery high on the hillside which he reached under cover of a wall. Up this he used to creep and using the corridor much as one would a shooting butt, he could lie in wait for the unsuspecting ibex that once were so plentiful among these hills.

Some time in the later afternoon when the setting sun had withdrawn abruptly from the gilded peaks, leaving the air damp and chill, we all dismounted in a village which we mistakenly took for the goal of our journey. We still had twelve miles to go. However the porters lit a huge fire, water was boiled and sweet tea handed round. The villagers gathered and exchanged the latest news with Jan Badshah, staying to marvel at the Begum Sahiba and her handsome son – hurrying away to return with platters of walnuts which they obligingly shelled for us, turning the horses loose to graze, and exclaiming over our anoraks.

The entire police force at Lotkhuh Tana came to covet these anoraks and it was with sadness we had to explain that they had been given to us by a generous manufacturer across the seas in Scotland, in order that we might have our photographs taken while wearing them, against the setting of their beautiful country. It was almost cruel not to be able to hand them over for one only has to admire anything a Pakistani owns for it to be thrust willingly and embarrassingly upon one. Had I known that my precious anorak was going to end up in the Lotkhuh River, I would have given it away to the first admirer.

We compromised by undoing one of our saddlebags and distributing pills, cough mixture, sweets and bandages indiscriminately. In spite of so much bounty materialising like manna from heaven – which I bought once in Baghdad in the most ordinary way to find that it was a popular sweetmeat made up in little round boxes ready to post to one's friends – the people were extraordinarily patient and forbearing. They had a natural dignity and the ones who were ill were usually pushed forward by a relative for attention. They came and went in the semi-darkness, almost unseen except when a flicker from the fire lit up a face or a hand shyly offering whatever food they had.

Although Prince Burhanuddin had insisted that we stay in the Royal Rest House at Garam Chashma, he had reckoned without the police force, and our friends at the *Tana* were equally determined that they were not to be cheated of one moment of our visit. Thus it was that thirty miles and twelve hours after we had set out, frozen, tired and hungry and partially paralysed in our lower limbs, we painfully and laboriously climbed down from our saddles – no other word could describe our slow descent, Jan Badshah practically lifting me off mine – and hobbled into the headquarters of Lotkhuh Tana.

A room was made ready for us by the simple expedient of hurriedly ejecting its present occupant who kept returning every now and then for some article of clothing left behind, and a couple of strong armed sepoys were detailed to massage our aching limbs. *Malish* is an art in which the Pakistani excels but the exquisite pain of those hard fingers digging into our knotted muscles was almost unendurable and we lay grinning foolishly at each other through tears, forced at least out of my weary eyes by this new form of torture. After fifteen or twenty minutes we were miraculously restored and able to walk next door to the *Tehsildar*'s room for supper.

A tablecloth was spread on the floor and our host excused himself from rising as he had hurt his foot during the polo match we had attended a few days before leaving Chitral. This broke the ice and after unravelling yards of grubby linen we discovered a badly-swollen ankle, which we were able to treat and strap up professionally. Cushions were brought for my greater comfort and a sepoy circled round with basin and ewer, a towel which had definitely seen a great deal of service draped over his shoulders.

Stewart had already been initiated into the complexities of eating with his fingers and the use of his right hand only for handling food, a sensible rule of hygiene laid down by the Prophet and adhered to long before Marco Polo described the custom as: ' Whatever is clean and fair they do with their right hand, believing that the function of the left hand is confined to such needful tasks as are unclean and foul, such as wiping the nose or the breech and such like . . .' A whispered consultation in the background produced a couple of battered knives and forks, which to everyone's delight we waved aside.

We obediently used our right hands, we mopped up the delicious chicken curry with massive pieces of *chapatti,* thick like the *nan* of the North West Frontier, and being asked anxiously if we would prefer ordinary tea to the green tea or *Kabuli chae* drunk after the meal we were both able to say with honesty that green tea was one of our favourites. Much depends on its preparation, the absolutely boiling water, the right amount of cardomum. We pronounced it excellent, there were smiles all round, everyone relaxed and we were accepted.

Garam Chashma lies just twelve miles from the Afghan border, a tiny enclave in the mountains, the polo field like a strip of green baize spread out along the only flat piece of ground in the valley, fringed with walnut trees just turning colour. Against the dark flanks of the enclosing shingle and scree they blazed out in a brilliant splash of orange, poplars feathered like quills in palest yellow stretched upwards sentinel straight among mulberry, apricot and chinar. The low, flat-roofed houses huddled halfway up the hillside turning blank faces to the snows of the passes, the walls built like dry stone dykes buttressed with stout wooden joists of pine and juniper.

Hot sulphur springs gush perpetually out of the hill slopes and every here and there are groups of women washing their clothes in small, steaming burns, dammed up with a few boulders, with no thought of the water ever running cold or their own good fortune in having this endless supply just outside their doors. From Afghanistan to Hunza volcanic influences are manifest in sporadic outbursts of these sulphur springs. Babur came to one further south on the Kunar River having ridden over the Jagdalik Pass between Kabul and Jelalabad. He dismounted at Qush-gumbaz, 'the bird's dome' opposite the mouth of the Kunar water and marching on from there stopped at the hot spring which even then was known as ' Garam Chashma.'

Imit, the chief village of the small state of Ishkoman in Gilgit is famous for its hot springs where Schomberg of the Seaforth Highlanders bathed joyfully and his servants reluctantly. His cook was urged on the return journey to have another bath. ' Ah!' said the bearer, ' your face is all shining from the last bath, a second one will do you good.' Aziza giggled and blushed looking at once sheepish and annoyed. ' A second bath,' chimed in Schomberg, ' will make you ready for a second wife when you

A young markhor like a Walt Disney fawn.

Girls gathering firewood.

Old man with goshawk.

Rest House at Bumboret.

Swing bridge Swat.

Gujar woman with baby.

Kalash girl laughing.

reach home '; a remark which infuriated him more than ever.[1]

Inside the Rest House, a strange, barn-like building, sad, and occupied only at infrequent intervals, an imposing, twelve-foot square bath like a small swimming pool fed by a continuous stream of extremely hot water awaits the few visitors who hazard the ride from Chitral. We were shown round the echoing rooms by Jan Badshah who was deeply conscious of his responsibilities as host, while the others slouched about, curiously like small boys exploring forbidden territory. The main hall was laid with an intricate tessellated floor, which together with the bath gave the whole place an exotic air of grandeur quite out of keeping with the remote wildness of the valley.

Finally they all withdrew and I was left in the silent building in eerie solitude, the splash of water in the vast, steaming bath echoing like some subterranean waterfall. A step at a time I lowered myself into an opaque blackness, just able to touch the bottom with my toes and fearful lest I lose the soap. It was heaven to feel the hot water giving such ease to my still tender limbs but almost impossible to really wash in it. Tentatively I floated around in the Stygian gloom, watching what appeared to be a kind of lion obligingly spouting forth this interminable supply and with an uncanny feeling that at any moment I might be sucked down into its depths. Stewart followed me and then together, looking like rather well-boiled lobsters, we joined our hosts for a walk round the village.

We had been escorted to the bath by half the Lotkhuh Tana police force, not out of anxiety for our safety but simply and solely to enjoy every possible moment of our company. I doubt if there was much official business for them in Garam Chashma where time drifts by in a leisurely cycle measured by the solar year. Beginning with the winter solstice the months take their names from the seasons or their activities, a familiar practice in rural communities and still used in Shetland where the spring ploughing is done in the *Voar* followed by the *Beltin* when the

---

[1] R. C. F. Schomber: *Between the Oxus and the Indus.*

cows are put out to the sweet grass after the winter, the fresh winds that blow called the *Beltin ree*; the *simmerdim* of the long midsummer nights that lead on to the *hairst* and when the crops are gathered in *at the back o' Hallamass* the animals are taken in to shelter again. In Chitral the *long nights* that follow the *leaf falling* or *Chunchoori*, give way to *the extreme cold; the wild ducks; the black earth* when the snow is melting, to *the sparrows* signalling the return of spring and *the trembling* of the growing corn, to full summer, the threshing and the sowing.

Here, where possessions are few, no one has more than his neighbour, there is nothing to steal and although nowhere is there a superabundance of food, there is enough. A small trade in ponies from Badakshan is still carried on during the summer when the passes are open : the men and boys play polo on the *Janali* or exercise ground which is also used by the school for drill and games. Living in a close-knit community crime is rare; after all where could a man go to escape from his sins? And once again one is faced with the damage done by indiscriminate thrusting of western standards and ideas on simple people such as these. Social medicine, higher education, better standards of living, unfortunately never seem to come alone and the recipients finish up their indigenous culture strangled in the strings which are inevitably attached.

It did seem something of a paradox that with free running water pouring in scalding streams out of the hillside, the Police Tana, a few hundred yards from this liberal bounty, while neat and tidily demarcated with rows of carefully-whitewashed stones, was innocent of one drop of it, hot or cold, within its precincts. A snowstorm which delayed our departure for several days owing to the disintegration of parts of the path back to Chitral town drove home to us forcibly the lack of even the most primitive conveniences. But then, never having known them, nobody felt anything was missing, and we were probably the only people in the valley who found it extraordinary or discomforting to charge around in the teeth of a gale seeking some boulder large enough to afford a moment's privacy.

Through the heart of Garam Chashma tumble the ice-cold waters of the Lotkhuh River, stocked with trout by an English-man, Captain Cobb, once Political Agent in Gilgit, who, like so many of his countrymen before him, endeavoured to bring into his alien surroundings something of his homeland at once ornamental and practical. Borrowing an old-fashioned rod from Jan Badshah, who helpfully indicated all the most likely pools, we landed several of these delicious fish, running from a half to three-quarters of a pound each, and differing not one whit from Loch Leven trout in Scotland. They were grilled for us at night and appeared on our plates crisp and brown so that the bones seemed non-existent. Our lure consisted of live grasshoppers, recommended by Jan Badshah and obligingly caught for us in the fields by a couple of small boys from the village.

At the school, where we were received like visiting dignitaries, all the pupils from the age of five to fourteen were paraded for our inspection in the compound amid a profusion of pink and red pyrethrums three or four feet tall, so that the children moved Lilliputian amid the feathery fronds of their foliage. The class-rooms were bare and dark, the few books earmarked but valued highly as the magic key to learning. The smaller children, the only stage at which girls are also admitted, had boards like slates and their clear eyes and fine features were entrancingly solemn under a variety of Chitrali hats, small embroidered skull caps or formidable Kashgari hats like muffs with ear flaps. There was also, across the river, a dispensary newly-built of yellow pine where an Ismaili *dhai* or midwife had just arrived from Lahore, and sat for her picture holding a very new baby, tightly swaddled in a dark green silk shawl, its little red face screwed up under a yellow knitted bonnet. We were informed proudly that the dis-pensary had been built with funds provided by the Agha Khan.

There is a great advantage in belonging oneself to a small country and one in which history can produce such splendidly convincing examples of the kind of behaviour expected and understood by all highland peoples, especially poor ones. The background is the same and if ours is a little further removed, it is not too far away to be real and remembered. The crops, the cattle and the sheep, the small stone houses with tiny windows or none at all, are familiar to both of us.

The evenings were spent round a fire of sweet-smelling juniper wood, the old *Tehsildar* wrapped in his brown *chogha,* the Chitrali coat made of soft wool woven on foot-wide looms and lavishly embroidered in a Paisley shawl pattern. With sleeves reaching almost to one's knees, its warmth is a vital necessity in the bitter cold of winter. Everyone was naïvely interested in our home, our habits, our family. All conversation was carried out in *Urdu,* translated into *Khowar* by Jan Badshah for those whose *Urdu* was scanty and liberally supplemented by drawings either by Stewart or myself when *Urdu* failed us.

The *Tehsildar* recalled the days of his youth, although he still played an impressive game of polo, and the long hunting trips after markhor and ibex, both of which live at about 14,000 feet. In summer the ibex retreat to the snow line only leaving it to feed, while the grass and juniper slopes immediately below the snow line are, at the same season, the home of the markhor. I still possess the drawings we made for them of the fauna of Zambia which we had both known so intimately and we found common ground in comparing the leopard, *Panthera pardus* with the snow leopard or ounce of the Himalayas, *Felis uncia.* They continually demanded more and the book with our sketches passed from hand to hand as the sparks flew upwards and apricot kernels, apple pips and spit shot downwards like grapeshot all over our floor.

Whether they believed our stories was another question. Perhaps they had their reservations like Aman-ul-Mulk when his son came back from Calcutta in 1893 with fearsome tales of the sights he had seen. The old *Mehtar* believed him up to a certain point : ' he believed about the railway and the telegraph for he thought it possible that men who could make rifles as the English did might also be able to invent some arrangements for sending men and messages rapidly along; but when his son told him that they made ice in the hot weather he said he could not possibly believe that, for only God could do such a thing. He said he drew the line there, and told his son that he need not tell him any more of his stories!'[1]

One night we had a visit from some itinerant musicians and we all crowded into one tiny room to watch the performance. We ourselves might have been inclined to dismiss the artistes as a third-rate touring company, but their simple-minded audience was mesmerised. There was a small, wizened man with a flat nose and a lecherous leer who played the *surnai*; a kettledrum player, another *surnai* and a *tubla*. In addition two younger members of the troupe did some dancing, the *pièce de resistance*, inevitably in these regions, consisting of a man masquerading as a woman being more or less seduced by her opposite number. This is just about the bawdiest *divertissement* possible, but when words are added, in this case in *Khowar*, one is placed in the unenviable position of not knowing when to laugh, like Herr Slossenn Boschen singing his supposedly famous German comic song in *Three Men in a Boat*, which reduced the entire audience to agonies of mirth and turned out to be one of the most tragic and pathetic songs in the German language.

But one of the men sang with great feeling a romantic song from Upper Chitral called ' Yoormun Hamin ' which later in the evening we begged Jan Badshah to translate for us. We did our best with the result of this and by comparing it with a similar song from *Tribes of the Hindoo Koosh,* we evolved the following lines :

' I wander over the mountains as though I walked on hot ashes,
The sword of love has stricken me : I made me a shield of the
bones of the ibex,

Oh Yoormun Hamin !

---

[1] Francis Younghusband : *The Heart of a Continent.*

Oh beloved I swear by God that having seen you there is no
light,

Night and day are alike to me, no dawn comes to me,
Oh Yoormun Hamin!

The curls of my beloved are like roses and ferns,
Come sit with me and sing like the bulbul or mynah,
Oh Yoormun Hamin!

Still I gaze upon you; you turn from me and look away,
My life is yours, why do you smile at my enemies?
Oh Yoormun Hamin!

I sigh night and day for my nightingale,
I kiss her black ringlets in my dreams,
Oh Yoormun Hamin!'

The evenings nearly always ended up with Jan Badshah, the last to leave, fiddling away with his portable radio on which we listened shamelessly and with illicit glee to telephone conversations between gentlemen in Malakand and Swat, while we handed round steaming cups of Bovril, the only contribution we were allowed to make to the commissariat, and which they all insisted on describing as ' very hot tea '.

6

Kafiristan

The country of Hindustan is extensive, full of men and full of produce. On the east, south and even on the west it ends at its great enclosing ocean. On the north it has mountains which connect it with those of Hindu Khush, Kafiristan and Kashmir. North west of it lie Kabul and Kandahar. Panjhir (Panj-sher) is another tuman: it lies close to Kafiristan along the Panjhir road and is the thoroughfare of Kafir highwaymen who also being so near, take tax of it. They have gone through it killing a mass of persons and doing very evil deeds since I came this last time and conquered Hindustan.

Babur-nama : A.D. 1526

The snowstorm which had allegedly made the track back to Chitral impassable, was greeted with unconcealed joy by everyone at the Police Tana, ourselves included. The only inconvenience was to the displaced sepoys whose room we occupied, who simply grinned and shrugged with the *Khowar* equivalent of ' It couldn't matter less !' This we believed, for a room of one's own in Pakistan is seldom regarded as a luxury. Gregarious by nature, the men will sleep cheek by jowl in compound and on rooftop in summer and sit up chatting in a companionable huddle round the fire in winter, while in the women's quarters, to be alone is to be utterly and acutely miserable.

Jan Badshah, our self-appointed public relations officer,

rubbed his hands happily as though he personally had been responsible for the sudden change in the weather and bore us off to visit a nearby *kila* or fort. It was a bitter, blustery day with fine snow blowing in gusts, the mountains dusted with white against which the rich burnt sienna of the walnut trees and the bright, yellow-green blaze of almond and poplar flamed splendidly.

At one corner a squat watch tower brooded, reminiscent of the North West Frontier and the fort had a grim starkness about it not unlike a Scottish keep with its soaring outer walls and inner courtyard, a design that has proved its usefulness down the centuries, large enough to accommodate cattle and sheep and having its own natural spring for water. The *kila* had been built of stone faced with clay which was flaking off in places like old harling, bristling with wooden joists that peppered the walls haphazardly, sticking out like pneumatophores. It was so close to the mountainside as to be almost part of it, the rock and shale shoulders leaning over it as though one day they might overbalance and engulf the whole edifice.

Surprisingly its boundaries of dry stone walls enclosed a sizeable orchard through which we wandered coldly, under the damp branches of apple, peach and apricot trees, a few of the fruits still hanging forlornly like small Christmas decorations that someone had forgotten to take down. Inside, the rooms were large and draughty and we sat around awkwardly on tatty velvet upholstered chairs until the owner appeared looking uncomfortably sleepy as though he had just been roused from his afternoon siesta. However he welcomed us warmly enough and soon someone brought in tea, what could only have been a kind of pancake made with eggs, and a platter of walnuts.

The *Khan* or *Lal* as the elders are called in Chitral, was anxious that we should see everything and our conducted tour included a perilous climb to the roof up an open wooden stairway from the central square, its single handrail poised delicately on two or three uprights but still functional for those whose legs were long enough to span the missing step or two. Here the owner, in ample homespun *chogha* posed with Jan Badshah, and a sepoy in an army greatcoat who had come along for the fun. They were joined, just before the shutter of the camera clicked, by two other gentlemen who had seemingly appeared out of the thin air, breathing heavily in their rush to be registered for posterity, but whose identity was never disclosed.

Then, after a hurried conference, one of them shuffled off and came back carrying an ancient flintlock, carefully wrapped and tied up in a piece of cloth, which the old *Lal* hoisted on to his shoulder just as it was and stood there, rigidly self-conscious on the flat roof, his figure giving scale to the lowering mountains of the Hindu Khush, hung like a backcloth behind him.

Next morning 'bed tea' was brought to us by one of the sepoys at 4.30 a.m., although it seemed to us like the middle of the night. Fortunately both Stewart and I are of one mind as far as morning conversation is concerned. By tacit agreement a decent period is allowed to elapse before we expect any discussion of the day ahead. By six-thirty and the arrival of the horses, only an hour later than arranged for, we had had ample time to surface quietly and watch the rose coloured dawn flush the highest peaks above the black cleft of the valley.

The return journey was probably even more terrifying because we knew what lay ahead, having to endure it twice over as it were – in retrospect and in actual fact. Somehow we stuck to our horses and they, splendid creatures, stuck to the ribbon of track and we stopped at last in a flat green pocket in the great massif of mountain for tea and fruit with a hospitable landowner, the horses grazing, tiny beside the pale grey boulders. The only untoward incident of the journey had been the accident at the stream when, instead of fording the river, the younger of the 'grooms' stupidly tried to lead the horse across a single plank bridge, obviously to save his own feet getting wet. Half-way over, the animal, quite unable to sustain his balance, fell in, and all our luggage sketchily looped upon his back simply took off down the racing torrent of the Lotkhuh River.

There was a mad scramble to snatch as much as possible before the icy waters carried the bags bobbing and tumbling beyond our reach, and men and horses splashed around shouting and yelling and enjoying every minute of the diversion. Finally all was recovered except my anorak, in the pockets of which reposed my light meter, spectacles and favourite lipstick. I often wondered afterwards whether anyone ever found them and if so what they made of the odd collection.

I suppose we were lucky that our pony did not choose to fall from a greater height; apparently such an occurrence is not unusual but fortunately we did not know about this until we were safely back in Chitral. Durand had met a *kafila* on this same road, *en route* from Bajaur to Badakshan and found one of the Hindu traders bewailing the loss of a fine mule killed by a fall from a cliff, the second lost since they had left Chitral, and half his load washed away in the stream.

About thirteen miles short of Chitral we had an unexpected and delightful meeting with the Political Administrator, Mr. Idris and his small cavalcade, setting off on a tour of the district. An exceptional officer, who got out among his people as often as he could and met them on a friendly, man to man basis, the importance of his position was respected and no advantage taken on either side. Younghusband would have approved of him I feel sure, he himself deeply conscious of the need to give these ' virile and attractive people . . . both independence and protection . . . Even from the point of view of picturesqueness it would be a thousand pities to destroy the freedom of these mountain peoples; to break up these primitive courts where the ruler meets his people face to face, and knows each man among them as they know him; and to wither the simple customs as the grass is withered by the frost, by introducing the cold systems of British administration . . .' Idris continued during his term of office along these lines and was greatly liked and deeply missed when he was moved to another district as good Political Officers are only too frequently.

We stopped and chatted and he pressed upon us some packets

of cigarettes, for our long evenings round the fire and extra days had sadly depleted our store, and showed us the old entrance to the antimony mines at Krinj where quartz veins traverse slates of the Palaeozoic age. Mining was begun in Chitral in 1939 he told us, but stopped after Partition. It was scarcely surprising that the venture should seem uneconomic eight thousand feet up in this wild region inaccessible to heavy transport, the long haul to Dargai and the railhead over mountain passes closed in the winter months.

From antimony comes the *sur'ma* which is used as a cosmetic throughout India and Pakistan, the mascara that even tiny babies have applied round their eyes; the black that makes the dark eyes of the beloved even blacker and inspired all Persian and Pakhtu poets with a strange sense of symbolism to write of its killing power. More prosaically, but in the same deadly manner, antimony is incorporated in the charges of shells producing a dense white smoke when they explode.

We arrived back at Burhanuddin's house about half-past five that evening to be greeted touchingly by the Shahzada with: ' Welcome home !' His small granddaughter had been brought from his private dwelling behind the bachelor quarters used to entertain his guests, an enchanting little creature in miniature *shalwar qamiz,* a pale green lace *dophatta* over her head which she managed perfectly. He carried her around in his arms, obviously very proud and fond of her. Children in Chitral were charmingly behaved and always treated with the greatest affection.

Burhan miraculously settled up with the owners of the horses to everyone's satisfaction. Jan Badshah bade us a reluctant farewell and we settled down round the fire to discuss ways and means of attaining our next objective. The thin sliver of land marked Kafiristan, wedged like a narrow corridor between Chitral proper and the southernmost flanks of the Hindu Khush, appears on the average map as barely wide enough to contain the letters of its name. This insignificant strip of territory however, is inhabited by the last survivors of a fair skinned, pagan

75

race, whose origin has confounded travellers and ethnologists for the best part of a hundred years.

They were there before Alexander and were noted by Ching-his Khan : Marco Polo spoke of them as the people of Belor, being ' idolators and utter savages, living entirely by the chase and dressed in the skins of beasts.' Tamerlane had various un-resolved skirmishes with them in the fourteenth century and is reputed to have acquired a Kafir wife. Like the Scottish border reivers, they spent most of their time harrying their neighbours. They were the scourge of travellers in Babur's reign, although he never failed to enjoy their wine, and waged a remorseless and bloody war against all Muslims and each other with impartial zest up into the early days of this century.

In spite of being surrounded on all sides by fanatical Muslims, they have contrived to preserve their faith, independence and unique culture and have earned the name ' Kafir' meaning ' Unbeliever'. Lying thus on the fringe of West Pakistan, Kafiristan consists of three separate valleys, Birir, Bumboret and Rumbhor, each one more inaccessible than the other and wear-ing like a garment, the spell of remote, unvisited places.

Although the ruling family of Chitral is believed to have Kafir ancestry, or perhaps because of it, our interest in the Kalash Kafirs was slightly deprecated. No one would have dreamed of putting obstacles in our way but when we told Burhan that a couple of American girls staying at the Rest House had invited us to join them on a picnic to the Kafir valley of Birir, where they had been told that the women would dance for them, he laughed and asked what we expected to see. ' It is very boring,' he went on, ' they simply go round and round in a circle, back and forth singing " Ho! Ho! Ho! Ho!"' and compared it un-favourably to the performances of the men we had seen dancing in Chitral.

There are other Kafirs, often related we were told, across the border in Afghanistan, but having yielded to pressure, they have turned Muslim and the land they inhabit has been virtuously renamed ' Nuristan ', ' Land of Light '. In Pakistan the Kafirs have not been subjected so far to any form of coercion, and remain for the most part intriguingly and delightfully heathen. These true Kafirs are usually known as the Kalash or Black Kafirs to distinguish them from the Kati or Red Kafir, who, either owing to the awkwardness of belonging to a different persuasion to that of their visiting relatives, or because of intermarriage with Muslims have embraced Islam, losing their identity in the process. It may be only a matter of time before the Kalash too succumb to orthodoxy and disappear into the limbo of forgotten things.

Of the three valleys, Birir is the only one to reveal any apparent consciousness of its attractions for the outside world, for it is accessible during summer and autumn to the ordinary tourist, who can now travel at least part of the way by jeep, as we did. Visitors are naturally anxious to see and photograph the Birir Kalash and the curious shuffling dance common to most of the Kafirs. The women of Birir have been quick to exploit this pleasant and effortless source of revenue, for they are now ready to appear automatically and dance to order at the rate of one rupee each.

As about twenty dancers may be involved, this becomes quite a costly business, but the picturesque costumes, the beautiful cowrie shell headdresses and the loveliness of some of the women made it well worth while. For us it was a kind of introduction to the people we were to come to know later in our travels, although frustratingly short, like reading a paragraph on the dust jacket of a book and being unable to get at the material inside.

Dancing appeared to be the sole concession to the outsider, an almost tongue-in-the-cheek affair, as the women emerged as though by magic from among the almond and walnut trees to gather in little groups by the dancing floor, a green patch laid like a handkerchief in the narrow valley. Below us the river tumbled noisily over the smooth boulders, a coolness rising perceptibly from its glacier fed waters. They danced with solemn concentration, withdrew giggling a little and no doubt discussed our curious dress, disappearing in the same way as they had come, leaving the grass bare and empty except for the fluttering leaves disturbed by their stamping feet.

They had been accompanied by two men each with a huge *tubla* slung round his neck on which they drummed out the rhythm which did, in effect, sound exactly like Burhan's imitation. A ragged boy about five years old, seeing us filming, picked up an empty cigarette packet and cleverly opening it up, fashioned it into a mock camera, holding it gravely to one eye as he had seen us do, and wholly engrossed with his new invention.

On the outskirts sat an extraordinarily good-looking young boy watching us, like some Grecian shepherd lad, taking time off from the desultory guarding of a flock of long-haired, silky goats, which seized the opportunity to climb everything within sight, devouring all they could reach. Before we left, one of the men approached us shyly, with a great oval plate heaped with small, sweet and seedless grapes for us to eat.

Pakistanis, when they have heard of them at all, vary in their reaction to the Kalash. Slightly ashamed of their pagan ways, they are at the same time reluctant to relinquish claim upon a people whom ethnographers regard with such reverence. Like eccentric but distant relatives, the Pakistani apologises for this uncouth tribe on his borders, hastily disclaiming all responsibility for it and puzzled that others should find it interesting. So they leave the Kalash largely alone and occasionally do odd things like building a trout hatchery at the head of a valley. A few fanatical Sunni Muslims in lower Chitral speak loudly of summarily converting them, but the arduous journey involved and the patent discomforts they might have to endure, no doubt deter them.

When diminishing species, even of fauna, cause us so much concern, it would be a pity if such a unique people as the Kalash were allowed to disappear or undergo the same treatment meted out to their counterparts in other parts of the world. It is common knowledge that the Red Indian, Bushman and Aborigine of Australia, gained nothing but disease, dissipation and eventual decimation from the unending endeavours of more advanced races either to destroy what they could not understand, or insist on conformity with a way of life which they assumed must be the right one.

It is difficult to know at what point help becomes interference, and how much change is justified. Very often, with the best of intentions, we give the wrong things, either too much or too little, and seem incapable of looking forward to the ultimate end of our labours, leaving behind us a vision of Paradise unattained and I am reminded of the old lady in the north of Shetland who was asked if she wanted electricity. Reluctantly she agreed to accept this marvel of modern science and at great expense a line was run for miles across the country to reach her tiny croft. In the end all she wished for was one bulb by which she could see to light her oil lamp.

Like so many other ancient peoples who once held sway over great stretches of country, the passing centuries have slowly diminished them, but there was a time when Kafiristan extended from Kabul to the Indus, taking in Badakshan, Chitral, whose Kator dynasty may well have sprung from one of them, the Kunar and Swat valleys and the mountains of the Indus itself. The Kalash Kafirs of today firmly assert their descent from Alexander the Great and that they must be largely of mixed origin can scarcely be disputed, for the great tract of mountainous territory that split their original lands in half, has formed the crucible of innumerable and divergent cultures. When Alexander did finally cross the Hindu Khush, the plains of Kabul and the passes over the mountains were already held by Greeks, their forbears transported to Asia by Darius Hytaspes after the fall of Miletus.

The admixture of Greek and Persian blood could well have been strengthened at least in part by the arrival of Alexander's weary mercenaries; Iranian cavalrymen, Bactrians, Sogdians, Arachosians and Scythian horsemen, the famous archers who had marched with him from Ionian Greece and Samarqand. Perhaps the fires of conquest were burning low, dimmed by the gruelling trek across the plains from Babylon and the bitter mountain winds against which the *toplites'* heavy armour offered no warmth.

Looking down on the enchanted valleys of Kafiristan, rich in walnut, wild almond, white mulberry and vine, there must have been some who gazed with longing on the clear rushing waters that scoop out their channels between deep clefts of hills thick with pine and deodar, found them good and settled there, to drink the yellow wines and beget a second strain of Greek or Persian children out of the wild and hardy tribeswomen.

Although much wiser and more learned minds than mine have speculated upon the Kalash ancestry, no definitive solution has been reached. The field remains open and anyone may conjecture or pursue the elusive threads of their origin, but two indications seem valid, one in the light of history and one a personal hypothesis, and both involving the most simple, everyday objects, the vine and the horse.

Alexander, having turned in his march of conquest towards the Indus, then made for a city called Nysa which Arrian, the great historian of his time, tells us was founded by Dionysos, the original Greek name for Bacchus, the god of wine. This Dionysos, apart from introducing wine-making to the local inhabitants, had built the city as a kind of prototype of our Chelsea Hospital, expressly ' for an habitation for such of his soldiers as age or accident had rendered unfit for miltary service . . .'

It is pleasant to digress in imagination and think of these old Greek warriors taking their ease beneath the vines, their shields beside them, drinking the wine and talking of youthful battles, remembering perhaps with Hafiz, the

> ' Songs of dead laughter, songs of love once hot,
> Songs of a cup once flushed rose red with wine,
> Songs of a rose whose beauty is forgot . . .'

The sudden appearance of the great conqueror however struck terror into the Nysaeans and as soon as they had recovered, a deputation presented him with a petition to spare their city ' for the reverence thou bearest to Dionysos their god . . .' Alexander received them graciously and leaving the city unscathed, made sacrifice to a god he could scarcely refuse to ignore, while his soldiers, singing hymns indulged in a truly Bacchic orgy.

Centuries later this same city of Nysa was epitomised with startling clarity in a war hymn of the Kafirs of Kamdesh as they danced and sang :

' Oh thou who from Gir-Nysa's lofty heights was born . . .' linking through the centuries the worship of Bacchus in the city of Nysa with the inhabitants of the small remaining valleys of Kafiristan.

From this it could be deduced that the Kalash may be originally of Greek descent and learned their wine-making from Dionysos himself, but there remains a second clue in this fascinating voyage of ethnographical discovery. The Kunar River, whose upper reaches are in Chitral, was called by Aristotle and others, the Khoaspes, ' The River of the Good Horse '. Which forgotten quadruped gave its name to this river we will never know, but like Bucephalus, Alexander's own favourite charger, he must have been remembered for his valour, and the word Khoaspes compounded in his memory from the Persian word for a horse – *aspa* and the local usage of the Pakhtu *kho* meaning good. It is significant that both the tribes Alexander encountered in this area, the Aspasii and the Assaceni, have names derived from the same root.

It seemed to us that there must be strong Persian roots in the Kalash, for we discovered that the name for a horse in Bushgali as spoken by the Bushgal tribe of Kafirs who lived around Birkot, about forty miles from Chitral, is *Ooshp* and in the Yidgah tongue of the Kafirs inhabiting the upper part of the Lotkuh valley not far from the hot springs at Garam Chashma, it is *Yasp*.

Moreover, in Kafiristan today, few people have ever seen a horse, but horses figure largely in their ancestral effigies, chief-

F   81

tains being represented on horseback and rows of wooden horses' heads adorn the altars overlooking the threshing floors. Sir Olaf Caroe sees in the Aspasii the prototype of the Isapzai or Yusafzai Pathan of the North West Frontier. I would not quarrel with his superior scholarship, but I like to think that the wooden horses, the *yasp* and *ooshp* now weathered by innumerable snows and burning suns, the vines that Dionysos turned to wine and the strong Kafir leaning to Zoroastrian rites, means that he too is of Graeco-Iranian stock.

In such a wild and mountainous region, where wine must have been an unexpected luxury, there were few who passed that way but did not remark upon it and Kafiristan has been well documented because of it since the sixth century when Chinese pilgrims speak of the country on their long journeys to the Bhuddist shrines of India. Sung Yun crossed the Pamirs to the Oxus in A.D. 519 and entered the sub-continent by way of Kafiristan to avoid, so we are told, an even more fearsome crossing of the upper Indus by a bridge constructed from a single iron chain.

Babur, who in his earlier years confessed an addiction both to wine and *majun,* a drug like *bhang* or *charras* used on the North West Frontier, frequently wrote of his parties with obvious enjoyment :

' Chaghan sarai, a single village with little land at the mouth of Kafiristan . . . its people though Musulman mix with the Kafirs and consequently follow their customs. A great torrent (the Kunar) comes down to it from the north east behind Bajaur and a smaller one called Pich comes down from Kafiristan. Strong yellowish wines are there, not in any way resembling those of the Nur-valley however. The village has no grapes or vineyards of its own; its wines are all brought up the Kafiristan water and from Pich-i-Kafiristan . . . The Pich Kafirs came to help the villagers when I took the place. Wine is so commonly used there that every Kafir has his leathern wine-bag, (*khig*) at his neck and drinks wine instead of water.'

Without knowing it, these Kafirs are safeguarding themselves against many troubles caused by drinking water from the mountain streams contaminated by sheep or goats and which we were warned could contain all manner of unpleasant things from animals suffering from liver fluke, lung worms and stomach worms. Indeed in the Gilgit area we came across many such cases especially where no wine was drunk.

In 1602 a Portuguese Jesuit, Benedict de Goa, coadjutor to the Superior of the Order in the Moghal's Empire, set off from Lahore to China, where he died, attaching himself to a caravan of five hundred merchants and passed through a part of eastern Afghanistan which he called ' Capherstam '. He says the soil was fertile and yielded plenty of grapes; offered a cup of wine he found it very good.

Then came Fazl Huq, a Pathan, son of a *mullah* or priest, who had been converted to Christianity at Peshawar, a fairly rare occurrence. Joining the Corps of Guides as a Sepoy, he set off for Kafiristan in September 1864 at the invitation of a Kafir soldier. Reaching the Kunar River, they floated down on a raft of inflated skins and entered Jelalabad disguised as women. At the village to which they had been invited, Fazl Huq and his companion, an ex-*mullah* called Narullah, carried on their missionary work for twenty days and were very well received, although it is doubtful if they made any converts. Huq kept a journal using lime juice as invisible ink and reported the customs of the Kafirs.

In 1883 N. W. McNair, an officer of the Indian Survey, against orders of the Indian Government, penetrated the Bashgul valley disguised as a Muslim *Hakim,* taking with him an enormous book with cabalistic signs which concealed within it a plane table for mapping and other surveying instruments. He reported the Kafirs were celebrated for their beauty and their European complexions; that they worshipped idols; drank wine out of silver cups and vases; used chairs and tables and spoke a language unknown to their neighbours; that brown eyes were more common than blue; that their complexions varied between pink and a bronze dark as a Punjabi; that the infidelity of wives was punished by a mild beating and that of men by a fine of cattle, which still holds good in the Chitral area of Kafiristan today. He also noted one of their prayers:

> Ward off fever from us.
> Increase our stores.
> Kill the Mussulmans.
> After death admit us to Paradise.

Two years later the Bashgul Valley was more fully explored by Colonel Woodthorpe of the Indian Survey when he visited it with Sir William Lockhart on a mission, the object of which was to examine the passes of the Hindu Khush, but the sole complete picture of the Kalash living in their pristine state of paganism is given by Sir George Robertson, whose path we followed, and who made his journeys into the country in 1890 and 1891. He should have gone as Agency Surgeon to Gilgit, but 'wild to go into Kafiristan and utterly dissatisfied with his appointment at Gilgit' off he went and visiting the upper reaches of the Bashgul, penetrated further westwards than any other explorer. Even he was already encountering tribes who had been converted to Islam and his was the last opportunity that any European was to have of observing the Kafirs within the boundaries of Afghanistan before they became Muslim.

By the later nineteen hundreds Kafiristan was shrinking visibly, its borders Badakshan on the north, the Lotkhuh valley of Chitral on the north-east; Chitral proper and Lower Chitral on the east and the Kunar valley on the south-east. By 1896 the Afghan had already appeared on the Kafir borderland 'and the process of proselytising at the point of the bayonet' had been commenced.

'What will be the end is curious to speculate on' wrote Durand, 'the Amir (of Afghanistan) is evidently anxious to conquer the country; the Mehtar of Chitral has brought certain parts of it under his sway: the Pathans across the mountains in Bajaur all want to wipe the Kafir out. The end will probably be gradual annexation, incorporation in the neighbouring states, and Mahomedanism.'

But Durand had little patience with the Kafir himself and his sweeping and dogmatic appraisals, so far removed from Younghuband's firm yet kindly tolerance, tend to distort the image, making it difficult to assess the real situation in such a distance of time.

The whole unfortunate history of these strange people up to the drawing up of the Durand Line and the subsequent elimination of Kafiristan except for the three valleys within Chitral, according to Durand, has been one of murder and strife and the only good thing which apparently has emanated from the country is their wine. R. C. F. Schomberg who visited Kafiristan in 1936 appears to have found the Chitral Kafirs interesting but far from warlike and during our visit, we not only got along extremely well with them but discovered that they were regarded by their Chitrali neighbours as the soul of honesty.

Naturally with such a background we wanted to see them for ourselves and our visit to Birir only whetted our appetites for more, but the valley was too easy of access to be really cut off. We settled therefore for a journey to Bumboret, which, in spite of a small Rest House at the head of the valley, our ultimate goal, is rarely visited for the path is not an easy one. Our first step was to find some form of transport to take us to Ayun where the track takes off from the main Chitral valley road.

7

To Bumboret

There arose memories of the fanfares of old heroic days—which
still attack our hearts and our heads—far from assassins of old.

Rimbaud : Les Illuminations

' Eighty rupees Sahib, first class Jeep. Ayun is far away and I
am a poor man Sahib !' With the plaintive moan of the shrewd
expert that betokens a long bargaining session our prospective
driver waved his arms as though to indicate the immense distance that we were demanding he should cover. Our counter
suggestion that he must be mistaking us for rich American
tourists was met by a gale of laughter from the crowd. We were
comfortably seated in one of the open-fronted shops in the
Chitral bazaar amongst a colourful display of miscellaneous
objects ranging from rock salt to hand-knitted woollen socks of
intricate and startling design. Around us, jockeying for position,
shuffled a keen and lively crowd, business happily forgotten for
the afternoon.

Our host poured another cup of sweet, sticky tea, pressed upon
me a pomegranate which he dusted off with a corner of his
chaddar draped conveniently over his shoulder, and settled down
to enjoy the bargaining. At 60 rupees, nonchalantly spitting
pomegranate pips in the approved manner, we announced

pleasantly that we had decided to walk to Ayun, which temporarily nonplussed the owner of the Jeep and sent the shopkeeper into a fit of hysterical coughing over his hookah. Half an hour and several cups of tea later, the bargain was clinched at 45 rupees and we stepped forth to inspect this Rolls-Royce among Jeeps.

At first glance we were conscious only that the vehicle had once been a Jeep. Our protest that it was entirely without covering was met by an immediate response from half a dozen bystanders, who pounced upon it in unison and after unravelling yards of knotted goat-hair rope, succeeded in dragging over the top the remains of a hood, which, when tied down, was then fitted, if such is the word, with two opaque and jagged squares of perspex. Although primarily intended to serve as windshields, like a pair of blinkers, they effectively obscured the sides of the road from the driver's view. At the point where the bonnet was raised and a large stone wedged in between the generator and the engine in lieu of bolts became apparent, we hastily averted our eyes and felt it would be better not to see any more.

Evening was far advanced by the time we had packed and routed out the driver's mate, who happened to be saying his prayers at the local mosque. We could only hope after such prolonged devotional exercise that he had included one for us. It was pitch dark when we finally reached Ayun after a perilous ride during which, in the interests of safety, we were forced to jettison the side windows.

In spite of a slight tendency to disparage the customs of his heathen neighbours, Prince Burhanuddin humoured us in our odd desire to visit the Kalash, and sent a message for us to the Chitral police requesting that they inform their opposite numbers in Ayun of our inpending arrival. The telephone message needless to say had gone astray somewhere along the line, and we arrived cold and hungry in a maze of dimly seen and narrow lanes angled between the sleeping houses.

Our driver was just as anxious to get rid of us as we were to dispense with his dubious services and find ourselves a bed for the night. Leaving us huddled in the Jeep, the wind whistling through the shrouds of the flapping cover, he and his mate disappeared into the darkness. Finally they succeeded in knocking up the occupants of the local police Tana and returned in triumph with the Chief Constable, a tall, handsome and burly Chitrali with the most imposing black curling moustache, buttoning up his greatcoat and utterly confounded by our arrival out of the night. In spite of the fact that he had obviously been dragged out of bed he rose to the occasion in the most business-like way and led us straight to the Rest House, once having justified its title as a country retreat for the rulers of Chitral, but long since abandoned and crumbling quietly away for want of repair.

The Constable solemnly unlocked the door and throwing it open with the flourish of a West End majordomo, ushered us into a room about the size of an average barn and almost as high. A sepoy followed, shielding a flickering oil lamp with his hand and revealing to our startled eyes something akin to the stage-set for The Sleeping Beauty. Cobwebs festooned everything within sight, although hastily flapped away with the Constable's *chaddar*. It was innocent of furnishings save for one brokendown chair, the remnants of a rickety table and a couple of *charpoys* or string beds just discernible in one corner under a heap of dark and musty *razai*. The steps of the surrounding veranda led optimistically down to the river, but ceased abruptly after the fourth tread, as I found later when forced outside because no one had thought to unlock the bathroom.

In spite of the almost total absence of creature comforts, everyone was kindness itself, fetching wood for the fire, producing water for tea and, miraculously, half-a-dozen warmed-up *chapattis*. Chairs were brought and dusted off and our new friends gathered round to enjoy the unexpected entertainment. Indeed they were quite prepared to sit the night through, our arrival a godsend in the middle of autumn's dull monotony, and we were obviously providing such a fund of innocent enjoyment that we had not the heart to send them away.

About three o'clock in the morning we pleaded extreme fatigue and they reluctantly withdrew, leaving us to crawl thankfully into our sleeping bags fully clad, to be awakened at dawn by the entire police station, now reinforced by numerous villagers to whom the news had somehow got around that free amusement was going at the Rest House. Stewart, although still uncertain of his Urdu, floundered manfully through complicated conversations, his irrepressible sense of humour coming through to our hosts even in the most elementary phraseology. Our relationship was invariably a mystery. It seemed quite inconceivable to these men that a mother and son should team up on such an adventure, but whatever their private thoughts they politely, if sceptically, accepted our explanations, together with all our other eccentricities.

A young sepoy was detailed to accompany us into Bumboret as he spoke both Urdu and the local Kafir tongue. Two men materialised as porters and after photographing the Constable at his own request, together with everyone else in sight, standing stiff as ramrods and drawn up in rigid formation from which nothing we could say would move them, we finally succeeded in saying our farewells.

It was a relief to find ourselves an hour later, the sun slanting through the chinar and willow, the river clamouring noisily at our feet, stepping out along the edges of the terraced fields leading away from Ayun, up through orchards of apricot and mulberry on our long trek to Bumboret. The track takes off from the main Chitral road at Ayun and the distance between this point and the head of the valley is a mere 14 miles. Within this space, however, the path climbs breathlessly from about 4,000 to 7,000 feet, running crazily through sun-baked, boulder-strewn stream beds; shooting tortuously upwards in narrow funnels cut into the living rock; meandering lazily along under a fine mesh of wild almond, laburnam, walnut and chestnut and involving no less than twenty crossings of foaming, ice-cold water. Nineteen of these are achieved by means of the narrowest of planks poised precariously above the green torrent roaring giddily beneath one's feet, to tumble in white wave crests over elephant-grey boulders worn smooth as silk, and the remaining passage involving an undignified scramble over the slippery bole of a fallen tree.

We were following, almost bridge for bridge, in the same month of the year, October, in the footsteps of Sir George Scott Robertson, with only a matter of 60 years between us. Conditions can scarcely have changed since his own description of the journey, for he says, having left Ayun: ' we followed the Bumboret River track the whole way, the coolies going by an upper road. We must have crossed and re-crossed the river at least twenty times, always by means of a single pole bridge. It was difficult to preserve the balance on the narrow, slippery pole which was continually shifting about. The water was running down at a great pace washing over the frail bridge. It was impossible for me to maintain my foothold on it at all and there had always to be a man in front of me and another behind to get me across. The Kafirs and Chitralis were as much at home on the single pine branch as if they were on solid rock and we passed over every time without mishap.'

The only alternative route to Bumboret – which Robertson's carriers took – although shorter, climbs clear over the mountain, but every other day small figures staggered patiently up and down the trail like ants, laden with bulging sacks of walnuts or bent double on the return journey from Ayun, carrying rock salt, kerosene and even sacks of cement for the trout hatchery then under construction at the head of the valley. Everything must be manhandled in, for horses and donkeys are useless in this kind of terrain.

As we trudged on slowly, ever upwards and both of us frequently pausing for breath, it was like stepping back in time into an almost mythical world where each landmark had been plotted in a past that threw up only an imaginary glimpse of figures moving against a background of snow-streaked mountains; whose feet had cooled as ours did, half-way through the march, in the deliciously icy milk-white waters and whose shades still lingered as they must have done so often, against a rock for shelter from the heat of the day. Now all was peace, the wild tribes tamed perhaps by the very beauty of their surroundings and the belief that when the Creator made the world, He kept the valley of Bumboret for Himself and then graciously decided to give it to the Kalash.

The sun glanced off the rocks like a burning-glass and we soon gave up even trying to wipe the sweat from our brows, the salt trickle making our eyes smart, our breathing becoming perceptibly more laboured as we climbed ever higher. Soon we began to catch glimpses of the Kalash, a few women gathering corn cobs, who looked us up and down frankly from under straight black brows, their glances lingering perhaps a little longer than necessary on Stewart's bronzed face and fair, sun-bleached hair. An old man herding some cattle greeted us courteously. The herds had now returned from their summer pastures up in the mountains where they are tended by the young men of the village, fully armed, for brushes with the Afghans across the tenuous frontier are not unknown. Bears and snow leopards are their only natural enemies, the former lumbering down from the hills in the autumn to feast all night long on a field of maize.

At first glance it was almost impossible to distinguish the Kalash village of Bumboret from the neighbouring rock, for the houses seemed almost part of the hillside, climbing dizzily up the sheer slope, leaning over at impossible angles so that the roof of one house becomes the threshing floor of the one above. The streets are narrow alleys running below the projecting balconies which are often intricately carved in a variety of forms, surrounded by wedge-shaped incisions and like some ancient hieroglyphics there seems to be no key to their origin. How did the Celtic braid pattern come to feature so widely, either contained within a square or as an over-all design ornamenting a pillar; was the acanthus leaf introduced by those early Greeks or was it brought across the Hindu Khush by the ancestors of the Kalash to whom it was a familiar, everyday object?

The wooden pillars supporting the *handts* or temples such as the *Jestakan,* housing the symbolic representation of the *Jestak,* spiritual protector of children and women in labour, are partly carved and partly surrounded by a painted frieze of tiny, pin-men figures, like a child's first impressions of a human being and bearing a curious similarity to the simplicity of decoration on pottery used in Athens about 750 B.C. Some of the animals are stylised conceptions of the familiar ones of the high mountains, markhor and ibex, the latter hunted throughout south west France and Spain by Upper Palaeolithic man, venerated because of their beauty, strength and courage, and found in Cretan peak sanctuaries of 1500 B.C., where the ibex with its sweeping horns appears to have served as a substitute for the ritualistic bull culture of the lower Minoan valleys. In Chitral's neighbouring State of Swat, during the excavations at Gogdara, a rock face was revealed carrying prehistoric *graffiti,* or more accurately carvings of animals which include an ibex, which bear a distinct resemblance to Iranian prehistoric pottery. Although the ibex, like the markhor, has been sadly depleted over the years, it still maintains a symbolic veneration, as the mascot of the Gilgit Scouts and as a model for the sculpture on a memorial pillar to the men who died in the fighting for Azad Kashmir, appropri-ately placed in Gilgit's Chinar Bagh.

As with all pastoral peoples, animals play an important part in their daily lives and often in their iconography. Other friezes in the Kalash temples depict cattle being driven off to the summer pastures, ceremonially repainted every year, and the wooden horses' heads that arch stiffly out from the altars above the threshing floors, the effigies of past chieftains on horseback, point to some dim background of half-remembered animism. The outward traces of their ancestry are all but invisible; no ancient monuments exist to give a lead to the archaeologist. The valley of Bumboret might have stood thus since the beginning of time, and the proud people who once ruled from Jelalabad to Gilgit, without identity, carrying their past within them in a tangle of myth and legend as yet unravelled.

8

The Kalash

Who possesses much silver may be happy,
Who possesses much barley may be happy,
But he who has nothing at all can sleep.
                Cuneiform tablet from Mesopotamia

The Rest House at Bumboret looks back down the valley; behind it, still and unreal as a painted landscape, are the pine-clad
slopes and white snow peaks that separate it from Afghanistan.
Between all our detours, filming and photographing, we had
now been 12 hours on the road and the two or three steps leading up to the veranda tore at our aching muscles and bursting
lungs, sorely tried by the long climb. Afzal the sepoy disappeared
in search of food and, more important, someone to cook it. We
had almost fallen asleep when a gentle cough aroused us.

' Good evening. My name is Hidayatullah. I am contractor
here.' In our bemused state we had sudden visions of plush
hotels, hydro-electric schemes, factories . . . but Hidayatullah
was superintending the construction of the trout hatchery, a few
hundred yards from where we sat. Looking up we were aware
of a pair of flannels, athletic shoulders under a striped pullover
and a neat tweed jacket, carefully brushed thick black hair and
a shy, almost apologetic smile. ' I hope I do not disturb you,' he

went on . . . ' Of course not . . .' replied Stewart, struggling to his feet. ' Oh please, no formality. I only wish to welcome you here to Bumboret,' and as we shook hands we felt again how fortunate we were to be greeted thus, only seconds after our arrival. Travellers in Pakistan are invariably accorded the greatest respect, often much more than they deserve, a courtesy that harks back to tribal tradition in lonely places and still surprising and touching in this casual, materialistic world.

Hidayatullah's home was at Drosh, about ten miles or so south of Ayun, but he had lost his heart to the Bumboret valley and was full of a naïve enthusiasm about the place and its inhabitants. We have corresponded with him ever since our visit and in his first letter he told us that he had been able to complete the hatchery before winter set in. ' I may start some more work there this summer,' he wrote in the spring of the following year, ' as I like the place, particularly because there one has a chance to see many good and kind visitors from different countries. You can easily see our liking for such people from our physical environment. Being almost on the roof of the world we have few opportunities to see such people here in this corner. It is their kindness to come here and see us, their fellow human beings.'

He took us under his wing and introduced us to the village. We would wander round, welcome because we were in his company and as we went he told us many of the Kalash customs and beliefs.

Houses are built usually on two storeys, largely to escape the heavy snowfall in winter, the ground floor being used for storing grain. Reached by the simplest form of ladder, consisting of notches cut in a plank of wood, effective but extraordinarily difficult to negotiate in an upright position, the outer room or veranda where the Kalash sleep in the hot weather leads to the living quarters. Although most of the Kafirs in Bumboret are tallish people, the lintels were so low that we all had to stoop to enter, the doors opened by means of an enormous looped wire key about the size of a badminton racquet.

The inside of the house is of the starkest simplicity, devoid

94

of windows, only a hole in the roof for the smoke to escape from the central fire, smouldering constantly between two stones. On either side of the room are the sleeping quarters set on slightly-raised platforms; *charpoys* for the married couples and hard boards covered with well-worn blankets for the old people and children, which seemed to us a little unfair.

In the first house we visited, and where we always felt free to drop in at any time, lived Murayik, her husband and their four children, her mother and father and an aged aunt. Like most of the Kalash, Murayik had beautifully modelled, almost patrician features; her nose just delicately tilted; a full, heart-shaped face; a mouth that curved deliciously and dark eyes, although hazel eyes are not unknown, almond shaped, but straight set under her black brows. Both men and women had an entirely different caste of features to those of Pathan or Afghan and many of the men could have passed for Chitralis.

Standing aside, she signalled to us to enter with a graceful wave of her hand. After our eyes grew accustomed to the dim light inside, we were able to take stock of our surroundings. Hanging from the soot-blackened rafters was a goatskin of milk and a gourd of honey and standing in one corner a bin of maize. A few primitive utensils are kept between the hearth and the wall behind it and no woman can put her foot in this space without contaminating it. A conical basket made of willow and bound with strips of grey and black goat hair, which is carried on the back like a creel, is used for collecting fruit, maize and nuts. A wooden mortar for pounding walnut kernels, one of the staple foods of the Kalash, along with a shallow wooden trough for mixing dough for the *chapattis,* the thin cakes of unleavened bread, together with a few cooking pots and a beautifully shaped water *chatti* completed the domestic arrangements.

Tobacco is grown but is pounded into a black paste and chewed rather than smoked. The one luxury is the potent wine distilled from the grape or the wild white mulberry. Robertson remarked that he found it mostly poor and even then diluted with water. When kept two or three years, however, it becomes clear and sometimes strong, although neither he nor anyone else for that matter has ever reported seeing a Kafir drunk. In 1857 a missionary, the Reverend Ernest Trumpp, wrote that three Kafirs (from Nuristan) sent by a Major Lumsden as recruits for the Corps of Guides, whose headquarters are at Mardan, demanded and apparently got a *mashak* of wine a day, a leather water bag holding the equivalent of six English gallons, yet they were never intoxicated.

The children were shy and well-behaved, the little girls clinging to their mother's skirts as she handed us plates of walnuts and roasted maize and tiny, sweet, seedless grapes, and between Afzal and Hidayatullah we were able to talk in a roundabout kind of way and ask questions. As in many isolated communities, farming is largely conducted on a communal basis and everybody lends a hand with the major operations such as sowing, reaping and wine-making. The Kalash are also noted engineers and Hidayatullah pointed out the slender water channels that laced the mountainside, straddling the enormous fissures in hollowed-out logs like giant rhone pipes and running for 20 miles or more from above Bumboret to irrigate fields around Ayun. Apart from irrigation, water is also used to turn the mill wheels for grinding corn and within the tiny stone houses, where the women squat in almost total darkness, the whirring noise of the wheel and the spatter of grain sounds as though the entire house was filled with the clatter of birds' wings.

I never tired of watching the Kalash women. Slow-moving and incredibly graceful in all their actions, they still wear the traditional dress although the men keep theirs for ceremonial occasions and have adopted the flat Chitrali hat, baggy trousers and shirt worn outside, although often belted at the waist. The women's free, swinging walk sends the brown-black robes, the colour of fresh cut peat, flowing in long fluid lines like an Augustus John gypsy. It is strange that we women of the west, with all our cult of the body beautiful, have never learned to carry ourselves naturally with dignity and grace. We scurry, slouch or stride through life with unseemly haste. We are care-

Women working in fields.

Women and girls wash their clothes in small steaming burns pouring from hot sulphur sprin

Stewart with our police friends at Lotkhuh Tana.

PIA Plane landing in the narro valley of Chitral.

less with our hands, our necks, our arms. Murayik had never seen a lipstick and I cannot remember seeing antimony used on her eyes. Occasionally she and some of the other women plastered their faces with mud, either as a protection from the cold wind or the burning sun or to cure some minor blemish, but their only mirrors were certainly the river pools where they went to wash or braid their hair.

Outside the house a couple of girls were spinning goat hair, the pendulum of the conical spindles rising and falling in an hypnotic rhythm as they sat chatting together in the warm sun.

The dark, goat hair robes of the Kalash women are apt to look a little threadbare in summer but a new dress is woven every year, the old kept kept for the hot weather and the heavier, new one put on during the cold winters. The general design is a voluminous garment, tightly cinched at the waist with a woven *cummerbund,* fringed and often dyed red and above it the bodice is bloused like a monk's cassock, which makes a handy place for carrying things and into which they thrust all manner of objects. Numerous strands of thin chain are attached to the waistband, hanging down one side in loops like an old-fashioned châtelaine and the more prosperous ladies like to have bunches of keys jangling from it, which somehow gives them the air of a housewife busy about her stillroom.

Even the poorest woman will be adorned with innumerable strings of beads; white, red, blue, yellow; large beads, small beads and minute beads like tiny melon seeds, row upon row, so that the V neck of the garment is completely filled with a blaze of colour, and as I admired Murayik's heavy silver necklet that topped this bright array, I felt woefully under-dressed, my neck rising naked and unadorned from the open collar of my khaki shirt. Silver ear-rings hung from several holes pierced round the lobes of her ears, heavy bracelets clanked on her wrists and on the fingers of her strong, graceful hands were silver rings.

The main adornment of the Kalash is undoubtedly the strikingly beautiful headdress, heavily encrusted with cowrie shells. The cowrie, *Cyraea moneta,* once in demand as currency in

G

places as far apart as Africa, Asia and the Philippines, has been adopted as a form of decoration from the Hindu Khush to the northern shores of Lake Kariba, where we had seen the Batonga women wearing circlets of cowries as armlets or sewn on to their short leather skirts. In Marco Polo's time the cowrie was used in Yunnan where he says ' for money they use the white cowries, i.e. the sea shells that are used to make necklaces for dogs; 80 cowries are equivalent to 1 *saggio* of silver, which is worth 2 Venetian groats . . .' and he suggests that all the cowries used in these provinces came from Siam or Malaya.

Underneath the headdress which once might have been worth a fair sum of money in China, the women wear a bandeau consisting of a piece of material about two inches wide with two rows of cowrie shells, seldom removed except for occasional washing or dressing the hair. Then comes the hood which appears to be peculiar to the Kalash. A long strip of material is sewn to make a kind of hat with a continuing lappet hanging down behind to waist level, and on the point just above the forehead is a pompom of purplish or rust coloured wool. Rows of gleaming white shells are arranged evenly to just above the shoulders and below this point the pattern is composed of a central medallion of cowries surrounded by smaller circles made up of tiny pearl buttons, silver filigree discs and little brass bells, rather like the traditional bell on a cat's collar, with a deep fringe at the bottom. Murayik was continually collecting new ornaments for her hood much in the way that we might do towards a charm bracelet and she pounced triumphantly on the sweets we handed round, many of which were wrapped in gold or silver foil. Off came her hood, the paper was carefully smoothed out, and from somewhere she produced of all things, a large safety-pin, which she used to fix her new trophy in a conspicuous place among the shiny buttons and jingling bells.

It is not surprising that the hair is only dressed occasionally, so complicated is the arrangement of these thin, tight braids, a fashion common alike to the Ghilzais of Khorasan and the nomadic Gujars we met in Swat. One of the braids is carried from just over the left eye across the forehead in a loop like a black silk chain; long plaits hang down either cheek and from the longest one at the back, hanging well below the waist, is a bell which tinkles delightfully as the women pad along the paths in their bare feet. Often as big as a tea bell, its object is to frighten off the wild animals, the snow leopard and the bear.

It would seem that only the Kafirs in Pakistan affect this distinctive headdress, for even when there were other Kafirs across the Afghan border the women are described as simply wearing a kind of scarf over their heads. Two interesting variations are mentioned, one by Sung Yun in A.D. 520, who, in writing of the people in what must now be Sirikol or Hunza, remarks that ' the ladies cover their heads using horns from which they hang down veils all round.' Curiously enough, another Chinese pilgrim who seems to have covered most of our route, travelled through Badakshan in or about A.D. 630 and, writing of Himatala which name he applies according to Biddulph to the country about Kundoz, says that :

' The married women wear headdresses with a peak about three feet high decorated in front with two points which indicate the father and mother of the husband. The higher one represents the father and the lower one, the mother. If one dies before the other the appropriate point is removed. When both are dead this particular headdress is no longer worn.'

Robertson mentions this headdress only in relation to the Kalash he met : ' The Kalash women do not wear this headdress of horns but simply wear on their heads a sort of broad cap thickly covered with cowrie shells with lappets which hang down behind not unlike the headdresses of the Tartar women in Ladakh.'

And so once again the scent runs cold, and no one has hazarded an explanation of this extravagantly beautiful adornment; has not even remarked upon its bizarre loveliness seen for the first time like fishes' scales shimmering in the sub-aqueous light of the pale turning trees and carried proudly as a coronet by the Kalash women of Bumboret.

9

Funeral at Burish

Oh thou who from Gir-Nysa's lofty heights was born
Who from its seven fold portals did emerge,
On Katan Chirak thou hast set thine eyes,
Towards the depths of Sum Bughal dost go.
In Sum Baral assembled you have been.
Sanji from the heights you see; Sanji you consult?
The council sits, Oh mad one whither goest thou?
Say Sanji, why dost thou go forth?

Kafir War Hymn

The Kalash year is punctuated by numerous festivals of one kind
or another, the first being held in April or May and called
Chilim Josht, in preparation for which no milk is used during
the preceding ten days, but carefully hoarded by the various
households. According to Hidayatullah, after a few days of gay
and colourful dances, the spiritual head of the tribe, called the
Betan, deliberately puts himself in a coma or hysterical mood. In
this trance the *Betan* forecasts the weather, the spread of disease
or the fate of a sick man. There is such strong belief in his
powers that even the Muslims are reluctant to question the truth
of his prophecies. This soothsayer, in common with others of his
kind in different parts of the world, frequently orders the sacri-

fice of goats or cows in the case of illness and, Hidayatullah assured us solemnly, the patient recovers.

Chilim Josht seems to approximate to what Schomberg refers to as Jyoshi, although it is almost impossible to give firm dates for these festivities as the Kafirs are quite unconcerned with such trivialities as calendar days, months and so forth, so that the various celebrations are timed sensibly by the seasons and the weather. *Chilim Josht* is a strictly male affair and no women are allowed in the vicinity. The day begins with dancing, the men forming a circle, clapping their hands to the beating of drums and a high, singing lilt of ' Ho! Ho! Ho!' the exact counterpart of the women's dances we had filmed in Birir. Little boys caper around outside the ring in a curious prancing step intended to frighten away the snow leopard, while the ' Ho! Ho! Ho!', imitating the grunting sound made by the bears, is expected to keep these creatures also at a respectful distance.

Schomberg says that one of the boys then took some fire, probably a blazing torch and went up to the *Mahandeo Dur*, or house of the great gods. This is the shrine called *Malos* by Chitralis and *Malosh* by Hidayatullah. He told us that it was their sacred place where oaths are taken and sometimes a goat is sacrificed to propitiate the deities concerned in rain-making. A stone altar built into the hillside just above the dancing floor is adorned with horses' heads and there *saruz*, juniper wood, is kindled, a kid seized, its throat cut and the blood and milk that has been collected, sprinkled on the fire.

That there is a strong connection between the Kafir mythology and that of the Mazdaism of ancient Persia seems fairly certain, both possessing ritual but little theology. Major deities are common property and *Sajjigor, Sanji* or *Sajji* is the Kafir name for the god who looks after the world under the command of the Creator who is called *Dezau, Sajjigor* bearing some resemblance to *Saoshyans,* the Zoroastrian Saviour. Milk is used in both cults and sacrifices made in the presence of fire. ' The essential part of the cult, the sacrifice of *Yasna* (sacrificial liturgy) takes place in the presence of fire; the judicial oath is sworn by fire, shining in the night; fire hunts and destroys demons; and by the evidence of ancient geographers and archaeology Iran was studded with fire temples.' Sajji was in addition, according to Holdich, the oracle consulted before entering into battle, an underlying militarism also forming the basis of Mazdaism.

Wind and fire, water and earth are all personified in the old Vedic religion, and as the elemental forces of nature formed the basis of Zoroastrianism. Fire was the most vital, not only because it was an offshoot of the sun, but the core of life itself, burning through the ages since the first caveman created and kept alive the tiny flame. There is something in all of us that responds to fire like a child to light and, in a way, our modern form of living, often without its vital spark, means a denying to ourselves of a primaeval, atavistic necessity, the close-knit family circle, its epicentre the fire.

Hidayatullah was eager to expound on Kalash beliefs and as a Muslim extraordinarily tolerant of the idolaters. Perhaps, as in many primitive communities, there were perfectly sensible economic reasons underlying many of the *tabus* still extant. During the festival of *Uchal*, for instance, anyone found picking fruit from the trees is heavily fined. The villagers may even kill one of the offender's goats and eat it, which seems a pretty severe penalty. After *Poorsh*, however, when the fruits ripen, berries are plucked and the famous wine is made from the grape and the wild white mulberry. This is partly in preparation to welcome the young men back from the summer pastures with their herds, and when they arrive, usually towards the end of September, the festival of *Budalek* is celebrated.

On the eve of the cutting of the autumn crops comes the festival of *Rat-nut*. Hidayatullah was reluctant to go into too much detail in describing the events which obviously approximate to a kind of Bacchanalian rout with a great deal of wine drinking and *laissez-faire* between the sexes. He told us in a rather shocked voice that some of the girls and even married

[1] Larousse: *World Mythology.*

women run away with men and later when their lawful husbands protest, they can, by Kafir custom, claim twice as much money as they got for the wedding *dot*. Occasionally the local Don Juan may get off with a token beating, or he may be forced to ' gift ' one of his cows or goats. There seems to be no real rancour about such ' goings on '. The Kalash are lighthearted folk and take life much as it comes.

At the beginning of winter comes the ceremony of what Hidayatullah called *Chitir-mas* and Schomberg *Chowmas*, both uncannily reminiscent of the Christian *Christmas*. For three days the Kalash shut themselves in their houses. No one is allowed to enter and intruders are beaten and turned out. When the people emerge they send food to their relatives and the men visit the graveyards. Different valleys have different customs and not all the festivals are celebrated simultaneously.

In an area, however, where amusements are few, any excuse is sufficient for a gathering, feast or dance and on one occasion, we were fortunate enough to witness one of their most interesting and, as far as we know, hitherto unreported ceremonies. We had been making our way through the Bumboret valley and near Burish we became conscious of the sound of chanting, a thin, reedy call, shrilling above the rushing waters and dying away in small cadences, plaintive yet rhythmic. Suddenly, round the corner of a stone millhouse, a wide glade opened in front of us like a gigantic natural stage, across which figures flitted to and fro in a continuous pattern of movement.

Under a giant deodar, a group of women surrounded a *charpoy*. A little below them splinters of wood flew upwards from a primitive axe and slightly to one side below a steep, grassy bank shelving down from the houses perched on the hillside, was a wide semi-circle of cooking fires, wisps of pungent smoke drifting like blue gauze through the dapple of sunlight. We had stumbled upon a Kalash funeral.

Strangely enough our totally unexpected appearance, which could well have provoked resentment, was accepted as the most natural thing in the world. Formal permission was obtained from the oldest man present for filming and taking photographs and the Kalash carried on with their ceremonies as though completely unaware of our presence. The corpse, a woman who had died that morning, was laid out on a *charpoy,* her small body lying in state, infinitely moving in its ceremonial robe of rich, embroidered brocade, in exotic contrast to the rough rope bed.

Over her, like a high priestess, leaned the woman responsible for the chanting we had heard, intoning in a high wail like a dirge a kind of saga of the dead woman's life, her hands moving with poignant eloquence back and forth above the body, finishing always with a hand swept across her breast and up into the air like the release of a bird or the departure of the spirit. Round her women relatives sat grouped like figures in a Greek frieze, still and silent. Sometimes she was joined by another woman and the two in unison took up the song.

A few yards away from the *charpoy* and a little further down the slope, chips of wood flew upwards from a rough adze as the men bent over the fashioning of the wooden coffin. Small boys clustered round were happily hacking away at bits of wood with any tools left unguarded. One plump, solemn little chap, about two years old, clad only in a long, flapping shirt, on his head an embroidered pill-box hat, was making determined efforts to clamber on top of the half-finished box, watched intently by a little girl only slightly older, wearing an outsize striped goat-hair robe, girded at the waist. Soon their mother, moving unhurriedly down the hill, her dress swaying as she walked, swept the two of them up and away with the greatest tenderness. They made no protest and were removed to the background with the minimum of fuss. We never heard, during the whole of our stay, any voices raised in anger or impatience towards a child nor any youngster being cheeky or flying into a tantrum.

A funeral among the Kalash, as we soon grew to realise, is more of a social gathering than an occasion for extravagant demonstrations of grief, and a little way from the corpse and the coffin a row of women were preparing the *chapatti* with which to feed their guests at the evening's festivities. A long line of circular iron plates without handles like old-fashioned Scottish *girdles*, each with its small fire burning below, stood alternated with wooden troughs about two feet in length. One of the women, her wide sleeves pushed back, her arm encrusted with dough up to the elbow, would scoop up a handful of the mixture from the trough and squeeze it on to the hot plate beside her in a little mound, shaping and flattening it skilfully with the back of her hand. The next woman, armed with a long piece of metal like a fish slice, lifted the edges much as we do those of pancakes, and as soon as the underside was done, flipped it over on to the next plate from which it was conveyed by a third woman to an old man busily engaged in stacking a tall wicker basket with the finished bread.

The glow from the fires flushed their cheeks and the long braids swung in slender trellises of shining black. An old woman hastily wiped her nose, a young woman her brow with the sleeves of her robe in a careless, thrown-away gesture of natural grace. There was an endless chatter and at times the men would come up with more firewood, stir one of the cooking pots bubbling away with chunks of meat, and joke with the women or tease the girls. Children ran to and fro, the girls of ten or twelve miniature replicas of their mothers.

Meanwhile small groups had been trickling in from all directions to pay their last respects, long lines of women toiling up the hillside, silhouetted against the blue of the sky like a procession of nuns in their long brown robes, hands clasped below the waistband, together with their menfolk, ready to join in the evening's festivities. Babies were gathered into their mothers' arms, given the breast modestly but unaffectedly, small bare toes curling in contentment from out the warm folds of the dresses that sheltered them, little boys wearing hand-knitted socks with chequered tops. We were told, incidentally, that had a man died there would have been singing and dancing; apparently a woman merits only singing.

Amid all the poetry of movement, the women in their long dresses, the staccato notes of colour of their fabulous head-

dresses, one of the most charming sights was the greeting ceremony. The daughter of the dead woman, a girl of singular
beauty and a natural sweetness of expression, welcomed each
new arrival with gracious elegance, advancing towards each one
with the dignity of a society hostess. With children and men the
ceremony was fairly simple; an embrace, a kiss on each cheek,
then a kiss on the back of the hand. In the case of women or
close relatives the two first embraced, kissing alternate cheeks,
then kissing the backs of each other's opposite hands. Then they
embraced again and kissed cheeks in an uninterrupted sequence
of movement like a ballet, at once touching and graceful.

Biddulph describes a similar custom of salutation in Chitral
between equals meeting after a long absence. ' After clasping
each other, first on one side, then on the other, hands are joined,
and each person in turn kisses the hand of the other. Superiors
are greeted either by kissing the hand or touching the foot '
(something we never saw the Kalash do) ' both at meeting and
parting . . . When the meeting is between two of equal rank,
the inferior kisses the hand of the superior, who in turn kisses
the former on the cheek . . .' Then he goes on, quite unwittingly,
to give us yet another Iranian clue to the origin of the Kalash . . .
' A similar practice is said to have existed among the ancient
Persians.'[1]

Near the end of the long afternoon one of the guests developed
a headache and a request for medicine snowballed into a regular
clinic, holding up all proceedings for the best part of an hour.
I did my best with the help of one of the younger men who spoke
Urdu, to offer advice and pills, bandages and ointments.
Although we could not speak each other's tongue, we managed, as women will, to understand each other very well. There
was one old lady who complained bitterly that when she walked
up hills or did any hard work she got very breathless and laying
a hand on her heart she begged for medicine to make it strong
again. It seemed scarcely surprising that she should find herself

---

[1] *Strabo*: Book XV, Chapter 3, Section 20.

out of breath on such occasions, for she looked to me to be well over seventy. I comforted her by pointing out my own grey hairs and assuring her that neither of us was young any more and that her infirmity was just one of the less agreeable accompaniments of advancing age.

About five o'clock, when the shadows began to lengthen and the colour drain from the leaves, the covering which had been laid over the woman was partially removed and the older of the two singers who had chanted her requiem put on her the two headdresses, first the narrow bandeau and then the heavy hood studded with all the small, treasured ornaments of her girlhood and in which she is laid to rest. Her face was incredibly peaceful, almost unlined and might simply have been sleeping there among the green shades. I wondered what illness had suddenly overtaken her here, so far from any hope of medical aid and thought at least how splendid to be the means of such a pleasant gathering, and to know that all one's friends and relations would be assured of music and feasting to send one on one's way.

A couple of men picked up the rough coffin, now considered as finished, and followed the other four carrying the *charpoy* with its small burden, moved off slowly under the branches, the evening sun slanting through the pale lime and darker greens in an almost translucent light, to the *Mandajao*, the burial ground. The name comes from *mandeo* meaning a coffin, and *jao*, many. Unless actually burying someone or erecting an effigy, no one is allowed within its precincts.

The coffin is laid into place above ground, on the slope reserved. The blanket covering the woman was thrown away in an almost ceremonial gesture and the body tenderly and reverently lowered into the coffin. A goatskin filled with *chapatti* was then placed beside it, whether to propitiate the gods or as a symbolic form of sustenance for the spirit on its way to whatever Nirvana the Kalash aspire to, we could not discover. In fact, apart from a natural reluctance to intrude upon these final rites, I was not too anxious to draw any more attention to my presence than was absolutely necessary, for women are *tabu* in the vicinity of the *Mandajao,* so Stewart took the final pictures while I tried to efface myself in the background.

The lid of the coffin was weighted down with a large stone as a precaution against marauding animals, a few pieces of *chapatti* scattered on top and everyone moved off. After a funeral little attention is paid to the grave, such a sensible attitude compared to the macabre pilgrimages carried out, often more as an outward show and of no possible benefit to the empty shell mouldering beneath. As these Kalash graveyards are invariably built on a hillside unsuitable for agriculture, the spring torrents make havoc among the wooden coffins and we found many of them lying open, with cowrie shells, bracelets and trinkets scattered among the bones, but no one would dream of despoiling them.

Indeed, Stephen Halliday of the Cambridge Chitral Expedition reported that because of a bad harvest in 1960 many of the big fruit trees belonging to the Kalash had been mortgaged to men down in Ayun. The owner of the field however was allowed to keep any fruit he could reach with a stick of agreed length. When it was suggested jokingly to one man that he would be better off if he stood on a log, he was genuinely shocked. ' That wouldn't be honest!' It was understood in his agreement with the Ayun man that the stick would be used only from the ground.

There is much in the Kalash religion that is simple animism. Their lives are governed by a complicated system of *tabus.* These vary from valley to valley where sometimes women are segregated in a special house called the *Bashali* during menstruation and childbirth, the length of time of their solitary confinements varying among the different tribes. Schomberg notes that in Birir a woman has to remain apart for three months after her confinement as against a month in Rumbhor and fifteen days in Bumboret. The custom of erecting wooden effigies to commemorate the dead, like so many other customs, seems to be disappearing. We did come across several wooden figures outside villages representing the tutelary deity or guardian of the inhabitants but unfortunately only too many of these now rare specimens have been bought up or carried away by so-called archaeologists, and some of the finest examples will never be seen again in their native setting.

We hope to return one day and try to discover more of life among the Kalash and as we distributed the last of our sweets and small offerings among the children and took leave of Murayik and her family and our dear Hidayatullah, we felt that we had lived for a short while in Paradise. Contact with civilisation is not always the wonderful benefit we are led to believe, and the Kalash way of life still maintains, in marked contrast to many better developed areas, a childlike innocence and an honesty that has never known envy and we could only hope that whatever else may come their way, they will be able to preserve for a little longer the simple happiness they were generous enough to share with two visitors from the outside world.

10

A Royal Holiday

A very merry, dancing, drinking
Laughing, quaffing and unthinking time.
John Dryden : Secular Masque

Back in Chitral itself, through the kindness of Major (now
Colonel) Mumtaz Khan and the courtesy of the Commanding
Officer, Lt. Colonel Zia-ul-Haq (since retired), we were invited
to dine and spend the night in the Mess of the Chitral Scouts at
Drosh, 15 miles from Ayun. I only now realise the signal honour
that was done me, as women are not normally allowed into a
Mess except on special occasions, and whatever else may have
crumbled, deteriorated or simply suffered a sea-change with the
wave of nationalism that swept the country at Partition, Paki-
ston's fighting forces have yielded not an inch of the tradition
that was established by British officers. We were once again in
the tracks of Younghusband when in 1895 he made his epic dash
ahead of the main force to the Relief of Chitral.

It was becoming increasingly difficult to accept the fact of
Chitral's stormy past; that this pleasant Fort stood near the
scene of one of the bloodiest battles in the history of its Kator
Rulers. In 1894 Mr. George Curzon, future Viceroy of India, his
party in England being out of office, was touring in Hunza and

the Pamirs and visited the town of Chitral with Younghusband where Nizam-ul-Mulk gave them a warm welcome. We are told that they played polo and dined together and the Mehtar rode out with them for several miles to say goodbye. This was the last they saw of him. Less than three months later, this attractive young ruler was murdered by his half-brother and his country plunged into war.

The Fort at Drosh which we were now visiting was built during the following year and rises in a series of terraces surrounded by carefully-tended gardens, like an oasis in the barren hills. Dahlias, sunflowers, asters and blue nasturtium creepers flowered under the white-washed walls of the Mess and green lawns spread themselves beneath apple and walnut trees. It was all incredibly neat; the Gothic arch of the main door outlined in stone; the oriel windows standing out like small sentry boxes, the glass in square panes and the wooden beams inset above painted black like an old English country pub. Two shining cannon flanked the entrance to the Guard House. They were seized from the Afghans in the 1919 war and presented to the Fort by the then Mehtar of Chitral, and every time we moved in or out the Quarter Guard turned out with embarrassing speed and precision. From the terrace we looked north-east over the Chitral valley, clumps of trees like a Constable landscape surrounding the *Nagor* or palace of the Governor of Drosh, while due west the hills climbed steeply up to the Shera Shing Pass leading into Afghanistan.

Tea was laid on the lawn, presided over by Major Mumtaz Khan's pretty wife, and joined by her brother Abdul Rab and Ayuz, the Forest Officer, we revelled in the unaccustomed luxury of silver teapots, dainty china and deck chairs, while Zaib and Ghazala, the Agency Surgeon's two children, played with Colonel Zia's white Pomeranian, Timms. Naturally the talk turned to other Forts and legends of their past. It was exciting to learn that a Chinese administrator once lived in the fort at Chitral. Mumtaz explained that under the T'ang dynasty Chitral was subject to a Chinese overlord and that once the Chinese

Empire had extended across the Pamirs and even to the south of the Hindu Khush.

The place called Shosht, lying north of Mastuj near the Baroghil Pass, was apparently known as Shuyist, and is referred to in the T'ang annals as the chief place of the territory of Shang-mi or Mastuj, in the eighth century A.D. Chinese remains have actually been found at Gasht and there was also a Chinese fort at Brep. We also discovered that the orpiment (*Arsenical pyrites*) for which Chitral was famous was stored at the Brep fort. These mines are known to be of great age and are all between 10,000 and 16,000 feet above sea level. They were first worked, it is believed, by the Chinese and many of the people who then lived in Chitral were taken away as prisoners to Yarkand. There is a tradition that the Chinese used to levy a tax ' in a kind of glow-worm ' and one wonders what these little creatures could have been used for.

After tea we were taken up to our quarters in the Officers' Mess where we washed and changed in unusual comfort and then joined our friends in the Mess for drinks and – for Stewart – billiards. Looking round there was little doubt but that its former residents, whose ghosts seemed to linger in dining hall and drawing room, had been remembered with affection and certainly esteem. The regimental silver shone, mirrored in polished walnut and inscribed with the names of so many British officers long since gone.

The dining room was magnificent and I can only hope that if any of that gallant band who used to sit here remain, they will not feel it a blot on the Scouts' history that their Pakistani successors admitted a mere woman to their table. They will remember the silver candelabra, the walls hung with beautiful snow leopard pelts and mounted heads of markhor, oorial and ibex. To keep the record straight and to our almost speechless delight Major Mumtaz Khan presented each of us with the Regimental Crest, a silver markhor in the form of a brooch, which we treasure and wear as the most humble *ex officio* members of the Chitral Scouts.

Kalash women dancing.

On the road to Bumboret.

Women chanting over the corpse at the funeral at Burish.

Cooking for the feast after the funeral.

Prince Burhanuddin chats with Stewart and other guests.

Road over mountai

That night a message came through to announce the birth of Prince Burhanuddin's first grandson and we were all invited to the three-day feast to celebrate this momentous occasion. In the morning everyone who could get away piled into Jeeps, and driven by Major Mumtaz Khan we set off post haste for Chitral. Burhan's home was in a ferment. All day long servants rushed to and fro preparing food for the guests. Priceless Persian carpets were laid end to end on the green lawns beneath the walnut and chinar trees and tables spread with dazzling, white lace-edged cloths groaned with food and wine. Every few minutes another celebrity, a local Khan or a headman, came riding in from distant villages on spirited, curvetting stallions with much indiscriminate firing of ancient flintlocks, taller than their owners and liable to explode like a home-made grenade, showers of sparks shooting off in all directions.

One felt that they might almost have been the same weapons used with such pride by Babur's men when they came to the storming of Bajaur. They were certainly new to the Bajauris for Babur wrote: ' As the Bajauris had never before seen matchlocks (*tufang*), they at first took no care about them, indeed they made fun when they heard the report and answered it by unseemly gestures.' This rude reception must have been short-lived for Babur records with satisfaction that ' on that day Ustad Ali Quli shot at and brought down five men with his matchlock.' Babur here and in other places throughout his memoirs calls his larger ordnance ' *firingi* ' a proof that they were recognised as having their origin in Europe, *firingi* being used to describe a foreigner or infidel. It was evidently the Turks, who because of their constant intercourse with the nations of the west, excelled in the use of artillery and when heavy cannon were first used in India, Europeans or Turks were engaged to serve them.

A steady flow of Chitrali dishes emerged in an endless procession from the kitchens in gargantuan proportions, goat being the predominating delicacy, becoming progressively ' higher ' as the days wore on. Maize was pounded feverishly at the side of the compound in the same way that it has been for centuries,

H

the principle similar to that used by the Chakmas of the Chittagong Hill Tracts whom we watched, a thousand miles away, preparing their rice.

At night a roaring fire added its quota of fireworks, lighting up the circled figures, row upon row of hunched-up knees in grey *shalwar*, the faces sculptured by the flickering glow, reflecting starkly the bone structure of Greek, Tartar and Mongol. To the wild, insistent rhythm of *surnai*, drum and flute, the gay heart of the Chitrali people flowed out under the feet of the tireless dancers, all male, who whirled and stamped, singly or in pairs, arms outstretched, completely unselfconscious, graceful and proud. The moon soared upwards fighting its way through the fine mesh of apricot and almond leaves as we sat in state in the first row, warmed not only by Prince Burhanuddin's incomparable wine but by the friendliness that lapped us round.

In the middle of the evening, largely due to the diuretic effects of the wine with which Burhan kept our glasses constantly replenished, I was forced to excuse myself from the entertainment. This in itself posed quite a problem, first to cleave a passage through the tight-packed throng behind me and then to scramble over the rough terracing, my torch weaving a slightly erratic pattern up towards the house. There we had our private bathroom complete with stone bath and square concrete Pakistani toilet.

Throwing open the door an extraordinary sight met my eyes. In one corner a small lantern flickered uncertainly, lending a kind of dioramic quality to the bizarre scene. Every inch of the floor was stacked with teetering pillars of plates, bowls, dishes and cooking utensils. In the midst of this chaotic spectacle, a couple of servants crouched on the edge of the bath like bulls in a china shop, brown hands sloshing water with gay abandon over the greasy crockery, dish towels draped over their shoulders and grinning happily at the miniature sea that washed around them. They were no whit abashed by my arrival and it took a good ten minutes to impress them with the fact that ' I wanted to be alone.'

In the intervals between the dancing, our host kept us amused with a fund of historic and legendary anecdotes, one of which has its counterpart in the *halela zurd* that features in a similar tale told on the North West Frontier. Long ago, the Prince's story ran, there lived a princess who suffered continually from ill-health. A local *hakim* of some repute was at last called in and gave her a small dose of a potent medicine which he assured her would make her well again. A miracle ensued and the princess regained her strength and spirits and lost no time in telling all her friends about her remarkable recovery.

The news of this powerful drug reached the ears of one of her enemies, preparing at that moment to mount an attack on the princess' army. 'Well,' he thought to himself, 'if such a small dose restored her Highness's vigour so quickly, then we will order a double dose for each of our men, they will become like giants and emerge victorious!' So in secret he sent for the *hakim* and demanded a large quantity of the medicine with which he dosed his army. Burhan shook with laughter. 'Not one of the soldiers was able to stand on his feet long enough to fire a shot!' The *hakim's* remedy had been croton oil, one drop of which acts as a most powerful purgative. Far into the night we sat listening and watching, caught up in a dream-like sequence, the women of the household segregated in their own quarters, shut in behind high walls. Still sufficiently bound by tradition never to trespass beyond them unless wearing the all-enveloping *burqa* proper to their position as members of the ruling house, they nevertheless welcomed me unreservedly, with not the least hint of envy that I was free to come and go where they were not. They fed me with pomegranates and apples and our worlds met over the new-born infant asleep in his mother's arms.

After the celebrations, impressively mounted by Burhan, Stewart riding the horse that had won the *Buzkashi* and subsequently bought by the Prince, we rode out in style together to his hunting lodge. There across the Chitral river, spanned by a narrow wooden bridge, a tiny stone pillbox at either end, the house lay tucked into the hillside and almost smothered in vines.

Here the Prince made his wines. While we rested comfortably in the panelled living room, he busied himself decanting bottles one into the other to clear the wine. These he kept under lock and key, standing in serried rows in small cupboards beneath a carpeted *dais* which we regarded with some curiosity.

'That's where my religious friends say their prayers,' he twinkled. 'Do they know what's underneath?' Stewart asked. 'Oh yes, indeed!' he replied, 'but they drink my wine and get a little high, then they climb up there and pray to Allah and go even higher!'

Our last sight of Burhanuddin was on the airstrip just before our departure. We had ridden gloriously down from his house, galloping wildly the length of the airfield in a last medieval gesture before transferring ourselves unwillingly to modern transport. Leaving us under the trees with the horses, he hurried off to return bearing in his arms a magnificent carpet, brilliant in home-dyed wool, his parting gift. It hangs on the wall above me as I write and together with his latest letter brings back some of the magic of that enchanting State.

11

Uddiyana

In climate it is glorious, lovelier far than Kabul,
Bleak is Kabul. Swat is mild and gentle,
Its air and verdure are like unto Kashmir,
Though it spreads not out so finely;
In every home there are cascades and fountains,
Fine cities there are, fine dwellings and fair markets,
Such a country, with such a clime and such streams,
Wherein every place is by nature a garden of flowers,
Hath no homes, no gardens, no fragrance or freshness,
For the Yusufzais have made of it a desert.
Swat is made to give kings gladness.
Every place in it befits a prince,
But the Yusufzais have no such feelings,
And have made of it a desolate hostel.

Khushhal Khan Khatak : Tr. Sir Olaf Caroe

Although the Khatak poet Khushhal Khan's incursions into
Swat were largely occupied in waging an indecisive war with the
inhabitants the Yusufzais, who from the days of Akbar to
Aurangzeb had led the resistance movement against Moghal
aggression, he was too honest an observer and too much of a
poet not to be moved by the beauty of the country around him.
At the beginning of its civilised history it was known in Sanscrit

as Uddiyana – 'the garden' and the name of Swat was first given to its river system because of the quality of its waters which are white and clear, or ' *sweta* '.

Khushhal, weary of the pursuit of the elusive Yusufzais and their guerilla tactics among their native hills, must often have found a camp for his Khataks by the side of that milk-blue river, fed by the melting snows from Mankial. One can see him plunging his bearded face into the icy torrent, a hand resting on a slate-grey boulder polished smooth as glass over the centuries, wiping his brow with a corner of his *chaddur*, his eyes like a hawk scanning the pines and deodar rising tall above the banks, one half of his mind registering its beauty. Somewhere along these reaches Babur took to wife Bibi Mubarika, daughter of a Yusufzai chief; Alexander before him pursued the wild Assekenoi, and Huien Tsang, the intrepid Chinese traveller touring Peshawar and Swat in A.D. 644, perhaps like Ruth was ' sick for home' as he wandered under the apricot, peach and almond blossom flowering in some gentle valley, the sun warming his bones after the biting winds and bitter snows of the high Pamir.

Khushhal's family, the Khataks, feudal aristocrats of the time, occupied that part of what is now Pakistan, between Attock and Nowshera, where the Kabul and Indus meet in a great turbulence of whirlpool and current, blue and yellow like the Thompson and the Fraser. He and his ancestors before him were, by royal appointment, the hereditary chiefs who looked after the stretch of the Grand Trunk Road between Attock and Peshawar with the right of collecting tolls at Akbar's ferry across the Indus, where the Attock bridge now spans the river below the great fort. No doubt the Khataks were required to supervise the *Mallahs*, the boatmen Akbar imported from the Juma and settled nearby, bestowing upon them the revenue from a village for their support. Their descendants still live on the other side of the Indus at a place called *Mallahitola*, ' colony of boatmen '. He would also have to organise comforts and refreshments for the Moghals and their suite when that glittering retinue rested for the night on its way to and from Delhi, much as King

James V of Scotland commanded his subject Jock Howieson to do likewise at the ' Queen's Ferry ' on the River Forth.

The Khatak family background could well have been that of an early Scottish clan, a bloodstained tapestry of continuous strife against the Yusufzais, the aftermath of Akbar's attempt to bring them under Moghal rule, during which the opportunist Khataks quietly annexed parts of Yusufzai territory. Both Khushhal's father and grandfather were victims of the ensuing blood feud, espousing the Moghal cause. Then suddenly the Khatak monopoly of the Indus tolls was brought to an abrupt conclusion by Aurangzeb, the last of the Moghals, who granted an Imperial Mandate for the abolition of tolls on the river, an act greatly resented by Khushhal. Having served the Moghals for the best part of twenty years, he took it as a personal slight, an offence against his honour as a Pathan, a people who had little respect for authority as such.

Worse was to come. At the age of 51, the Imperial sun having set upon Khatak territory, Khushhal was despatched in chains to Delhi where he was imprisoned. For six long years he meditated upon the Moghal attitude and poured out in verse his longings for home

Oh gentle morning breeze, shouldst thou pass by Khairabad,
Or should thy way lead thee by the side of Surai's stream,
Whisper to them my greetings again and yet again . . .

Restored to his beloved Khairabad, he resigned his chieftainship in favour of his eldest son and became, at the age of 51, the moving spirit in a rebellion against his former Emperor. For the remainder of his life he sought to unite the tribesmen against their common enemy, even penetrating Swat again in peace, to seek assistance from his erstwhile enemies, the Yusufzais.

Generally accepted as the greatest of the Pashtu poets, Khushhal is said to have combined the qualities of Burns and Wallace and, strangely reminiscent of Babur the first of the Moghals, like him he was as mighty with the sword as with the pen. Gifted with the same keen powers of observation, the ability to interpret them and an equally hedonistic approach to life itself, both men in later life displayed a depth of religious oratory, manifested in a kind of poetic confessional. But where Babur rarely revealed any deep love of women, Khushhal found them irresistible. Nothing that Babur wrote could approximate to Khushhal's frank appraisal of the Afridi girls of the Kohat Pass so brilliantly translated by Sir Olaf Caroe:

Fair and rosy are the Adam Khel maidens,
Among them are beauties of every type,
Large eyes they have, long lashes, and arched brows,
Sugar lips, flowered cheeks, and foreheads like the moon,
Tiny are their mouths as pouting rosebuds,
Their teeth are even and white,
Their skin so soft and glossy, and hairless as an eggshell,
Their feet delicate, rounded the leg line and their hips
    magnificent,
Slender of belly, their breasts full and firm, and small waisted
    are they;
In stature straight as the letter Alif, and fair of colour –
Like the hawk has been my flight upon the mountains,
And many a plump pretty partridge has been my prey;
The hawk, young or old, seeks its quarry,
But the swoop of the old hawk errs not;
Love's affairs are like fire, O Khushhal,
What though the flame be hidden, the smoke is seen.[1]

Three hundred years after his death, his poems are still eagerly recited in the *hujras* of the North West Frontier, just as the battles in which he took part are remembered from father to son, and the past, in this word of mouth way, is conjured up and relived over and over again. The Yusufzais of Swat look back with pride on their unbroken independence. ' Never in all history,'

[1] *The Pathans*: Sir Olaf Caroe.

said the Miangul Gulshahzada Abdul Wadud, father of Swat's present ruler, ' not even in the time of Akbar or Aurangzeb, much less under the Durranis, were the Yusufzais of this country subjects of any empire.'[1] Perhaps it was this background of independence which has given to Swat its atmosphere of complete freedom, an intense inward pride and sense of purpose, which was finally welded into one under the leadership of the Miangul Gulshahzada, known as Badshah Sahib, the father of the State of Swat and grandson of Hazrat Abdul Ghafoor, Akund of Swat and chief of the Yusufzais.[2]

It is not merely the beauty of the landscape that attracts the casual visitor, but a deeper integrity, carefully husbanded and directed by its rulers. In the VISITOR'S BOOK of the fine State-run hotel at Saidu Sharif, capital of Swat, a long line of illustrious names from all over the world testify to the peculiar quality of fascination exerted by the country and its people, each page a growing miscellany of tributes to this ' paradise on earth '; this 'Shangri-la '; this ' Place to which one will always return ' Ten years had passed since I first sat in that garden, the mountain air sharp with the smell of pine, the splash of water in the fountain behind me and the heady perfume of the ' lily of the night' casting its own net of enchantment about me. It seemed important to me now that I should return, and yet I was reluctant lest the spell be broken. Places and peoples have a habit of diminishing in stature on second sight and disillusionment of this kind is one of the hardest things to bear. But somehow, in the way these things have, everything was arranged and I was on my way.

From Peshawar the road leads out across the Kabul by way

[1] Olaf Caroe: *The Pathans.*
[2] Since our visit, the Wali of Swat, H.H. Jehanzeb has handed over his powers as Ruler to Pakistan authority and an era has come to an end. Politics lie outside the scope of this book and I suppose it may be fitting that the State of Pakistan should take over the reins of Government, but to all of us who knew Swat under its previous unique system, it can never be quite the same; we can only hope and pray that its qualities in some measure, can be maintained.

of Charsadda, where in 1867 the Green Howard Hounds, precursors of the famous Peshawar Vale Hunt, hunted jack one day a week, the other at Nowshera; where in the early days subscribers from Jamrud hacked over from the Khyber with a cavalry escort, and as late as 1930 ladies were allowed to hunt for only one month in the season and revolvers were carried by order. That part of the country between the Swat River and the Kabul has been eloquently described in the Hunt Records of 1870, the writer affirming that ' the far-famed shires of the Eusafzai Valley have long been acknowledged to be the only real hunting country in India.'

There is something at once childlike and touching in the dedication with which these *aficionados* of the hunt pursued this peculiarly British sport under the very noses of the recalcitrant tribesmen, within range alike of the sniper's bullet or the dacoit's knife, lurking like the jackal in the reed beds. That they got away with it may be due in no small measure to the fact that the ethics of the sport probably appealed to the Pathan sense of humour and his innate admiration for audacity in any form, or perhaps simply to a petrified bewilderment at the whole mystique of the cult whereby a man pursues with equal zest an animal or a human being. Like Drake, the Englishman ' wouldst see the game out ' then play out the rubber with the Pathans.

Perhaps the most significant result is that the Hunt's most ardent followers, at least during my short experience, have been those very Pathans whose fathers, crouching above a rock-strewn *nullah*, an old *jezail* at the ready, listened to the huntsman's horn and the Master's cry of ' Gone Away . . .!' echoing as wildly and as shrill as ' the flying bullet down the pass.'

My own heart rose and sang, untunefully I feel sure, as we bumped along between the *khets,* the fields of sugar cane, the wide *nullahs* and the familiar sand-coloured villages where the small morning cooking fires sent their blue signals upwards like a prayer, that lead on to the tree-lined roads around Mardan. Eight miles or so from the Memorial Arch to the Queen's Own

Corps of Guides, still mirrored in its own reflection in that quiet garden, are the rock edicts of Asoka and nearby, crowning the hillside, is the ancient monastery of Takht-i-Bahi, dating from A.D. 19 when the Arsacid Parthian dynasty of Ctesiphon sat in government over Gandhara and the northern Punjab.

Such are the tricks of memory ' which often hazy as a dream about the most important events of a man's life, religiously preserve the merest trifle ' that I also remember at Takht-i-Bahi the pride and joy of a Pathan mechanic who showed me a lathe discarded by the North Western Railway Workshops in 1902, which he then ran with great success by electricity and a smith making uncanny replicas of what we call in Scotland ' girdles ' but elegantly patterned in a conventional flower design.

We passed the railhead at Dargai, the impressive Power House where I had photographed endless transformers; switchgear; the rich burnt umber of ceramic circuit breakers strung against a brassy sky, and the shining steel spider's web of transmission towers, beneath the suspicious eyes of government officials ready to pounce should I transgress the strict security precautions under which I worked and allow even the tiniest patch of surrounding country to appear in my films. We had taken tea that day with one of the Pakistani engineers who proudly drew my attention to an almost perfect Gandharan figurine of the Buddha, picked up during the excavations but almost unrecognisable. I stared in dumb horror. ' It was so dirty,' he beamed, ' so we painted it this nice shiny black, isn't it ?'

The Malakand Pass to which we were now committed is one of the three natural gateways through the mountains from the vale of Peshawar leading through Dir and Chitral on to the Pamirs and China. Far below the motor road, to the centre of which our Government transport bus clung with obstinate tenacity and a fine disregard for oncoming traffic, hairpin bends and the ever-increasing drop into the Yusufzai Valley, meanders the narrow track clinging to the skirts of the mountains, along which nearly 2,000 years ago Buddhist pilgrims trekked into India by way of Kashmir to pay homage at the shrine of the ashes of Buddha in the Kanishka Stupa outside Peshawar.

Above us at the head of the Pass, squarely planted on its summit like a cardboard cut-out, squatted the old Malakand Fort, built in 1907. Once noisy with the clatter of arms, commanding the valley and the sniper's bullet, it now looks down incongruously on the neat valve house and shining penstocks of Jabhan Power Station. Here the milky waters of the Swat River, gathered from the flat green rice fields above Amandara and tunnelled through the sheer rock, are harnessed to produce hydro-electric power, then spilling out from the great turbines are sent on in a slender thread of shining canals to irrigate the Yusufzai plain and once again be used as a source of power at Dargai.

Only the fort and eyeless picquets strung out over the hillsides, remain as eloquent reminders of the Malakand Campaign in which Sir Winston Churchill got himself involved as a war correspondent and whose letters from the Front for the *Pioneer* newspaper, were also to be published simultaneously in England in the *Daily Telegraph*.

The Frontier had become a kind of proving ground for young officers, a fact of which the Pathan *jawan* took full advantage. Like their counterparts in the Highlands, the Pathans were continuously and assiduously engaged in complicated and bloodthirsty family and tribal feuds. The slightest provocation or insult, real or imagined, to the *nang* or honour of the Pathan was enough, and vengeance was swift. Every house in tribal territory still has its watch tower; the only fleeting truce then observed was during harvest time.

' Into this happy world the nineteenth century brought two new facts; the breech-loading rifle and the British Government. The first was an enormous luxury and the second an unmitigated nuisance . . . a weapon which would kill with accuracy at 1,500 yards opened a whole new vista of delights to every family or clan which could acquire it . . .', the only fly in the ointment being the unsportsmanlike policy of Her Majesty's Government, which not only extracted fines for the unbridled use of this new toy, but proceeded to punish its users and build roads into country that had been a happy hunting ground for generations.

The whole character of the ensuing campaigns whether in Swat or the Tirah, Waziristan or the Khyber, engendered a kind of exhilaration on both sides and its heroes, British or Pathan, were equally respected. Churchill was no exception and recalls with marked enjoyment the singing of Kiplingesque songs before battle. No one was blind to what the morning might bring and one must remember that the young men who sang so blithely:

> And England asks the question,
> When danger's nigh,
> Will the sons of India do or die?

did indeed stand always 'on the lovely brink of death', that dawn more often than not rose on the spectacle of the auctioning of a comrade's clothes, rifles and necessities of war. Churchill himself was outfitted in this manner, an economic proposition that augmented meagre supplies often months late in arriving at the front lines and obtained for the officer's worldly goods the best possible prices.

In the Mess 'noble sentiments' were given free and appropriate rein in such rousing chorusses as:

> Great White Mother, far across the sea,
> Ruler of our Empire may she ever be.
> Long may she reign, glorious and free,
> In the great White Motherland . . .

a pointed reflection on the accepted attitude of the age. But if we imagine that in the twentieth century we have the sole monopoly of what we believe to be advanced thinking in respect of racial equality, listen to the lines of one of these Pathans, Khushhal Khan himself, written three hundred years ago: 'All thy creatures white and black bear witness that thou alone art God: thou, the Lord dost encompass all things, whether they be

fair or in darkness.' It is not always remembered that Queen
Victoria caused a proclamation to be made that once hung in
the Victoria Memorial on Calcutta's *maidan,* which was intended to be a kind of British charter of rights for her subjects
' regardless of creed or colour ' or that she celebrated her 70th
birthday by undertaking a course in Hindustani, corresponding
regularly with Lady Lansdowne, wife of the then Viceroy, in
that language, beautifully transcribed in Persian characters. At
that particular moment when the young Churchill was being
carried by *tonga* forty miles across the plains from the railhead,
then at Nowshera, and over the Malakand Pass, the Great White
Mother's subjects on the North West Frontier were in no mind
to be ruled by anyone and would have been the first to refute
the mere idea that any human being, be he son of India or the
Great White Mother herself, could be their equal.

On my first visit to Swat, in response to a request for an interview with the Wali, I was fortunate enough, along with a friend,
to be invited to breakfast. The Palace is an unpretentious,
spacious building divided into three wings. Stepping out of the
car, we were met by His Highness's Private Secretary and on
entering we were introduced without any pretence at ceremony
to the Wali himself who had come out to meet us and greeted
us warmly. He led us into his drawing room, a long, sunlit
lounge which reflected the character of its owner in unostenta-
tious quiet grace. There we sat and chatted about our impressions
of the State and of how we had found it so much more civilised
than many of the so-called advanced countries we had known
in our travels. The Wali modestly disclaimed any credit for what
we had seen, emphasising the fact that it was his people who
had made it what it was. My eyes strayed inevitably to the well-
filled bookshelves and I was struck by the truly catholic taste
that they displayed; the classics, administration, engineering,
gardening, the latest contributions to science, technology, travel
and biography.

Breakfast had been laid in the panelled dining room. Looking
back my memory is laced with unforgettable impressions of that

meal; of morning sunlight glinting on silver and napery of conversation that ranged over the world; of great dishes of fresh fruit grown in the gardens and of the vista of hills and valleys seen through the open windows. Perhaps more than all these however, was the impact made by the simple, compelling charm of the Wali himself; of his versatile and agile brain, his wide knowledge of world affairs and his quiet humour.

At first, naturally enough, we talked of the State and of plans for the future. The Wali rather wistfully remarked that he doubted whether all his schemes would come to fruition during his lifetime. With a population of nearly half a million and an income then of only three million rupees, the strictest and most rigid economy had to be practised and a budget adhered to that admitted of no luxuries. I reflected bitterly how the balancing of books comes in the way of real progress and how economic aid by more fortunate countries could go such a long way in the hands of a man of integrity and goodwill.

A decade later and Miangul Jehanzeb is welcoming me once again, his figure perhaps a little thicker, a few more lines here and there, but the same alert, quietly confident personality. Related by marriage now to Ayub Khan, his sons Prince Amir Zeb and Prince Aurangzeb are married to the daughters of that great soldier-statesman who controlled the fortunes of Pakistan with wisdom and justice at a time when the country needed it most. I had another link with Swat now in Prince Amir Zeb, who with his wife Jamila, was a frequent visitor to the home of our very dear friends, Iqi and Nishat Shahban in Rawalpindi, who gave us so unstintingly of their hospitality and to whom we repaired for comfort and relaxation between our various journeys.

How often did we arrive out of the blue, dusty, tired and unmistakably travel-stained, to find without fail the immaculate figure of Iqi's driver Najam, smiling a welcome as though we were important guests instead of the most ordinary travellers. When, as sometimes happened, their house was full, their friends would rally round and like Lieutenant General Latif Khan, accept us as we were and lavish upon us all the luxuries large and small which we had been denied for so many weeks.

Rawalpindi became for us a kind of Mecca. Had it not been for all the kindness, understanding and practical help we received there, I doubt whether we could have made these journeys at all. My old friends General Shahid Hamid and his wife entertained us, loaded us with advice and letters of introduction, and there we met Prince Aurangzeb and his wife, and sometimes Nishat, myself and the two sisters who were also sisters-in-law made expeditions to the cinema together. All of these simple pleasures helped to keep our sanity during many difficult weeks, when it sometimes seemed as though we would never get the required permission to visit or stay in the places on which we had set our hearts.

12

Of Gujars and Emeralds

'A fruitful countrey, inhabited with pasturing people, which dwell in the Summer season upon mountaines, and in Winter they remove into the valleyes without resorting to townes or any other habitations: and when they remoove, they doe journey in carravans or troops of people and cattell, carrying all their wives, children and baggage upon bullocks.'

Hakluyt's Principal Voyages: Anthony Jenkinson

Next morning the Wali most graciously set a jeep and driver at our disposal so that I could show Stewart something of the State and the enchantment of Swat Kohistan, the upper part of the valley, with its tiny villages set in a mosaic of stone walls supporting narrow ledges like a giant's staircase where small crops grow, meticulously husbanded. Gaudy heaps of orange maize were piled up on the flat roofs to be sent spiralling into the air in a cascade of golden rain from flat wooden flails. A thread of a suspension bridge spans the shining peacock blue of the Swat River, a man swaying like a tightrope walker back and forth from the sawmill on the opposite bank, a thick plank of yellow pine on his shoulders, while the narrow gorges are chequered with the pageantry of Gujar caravans, the nomadic herdsmen of the Kohistan, on their long trek south to winter pastures.

The practice of transhumance is a special and peculiar response to the environment and the only possible way to utilise limited geographical opportunities. There are thousands of these Gujars in the upper valleys of Swat, Dir and the Yusufzai Saman of Mardan, one of the latter's largest villages being called *Gujar Garhi*, literally ' the town of the Gujars '. The original Gujars are believed to have been helots of the White Huns or Epthalites. The only mention of these White Huns before they crossed the Hindu Khush seems to have been made by the Chinese, whose indication is that they were the only Huns to have white skins and regular features and did not speak either Mongolian or Turkish. As vassals of a people of Mongol stock and because of their wanderings in northern Turkestan there may well have been more than a hint of Turco-Iranian blood in their background.

We met the Gujars on the road, much as I used to encounter the Powindahs from Afghanistan streaming through the Bolan Pass, their flocks ambling before them, their family belongings on camel or donkey, in a long, dusty procession, endless, like a great migration. I sometimes wonder how we ever succeed in getting anywhere; half our lives seem to be spent in simply looking after our possessions and instead of owning them it is they who own us. Like tethered sheep, we can move only within a small, circumscribed area bound by a stranglehold of domestic ties we are too frightened to break.

Although the Ghilzai too are believed to stem from the White Huns and have much in common with the Gujars, the latter are herdsmen pure and simple, unarmed, carrying on an age-old way of life, an all-enduring race, thrifty and industrious with no ambition but to be left alone with their cattle and fields. The Ghilzai or Ghaljis are the most numerous and probably the most valiant of all Afghan tribes and not all are nomadic. They have preserved, unlike the Gujars, a pride and fierceness tacitly respected in Pakistan and although their women too are unveiled, it would be a brave man who would risk making any overtures. A family's goods and chattels, known as *kaddi*, are carried on camels, the women usually walking, the men armed and mounted on horseback. In addition came the *charra log* the unencumbered, who had come without their families to work as labourers or hawkers for the season.

The Gujar women, although perhaps lacking in the striking, barbaric qualities of the Ghilzai, are splendid creatures with the most upright carriage imaginable. As very small children the girls learn to walk with miniature baskets on their heads and by the time they are in their teens they balance enormous wicker ones easily and gracefully, stacked with all their household goods. Politely interested in fellow travellers, they are disinclined for conversation as they walk on their way with long, unhurried strides, a baby under one arm or a kid too young to walk. They wear baggy trousers made of coloured cotton, usually in dark reds or black and gathered in concertina folds on the outside of each leg. The *qamiz* or *kurta* may be black or patterned and often bordered or ornamented with silver discs.

Personal wealth is carried in the form of silver jewellery and one can guess their status by its richness and quality. Two of the women we met were resplendent in all their recent wedding finery and, giggling, they shyly covered their mouths with the corners of their *chaddurs* displaying wrists encased in six inches of solid silver bracelets. A *tika* shone on the forehead like a young moon and between the breasts glinted an elaborate festoon of silver about a foot in length and consisting of a number of medallions each fringed with silver chains like an outsize *pesha-waz*, the ornament that sometimes fastens the bodice of the *qamiz*. In additon, the *qamiz* itself was scattered with silver sequins that winked like stars under the dark *chaddur*.

Babies were carried in the most nonchalant way in a kind of sling passing over one shoulder vertically down to the waist where it is wound round the body, the baby cradled on one hip rather like a roll of bedding and parallel to the ground, its little head sticking out in front decked out in a padded tea cosy of a hat in muted reds with silver *tawiz* or charms sewn on it. The smaller children, too young to take to the road, are accommodated comfortably on the backs of the gentle ponies or donkeys, a head lolling between sacks of grain or bedding. One of the most charming sights was of two of these children on a white pony, a piece of cloth passing over their thighs and underneath the animal like a girth. The boy in front wore a little green cap, socks with a kind of Fair Isle pattern round the top and clung to the soft cerise, blue and white *numnah* placed over the thick *razai*, while the girl behind him, a white scarf covering her hair looked for all the world like a Dutch painting. They must have been twins and had such a solemn wise air about them although I doubt whether they could have been more than three years of age.

Each group seemed more fascinating than the last; a bevy of little girls, turning round to have another look at us, convulsed with laughter at the sight of me in my strange blue jeans and khaki shirt, giggling uncontrollably, blue-black hair cut in a straight fringe above shining dark eyes; a woman smiling, riding one of the ponies led by her husband, a young foal prancing skittishly alongside and a handsome lad of about 16 leading on a thick chain one of the great red-brown dogs used to guard the flocks from wild animals. The men walked unencumbered, occasionally carrying a sick or young animal across their shoulders, but with equally effortless ease the women bore on their heads *dekshis,* cooking pots and provisions.

' Where are you going ?' we called.

' To the sun . . . to the sun . . .' they waved.

Ten years ago the motor road came to an end at Bahrein, a strange little village whose houses straddled the rushing torrents of the mountain stream and whose women were famed for their beauty. Now Stewart and I were conveyed by Jeep to a Rest House at Kalam along an excellent metalled road, looking out over a great expanse of valley threaded with loops and ribbons of blue water where rice will grow in the summer, and thence on to the road-end at Ushu.

Perhaps one of the most glorious views in Swat is to look down from the Karakar Pass into Buner. It was the subject of one of several paintings I did during my first visit, sitting up among the rocks and the pines, the far mountain ridges standing up like jagged teeth, dividing the quilted valleys squared off into tiny fields. Here was the site of the Ambela campaign when in 1863 the Imperial Government had sent an expedition against the Yusufzais, profiting nothing by the fact that nearly 300 years before the Moghal Emperor Akbar had failed dismally trying to accomplish exactly the same exercise. History repeated itself and the life blood of several hundred British soldiers and sepoys spilled out over the ground already stained by that of 8,000 men of Akbar's Frontier Army, defeated by the Yusufzais of Swat and Buner in 1586.

By a happy coincidence, Prince Amir Zeb happened to be visiting Swat at the same time as ourselves, and as he had long promised to show us the State emerald mine which he runs, this was one of our first outings. Never having seen an emerald mine before, we had no idea as to what we should expect, and the sight of a slice of dusty biscuit coloured hillside being laid bare by groups of stalwart tribesmen was mildly astonishing. Below the swinging picks other men were shovelling rock into shallow containers which they bore off on their shoulders for sorting. There was a pleasant air of leisurely progress about the whole enterprise and what appeared to be the minimum of supervision. Close by in a grassy valley, a small square had been walled off, the bricks in a lattice-work pattern so that the cool air could blow through, and here under the shade of two enormous trees, the men rested between shifts, ate their midday meal and spread their prayer mats. Amir Zeb was also arranging for a mosque to be built for them nearby.

In the main building we were shown a basin in which pieces of rock lay soaking in acid which would eventually bite through to the emeralds inside and one of the men brought us some raw stones to look at, pale green and powdery-looking in the white, horne blende schist. On the veranda squatted a double row of young boys, each with a white plate in front of him, sorting emeralds into size, their fine-boned fingers deft and sure. It seemed incredible that these lads simply looked on this exciting task as a job of work and obviously never gave a thought to the small fortunes glowing in front of them. At rest time they pelted out to play in the courtyard. No one would have dreamed of not trusting them.

Amir Zeb kindly brought out a few emeralds on a piece of white paper so that I could photograph them in the sunlight, all £250 worth of them. Somehow he contrived to drop the lot before our horror-stricken eyes. His manager was definitely more than a trifle put out, but the Prince remained unruffled and we all got down on hands and knees and scrabbled around in the dust until we were assured that all had been recovered. Alas, it is highly improbable that ever again will I have emeralds scattered at my feet. This ancient open-cast mine is near Mingora and the output is the property of the State, sold by annual auction to dealers in gems. It is said to yield at least a million rupees a year.

The emerald, we learned, is the rare, richly verdant green variety of beryl; fine, transparent specimens of which are accepted as the most desirable of all precious stones and, like the best rubies, surpassing even the diamond in value. Emeralds have always been known and highly esteemed in India where there are several mines of great antiquity, whereas Pakistan's only emerald mine is in Swat. In the Mahabarata there are references to emeralds and indeed a treatise on gem stones dated earlier than the tenth century A.D. recognises eight classes of emeralds, the best of which must be transparent and without dust; 'pure as a drop of water on a lotus leaf', of a velvety reflection and so coloured that when exposed to the sun on the palm of the hand, it tints the whole surface.

The emerald mine, however, is not Mingora's sole claim to fame for the town itself carries in its homes and hearths tangible evidence of singular archaeological significance. Like the railway line from Sind to Lahore, much of it laid upon conveniently obtainable third millenium bricks looted from Brahminabad and Harappa, the Great Stupa of Butkara provided useful building material for the new town of Mingora. It is inevitable that one civilisation should be superimposed upon another, but the removal of vital evidence in the unravelling of past cultures for such prosaic purposes is like filching stonework from Canterbury Cathedral to build a garden privy.

From a historical and cultural point of view, Swat is now regarded as one of the most important countries of the Indo-Pakistan sub-continent and excavations by the Italian National Museum of Oriental Art and Pakistan's own Department of Archaeology reveal a historical background staggering in its immensity, and reaching from the prehistoric and proto-historic era down to the period of Muslim occupation. It is fascinating to note that the geographical horizons of the *Rigveda*, the Vedic Aryan hymns passed down from Brahman teacher to pupil, probably before 1000 B.C. and addressed to Indo-European gods, were bounded by the Gomal, Kurram and Kabul – tributaries of the Indus – and also *Suvastu,* modern Swat, the ' fair dwellings ' of Khushhal Khan's poem, and indicate Aryan settlements in Swat itself. Below settlements of an Indo-Iranian group have been found paleolithic implements, and further excavation is expected to yield more positive data.

We were greatly privileged to meet Dr. Domenico Faccenna and other members of the Expedition and see something of their discoveries which will eventually be displayed at the Museum in Saidu Sharif, capital of Swat State. Much work however, has yet to be done in this field, for near Mingora along the banks of the Jambil River there stands an almost uninterrupted succession of ruins, a chain of sites and ' Everywhere along the terraces or at the foot of the smaller valleys one finds mounds, stelae, rock-cut reliefs with the figures of Buddhas and Bodhisattvas (chiefly Lokesvara), the remains of inhabited sites and gravestones . . .'[1] In fact, the Wali once remarked to me that if every site in Swat were to be excavated there would scarcely be an acre of land left for agriculture.

The past magnificence of the Butkara sanctuary is slowly

[1]Domenico Faccenna: *A Guide to the Excavations in Swat* 1956-1962.

emerging, the chronology set by the numismatic evidence of coins once placed in the reliquary recesses by the hands of Indo-Greeks, Indo-Scythians, Parthian and Kusana, from Appolodotus II to Hormizd II. Sassanian and Kidarite coins were found in layers relating to the collapse of the Sacred Precinct, and the latest of these, Khusro II (591-628), times the destruction of the Great Stupa as around the seventh century A.D.

Grave sites in Swat indicate both inhumation and semi-cremation and yield up such diverse objects as accompanied the corpse; an iron spearhead; a naked female figure in clay; spindle whorls; copper pins; laurel-leaf blades; gold ear-rings and fragments of necklaces, each one a personal possession, a loved object surviving its owner through countless generations, and reflecting in time as in a mirror the men and women of Uddiyana ' the garden ', of Swat State.

13

Flight to Gilgit

Steep crags and precipices constantly intercept the way. These mountains are like walls of rock, standing up 10,000 feet in height. On looking over the edge, the sight becomes confused, and then on advancing, the foot loses its hold, and you are lost.

Fah Hian : A.D. 399-414

' The Captain's compliments Madam and would you and Mr. Stewart care to step into the cockpit?' Teeth chattering, limbs numb with the biting cold of early dawn, we struggled to our feet and clambered for'ard, clinging to the net strapped tight round the bulging pyramid of freight, our fingers scrabbling at the roof struts as the plane bumped and fell in the air currents, until, the envy of our less fortunate fellow-passengers, we gained the warm comfort of the cabin where we were revived with steaming cups of tea.

Below and around us hovered a fantastic landscape of tented hills, each steep as a turret roof, pierced by the dark green arrows of pines, terraces climbing the lower slopes in scallops of flat brown steps. Wheeling through the narrow valleys, spanning the deep clefts like a bridge, the Dakota's wing tips slid boldly along the mountain walls where gnarled olive trees clung to the crevices.

Soon knife-edge ridges rose up to meet us, black-streaked pinnacles dusted with the first snows, feathering down the rich brown shoulders to open out into yet another valley deep in pine sentinels, with saucers of snowlike whipped cream slipping down to the tree line. As the first streamers of dawn flooded the sky with orange and pink, saffron and lilac, the great Karakoram range unfolded itself before us, stretching away into infinity, a blue icefield furrowed and slashed into a vast landscape of crystal peaks tinged with all the colours of Aurora.

Suddenly Captain Mir's fingers stabbed the air, his voice lost in the roar of the engines, and there, far to our right, over-topping the snow crests, virginal and diamond bright, the great massif of Nanga Parbat lifted from her sea of ice. In that alien world of glacier, tower and precipice, 31 men have yielded up their lives, caught by blizzard and avalanche, from Mummery's first British attempt of 1895 until, over half a century later, Hermann Buhl crawled the last few hundred yards on his hands and knees to plant on the summit of the Silver Saddle a small Tyrolese pennant.

The corner bastion of the 1,500 mile long Himalaya range, Nanga Parbat towers over the surrounding peaks, at 26,620 feet one of the eight or nine highest in the world and one of the most formidable. Dominating the Indus Valley, we saw her later from the Haramosh plain and again from Astor and Chilas, but nothing could quite compare with that first breathtaking vision through the curved dome of the tiny cockpit, the noise of our engine a single note in the silence, the small plane vulnerable like a bird beating its wings against this immensity of space. Like lunar astronauts our loneliness seemed absolute.

Looking out over the frontiers of Tibet on the east, Chinese Turkestan (Sinkiang) on the north and Soviet Russia to the north east, the summit of Nanga Parbat lies within Pakistan territory. The south wall with Kashmir at its feet rising above the Rupal valley is one of the greatest precipices in the world.

The approaches of expeditions in the past must have been

dispiriting to say the least, for they were forced to take either the long climb across the Babusar and Burzil Passes, both routes over 150 miles long and of such height as to be impassable for the greater part of the year. Caravans of porters had to struggle through blizzards and deep snow before even beginning the ascent and it was not until the victorious German assault of 1953 that the climbers were able to make use of the same route as ourselves, by air from Rawalpindi to Gilgit, and thus save time and effort for the final climb.

The sun roared up above the horizon and the plane sheered down over Chilas while far below the Indus snaked dull chrome-green through broad, barren valleys, or streaked steely-blue beneath black rocks old as time; jagged spurs catching the swift current, the foam-flecked rapids like watered silk. Springing out of the same plateau in Tibet that has given birth to the Brahma-pootra, the Indus tumbles bright as a Scottish trout stream through its wild, rock-strewn bed between the Himalaya and the Karakoram. Coiling round the tip of the Himalaya it flows along the valleys of Shigar and Shyok in Baltistan to the broad basins of Kapalu and Skardu.

There in the distant past the glaciers of the Karakoram and Indus met, producing a vast lake and leaving in their passage the long dunes of white sand that here and there fringe the waters in the Gilgit Agency. Cutting through the Chilas gorges at the foot of Nanga Parbat, looping broadly across Indus Kohistan to plunge southwards skirting the Black Mountains, the Indus arrives at last on the plains, and joined by the Kabul above Akbar's Fort at Attock, gathering to itself the Ravi, Chenab, Jhelum and Sutlej, it flows uninterrupted to the Arabian Sea.

Over Bunji sand and scree slopes veined the hillside and plunging down to the river bed opened out on to the great flat Hara-mosh plain. Lower still and the valley floor became a mosaic of russet-edged fields in squares of donkey brown and grey. A splatter of orange from the turning walnut trees lit up under our wings and the Dakota dropped height to swoop swiftly downwards like a plummeting hawk between the mountain walls enclosing Gilgit. Flattening out, a billow of dust swirling in our wake, we taxied to a standstill.

Like Chitral, Gilgit is snowbound for six months of the year, the only means of communication by air. A regular service by Pakistan International Airlines operates daily, mainly by Fokker Friendship, occasionally by Dakota, weather permitting, between Rawalpindi and Gilgit and whenever possible to Skardu in Baltistan. Captain Mir told us that originally South American pilots were brought in to fly these routes. 'But after a couple of weeks they gave it up.' 'But why?' we asked. 'Too dangerous, they became nervous wrecks!' Mir chuckled. 'Since then well we just took it over ourselves,' and slipping back his headphones he reached forward to pick up a well-used pipe which rested on the instrument panel in front of him next to a large NO SMOKING notice.

The air route from Rawalpindi to Gilgit is said to be the most spectacular and hazardous in the world. Wild atmospheric disturbances are liable to develop suddenly above the great depths of the Himalayan valleys and the Dakota with its low ceiling, after climbing over the highest ridges, has to twist and turn within the narrow corridor of the Indus Valley. Flying a year or so later with the Bush Pilots of British Columbia's west coast in tiny float planes, Beavers and Cessnas, I would say that there is little to choose between the two areas, so far apart but with uncannily similar problems. After several trips under varying conditions we agreed with Captain Mir that no matter how many times the route was flown one still experienced the same thrill. Passing over an area not far from the Babusar Pass one day, he pointed a little to the right and said casually; 'We have to avoid that patch – they sometimes shoot us up!' Thinking we might be verging upon Indian-held Kashmir, we asked 'Enemies?' 'No, no, just local tribesmen having their little joke!'

Poised at the epicentre of Central Asia where the ancient caravan routes thread the mountain ranges like a spider's web, fanning out to Tashkent, Kashgar and Sinkiang, the Gilgit

Agency is bounded on the west by Chitral and Swat, on the north by the Afghan territory of Wakhan with Russia a mere forty miles over the Pamirs. On the south the cease-fire line between Azad and Indian Kashmir runs across the country in an uneasy truce, while for over 300 miles the Karakoram range marks the Agency's snow-bound frontiers with China. Until the advent of the air service, virtually cut off from the outside world, it was said that when the first aeroplane landed in Gilgit the people rushed to bring fodder for the Jeep it disgorged, exclaiming that the plane had given birth to a child and would fly away again – presumably abandoning its offspring !

Before the Partition of the sub-continent, the Gilgit Agency was administered by officials of the Maharaja of Kashmir with headquarters in Gilgit itself. Shortly after Partition, the Dogra rule was overthrown in a revolt led by Captain Babur, brother of the Ranee of Hunza. The Gilgitis, armed with picks, knives, farm implements and ancient muzzle loaders, fought their way to within 20 miles of Srinagar, before the Security Council of the United Nations ordered a ' Cease-fire '. In the light of subsequent events, one cannot but sympathise with the people of Gilgit in their belief that had they been allowed to march on Srinagar and free it also from Hindu domination Pakistan's relations with India would now be on a very different footing.

Although after twelve years of negotiations an agreement was reached on the supply of canal water through the Indus Waters Treaty, one must remember that three of Pakistan's rivers have their source in Kashmir and on the unrestricted supply of this vital commodity depends the prosperity of much of West Pakistan. Feelings over the entire issue still run high and the bitterness that has been engendered on both sides is too deeply engraved to be easily assuaged. And yet on an individual and personal level the links are amazingly strong. During the height of the troubles at Partition there were Pakistanis who risked their lives to save their Hindu friends and vice versa. Along with a Pakistani officer in the signals, whose entire family was saved from annihilation by the selfless devotion of two Hindus, we

visited the memorial to those who fell in the fighting for Azad
Kashmir. Unveiled by President Ayub Khan two days before
our visit, a golden ibex stands poised on a simple stone obelisk
in the Chinar Bagh just outside Gilgit, surrounded by the tawny
gold of the chinars and the lime yellow of poplars, the mountains all around and the grey Gilgit river rushing below.

' Sargun Gilgit ' – ' Happy Land of Gilgit ' as it is called in
the Shina tongue – would appear at first glance to be a singularly inappropriate epithet for a land whose 42,000 square miles
of territory have been torn by internecine strife and ravished by
the invader's sword all down the long centuries of its wild and
bloody past. In some areas today, still unmapped, rifles of ancient
vintage are carried by every male big enough to shoulder one
and tribal law matches only the intractable savagery of its
landscape. Its people are poor, isolated in deep valleys for as
many as eight months of the year. In and around Gilgit the
bright splashing streams are so deficient in iodine that they cause
a high incidence of goitre.

Roads, although miracles of construction, are mere shelves
cut out in the living rock, barely wide enough to hold a Willys
jeep, spiralling up in giddy curves or swooping breathlessly
downwards like a switchback. Indeed it was not at all unusual
to find one of our companions in a Jeep crammed with passengers becoming violently car-sick behind us. A new Indus Valley
road was then under construction which will link the Agency
with Pakistan by way of Swat and the Malakand Pass. Built a
hundred feet or so above the existing one, the old road was perforce closed to traffic at various points between the hours of
8 a.m. and 4 p.m. It was possible on occasion to arrange a signal
with the foreman of the labour gang and make a perilous dash
through, stones spattering on the roof of the Jeep, but scarcely
to be recommended.

One could not say truthfully that visitors are *encouraged* in
the Gilgit Agency. Its frontiers are as jealously guarded as a
Pathan's *zenana* and equally difficult of approach, moreover, a
morbid nervousness surrounds any object that could conceivably

be deemed to be of strategic importance. It may hardly be looked upon, far less photographed, except with special permission (in writing) from the local Political Agent, but when this ban is extended to a swaying rope bridge spanning the Gilgit River it borders on the ludicrous, especially as an excellent reproduction of the said bridge hangs in a prominent position in the Gilgit Rest House. A permit from the Government Ministry of Home and Kashmir Affairs is a vital necessity even for a one-night stay in the town itself and is doled out with the parsimonious reluctance of the proverbial Aberdonian parting with his last sixpence.

The trouble is that no one wants the responsibility of sanctioning the entry of itinerant visitors, no matter how innocent their motives and in such cases a man is deemed guilty until he is proved innocent which poses a nice problem for all concerned. During our stay a member of a Japanese mountaineering team from Toyko University, desirous of mounting an expedition to climb a peak in Hunza, arriving to do a preliminary reconnaissance was given a permit for a two-day stay in Gilgit.

All too often the *bona fides* of would-be travellers depend initially on the doubtful judgment of a lower echelon of departmental clerks, hidden away in dark offices, waging a half-hearted struggle with mounds of dusty, pink-ribboned files. Seemingly unopened from year to year, they bulge out of musty cupboards, overflow desks and tables and mount in sad, uneven bundles in IN trays and OUT trays alike. That the bulk of them ever leave the office seems improbable, and one imagines that some day an old, worn-out man, who has long forgotten why he sits there week after week, will suddenly be presented with a permit to visit a distant valley, his original reason for going there lost in the mists of memory.

It is possible, however, if one is endowed with the tenacity or stubbornness to sit it out for several days, or the influence necessary to by-pass the first layer and make straight for the top, that you will find yourself met with the greatest courtesy and understanding. A telephone will be lifted, a clerk scurry in with flustered apologies, a signature scrawled and you will leave, bewildered but happy and no questions asked.

Having spent so much of my time during previous visits to Pakistan in places well off the beaten track, I should have known better, but being of an inherently optimistic disposition and never having had the misfortune to come up against actual opposition I imagined that I was welcome wherever I went. So, lulled into a false sense of security by our complete freedom to come and go both in Chitral, Kafiristan and Swat, we believed what we were told, that as Government-sponsored travellers no permit was necessary and certainly no one asked us to produce one at the airport in Rawalpindi.

On arrival in Gilgit, after a slight set-back at the airfield, news of our visit having just failed to get there ahead of us, we were met by a rather breathless Adjutant of the Northern Scouts, hurriedly fetched from breakfast. Captain Zulfiqar Ali welcomed us warmly enough but his subsequent horror on finding that we had no written permission to stay in Gilgit shook us considerably. To say that he turned pale might be an exaggeration, but we gathered from his agitation that we might just as well have committed high treason for all the sympathy we could expect.

Hesitantly we murmured that we had an introduction to his Commanding Officer . . . that the Tourist Bureau, the Government Press Information Department knew we were there or rather here, and we waved our Press Cards hopefully. Of no account; he walked the floor. We would simply be sent back to Rawalpindi on the first available flight. Without permits we would have to rely solely on the mercy of the Political Agent and we gathered that he would not look lightly on our solecism.

Eventually it was decided that a wireless message should be transmitted that night to Rawalpindi asking for the appropriate permits and meanwhile we would be more or less confined to quarters in the Rest House. We could scarcely have chosen a less opportune moment in which to arrive. The cook had departed ostensibly to visit a ' sick relative ' in his native Hunza and any-

Indus on way to Chilas.

A little girl in Thalphen stares at us unbelievingly.

Woman and child with pointed hat.

Our loaded jeep at Jigalot on the way home to Gilgit from Chilas.

The small boy who accompanied us from Chilas to Thalphen.

one who knows what that kind of journey is likely to involve will realise that if he was restored to us within a fortnight we could consider ourselves lucky. The Rest House was full to overflowing so we agreed to share a room.

Although in the weeks that followed we may have grumbled intermittently over what became known as ' the permit muddle ' the authorities will never know the simple pleasures our enforced stay in the Rest House afforded us, and as we in due course became its oldest inhabitants we added considerably to our experience of life and our list of friends. Thanks to Zulfi (Captain Zulfiqar Ali) and Jimmie (Captain Jamshed) youngest brother of the Mir of Hunza, we always had a plentiful supply of Hunza Pani with which to entertain our guests and the weather conditions were responsible for marooning in our midst two of the nicest Americans we have ever met, Dottie and Joe Bartos, to whom we send our affectionate *salaams* wherever they may be. The characters that came and went varied from the mildly eccentric to downright dubious and our days were enlivened by their presence.

On that first day, we, being newcomers, eyed our fellow guests with caution but we found kindred spirits in the Crockers, an American Colonel and his wife, charming and adventurous and on their way to Hunza. At the next table, during our meagre lunch of omelette, biscuits and Zulfi's contribution of tinned butter and cheese, which the elderly bearer thoughtfully offered to ' warm up ' for us, was a middle-aged gentleman of undoubtedly German parentage, whom I shall call Willi. Willi had arrived in Gilgit by devious routes ' here to make films ' but his entire journey appeared to have been fraught with disaster, due in no small measure we felt to his own misanthropic attitude to life in Asia.

His mere presence was a perpetual blight on the Rest House in general and his guide in particular, a delightful but sorely tried young man from the Government Tourist Bureau in Rawalpindi. Aman acted as a kind of buffer state between Willi and the world outside with a selfless devotion to duty and the patience of a saint. The last and the oldest resident in point of time was Phemian, a depressed Swiss engineer who had been engaged to build ski-lifts for the training of troops in winter warfare. Poor Phemian had spent weeks in growing frustration over the non-arrival of vital supplies. His money was running out, he couldn't leave Gilgit and the night before, as far as we could gather from his painfully inadequate English, he had been ejected from his room, a double one, to accommodate the Crockers and in the process had lost most of his clothing.

Towards evening we realise that we have no wood for our little Quetta stoves with which each room is supplied. It becomes bitterly cold in Gilgit at night and somehow we all converge on the veranda at once. The cook's 'stand in', a shifty-eyed and truculent Shin who appears to be running the Rest House, is duly summoned from his quarters behind the dining room where his own fire is well-stoked and burning brightly. With the first smile we have seen on his face he announces blandly that the wood shop is *band* 'closed' for the night and won't be open until eight o'clock in the morning. I devote some few minutes to telling him in Urdu exactly what I think of him, the Rest House and the place in general, which he receives first with astonishment, then indignation and finally a grudging respect but the final result is negative – he grins – shrugs his shoulders and leaves us to our fate.

Willi at once turns on Aman: ' They ought to have here wood available . . . they have guests who want fires . . .' and adds this latest insult to the growing list of complaints that poor Aman is due to present to the authorities on his return to ' Pindi '. The Crockers go off for a stroll to warm up and return in a couple of minutes with the astounding news that vast quantities of wood are being weighed and loaded just opposite the gates of the Rest House. This rouses everyone to action. Aman shouts for a bearer. Stewart swears we will carry it ourselves. In a body we march down the drive. Balti labourers, whom we last saw sleeping in the sun, are now staggering around under great loads of orange juniper wood. A phalanx of donkeys stand patiently waiting for their owners, nibbling hungrily at the bark of branches strewn on the ground. The wood pile is enormous, towering over us like a small house. Aman, bless him, opens negotiations.

The foreman of the gang piously protests that it is forbidden to sell wood after six o'clock without the Political Agent's personal permission. It is as though we had demanded a drink after hours in the presence of an Excise Officer. We are all by now slightly hysterical at the sight of so much wood almost within our grasp. The Colonel quietly fumes, looking as though he might mount an attack at any moment. ' Damned if I'm going to ring up the P.A. and ask " Please may I buy some wood?" ' Stewart mutters in an obscure African dialect. Aman, who could, we feel sure placate the devil himself, restrains us and explains with great calm that he is working for the Government, that these are his guests, that they are shivering and will surely freeze during the night. He will take full responsibility.

The *lukri wallah*s go into a huddle while we stamp our feet to keep ourselves warm and try not to look at the wood they toss around with such nonchalance. Finally with a great show of reluctance they relent. We may have a *sehr*. Extremely suspicious that the whole operation is a put-up job, we explain that we all require separate fires and that two pounds of wood isn't going to be much more use than a box of matches. More wood is brought and weighed out on a kind of tripod with a stone as a balance. We have to take their word that the resulting heap is one *maund* which can vary from 28 pounds to the official 82 pounds. At last we succeed in buying at what I for one am sure is an exorbitant price a largish armful of thick logs which is carried off by the bearer to be chopped up.

We all wait patiently inside our room. Phemian has succeeded in impressing upon us the fact that he has lost most of his clothes and cannot go to bed. Aman again comes to the rescue and finds the missing garments in a wardrobe in the Crockers' quarters and departs to hasten the cutting of the wood. Willi once more relates his experiences in Skardu, where, having been entertained by the Forest Officer he returned to the Rest House to find it

147

locked. ' I shout . . .' he explains, ' I bang, so . . . on all the doors . . . all of them. The night is bitter. At last an old man dressed in such a *chogha* comes out of the dark. He has a lantern which then fails . . .'

Suddenly in the midst of this tale of woe, Aman bursts into the room staggering, one hand clapped to his head. A piece of wood has flown up and struck him on the temple. We rush to his aid. A minute speck of blood is revealed on his hand and he collapses into a chair. Mrs. Crocker produces sticking plaster. I find disinfectant and swabs. Stewart sensibly comes to the rescue with whisky which revives him almost at once. By this time the wood is ready and we all disperse thankfully to light our fires. At eleven o'clock we stumble into bed in the dark, the electricity supply being regularly cut off until the following evening.

The whole of that week in the Rest House the walls echoed to Willi's plaintive cries of : ' Amaa . . . aan! Amaa . . . aan !' Things went from bad to worse. Willi became daily more miserable, shabby and down-at-heel. Nowhere could he get any co-operation in the making of his film and we would see him wandering around, camera in hand, muttering as he passed : ' These cows will be eating all of the flowers . . . all, all will be eaten up !' A trip to Hunza with the Crockers completely broke his spirit. Part of the road had collapsed and they had had a few nasty moments crawling around some chasm. By the time we returned from our first trip outside Gilgit Willi had gone. We often wondered what had happened to him and his caseful of films he was afraid to trust out of his sight lest they be stolen or damaged and could never bring himself to consign to the post.

Two days after our arrival, on 3rd October, the permits were delivered. To our dismay they gave permission only for a visit to Skardu in Baltistan, which had never at any point come into our itinerary. They were made out to Mr. Stewart and Mrs. Elizabeth *Stobo*, our joint middle name, and were for one week's duration. A note added :

1. Photography in the Gilgit Agency/Northern Area is banned except of the objects which are permitted by the Political Agent, Gilgit/Additional Political Agent, Skardu in writing.
2. Arrangements for accommodation and transport cannot be made unless at least a week's advance notice is given to the Political Agent, Gilgit/Additional Political Agent, Skardu,

There ensued a hasty conference, another signal despatched and a second permit arrived, this time with permission for one week's stay in Gilgit and Hunza up to Baltit . . . ditto photographs, ditto accommodation. Clearly we must be possessed of the power of *djinns* to be able to give a week's notice of our intentions and yet remain mysteriously settled in the place to which we were supposed to be going. It would have given us great pleasure to visit Hunza – General Shahid Hamid had already offered introductions – but too many others had written and filmed in Hunza and what could we have done with half a week in that delectable State? We had made up our minds to keep to the untrodden paths of the Gilgit Agency, come what may. Finally Captain Jamshed, who acted as liaison officer to the Northern Scouts in Rawalpindi, extracted yet a third permit which allowed us to visit Gupis, Shandur, Phandar and Yasin and was, miraculously, valid for ten days. By this time we had spent a happy two weeks in the Gilgit Agency, confined to the town itself and four miles round, although strictly according to the files we were not there at all.

Gilgit town lies embedded between great walls of rock that seem to lean over the narrow valley and the straggling bazaar. High to the west rises Dubani, 'the smoking mountain', so called because of the mist that drifts endlessly, nimbus-like, around its summit, while from the Hunza road the white shoulders of Rakaposhi thrust upwards into a cloudless sky. In the bazaar where the November sun was already shrinking, barely penetrating the width of the street, Kashgaris in fur hats with ear flaps rub shoulders with Baltis from Skardu wearing round skull caps of rough cloth and loose robes, goat hair ropes coiled round their waists. There were tall, henna-bearded Shins and slant-eyed roadmen from Sinkiang in padded jackets and trousers.

On either side open-fronted shops sold garish cotton, pen-knives and onions, feeding bottles, pomegranates and bright red Hunza apples; dried apricots from which the flies are languorously stirred; shallow bowls of spices; shelled walnuts and small but reasonably fresh eggs. These we convert into omelettes on top of our Quetta stoves, having long since ceased to depend on the indifferent cooking of Mir Din. Phemian, whom we invite from time to time, contributes large quantities of spaghetti, all he has left from his initial stores, an *embarras de richesse* we could well do without as we have only tinned cheese, an expensive luxury.

Stuffed otter skins dangle pathetically from wire hooks; snow leopard and fox skins, called *shal,* hang next to embroidered waistcoats which Stewart optimistically tries on only to find they are several sizes too small. The local cloth, *putto,* woven on 16-inch looms, is used for making Gilgiti hats like the Chitrali ones, jackets and the ubiquitous *chogha,* the loose flowing robe with long sleeves reaching to the knees so that the wearer's hands can be kept warm in the cold weather.

Gay little Hunza hats, beautifully coloured and stitched in a kind of *petit point,* are perched below the shapeless knitted hose with elaborately-patterned tops designed to be worn under the knee-high boots of soft markhor skin called *pabboo.* For the poorer people however the traditional *taoti* is sufficient. A piece of skin or cloth is wound round the leg and foot and held in place by a complicated lacing of goathair rope or leather thongs. As we wander through this Aladdin's cave, deep in conversation with Yusuf, our police escort, delighted with his novel assignment, and who, since our permitless arrival has regarded us with the warmest friendship, a tiny child calls out in English : ' Good morning !' Yusuf claps his hands and shouts : ' *Shahbashai buttcha!*' ' Well done, little one !' and the boy's father, at once upset and proud, cuffs him for his impertinence and laughs at his erudition.

Horses caracole down the middle of the road and a young markhor like a Walt Disney fawn, wearing a bright cerulean collar round his soft, mole-coloured neck, agile as a cat leaps to the top of a six-foot wall the better to inspect us. Ponderous heavy-jowled bulls gently nuzzle a grazing cow and yaks meditate in nearby fields, great shaggy creatures with square muzzles and long flowing pony tails. Small boys in a pattern of Gilgit hats like pancakes rush wildly to and fro through the crowds, clutching the hooked sticks with which they play ' *gutta polo* ' at every opportunity, the thick dust muffling the padding feet. Our newly acquired Shina phrase : ' *La mishto!* ' ' Very good !' drawing forth shrieks of laughter.

Down to the woodpile opposite the Rest House come tiny donkeys on mincing feet with loads of bright yellow juniper wood swaying on the wooden saddles. Prisoners from the local jail, their ankles shackled to a rod of iron which appears to be joined to a metal ring connected with a kind of waistband, move slowly but cheerfully through the bazaar, enormous bundles of wood on their shoulders. A small boy in Karakuli hat squats in the middle of the road heating an iron over a little charcoal fire for the tailor sitting cross-legged at his Singer sewing machine inside his open-fronted shop. A cobbler is busy making *chappals* the open-toed Pathan sandals. Beside him stands his *chelum,* the hookah smoked on the North West Frontier, with the familiar pottery vase filled with water through which the smoke passes, drawn up the long *serak* or bamboo pipe bound with silver or copper wire, the tobacco smouldering in the *topi.* A customer sits smoking a cigarette cupped in one hand, drawing the smoke through his fingers so that his mouth will not touch the tobacco, thus adhering theoretically to the orthodox Muslim rule. Under the trees in the Rest House garden, a couple of children scrabble for nuts and kernels and boys climb the branches to shake down the few remaining leaves for the cattle.

As the days go by we become quite well-known in the bazaar. Stewart has made friends with an old gentleman who sells Kashgari hats and with great forethought buys one for each of us. We also fall for six porcelain bowls decorated with Chinese figures alternating with posies of flowers, rimmed with gold and with Chinese characters on the underside, and the shop owner, delighted with his sale, then proceeds to unearth from the dark recesses behind him one of his greatest treasures – a copy of the *Geographical Magazine* with an article by Peter Goodwin on Gilgit and its bazaar.

Riaz, our friend in the Signals, when he hears us bemoaning the fact that we have had no letters, marches us off to the Post Office and walks straight through to the 'sorting room'. The scene that confronted us would be, I should think, an ordinary postman's nightmare. Letters were scattered in unbelievable chaos on benches, tables and occasionally pigeon holes on the wall, but mainly repose in utter disarray on the floor where they occasionally got turned over, scuffed aside or, if difficult to decipher, simply abandoned. Riaz pokes with his swagger stick among the litter: ' That's for so and so ' he points out : ' *Wah! wah!*' ' This one should have gone to Baltit, isn't it?' and glares on the poor chaps scrabbling hopelessly among thumb-marked envelopes.

Then perhaps we may stroll along to the Bank—another open-fronted shop where one can chat to Jafri the Bank Manager at any hour of the day, where no supercilious clerks glare suspiciously from behind shining bars and no one is assailed by guilty thoughts of overdrafts or bouncing cheques. Jafri immediately sends out for tea and money changes hands lightly over ' custard cream ' biscuits or cigarettes. On his half day, an apparently arbitrary holiday determined solely by the exigencies of business, the Manager joins us for expeditions to the Kaghah Nullah.

The hospital is another port of call always open to us and we drink tea with Colonel Rashid, the Agency Surgeon who is a mine of information on the district and its medical history in particular and his young assistants come and go and describe with naïve pride and a wealth of detail their latest operation. I have had a bad shoulder, aggravated no doubt by carrying the heavy camera. It is expertly X-rayed and I am given radiant heat several mornings in the week.

In the evenings we are entertained by Riaz and Zulfi in their quarters at the Northern Scouts' Mess. Here we listen to records, consume vast quantities of almonds roasted in butter and taste Kashmiri tea which seems rather like a runny pink milk pudding with salt in it and not even to please our friends can we honestly say we like it. In our room at the Rest House, huddled round the Quetta stove, we write up our notes by candlelight and from our respective beds watch our own private family of mice struggling to carry away the walnuts in their shells and wonder how Beatrix Potter's Two Bad Mice would have fared under such primitive conditions. Ours are obviously peasant mice who have to toil for every scrap of food that comes into the home. No baby's bassinets for their offspring. They are courageous little chaps though and the firelight glints on their beady eyes and quivering whiskers as they push and heave at the slippery shells.

Whatever we do for the rest of the day, however, the afternoons are sacred and devoted exclusively to the week's polo organised following on President Ayub Khan's visit to the Agency two days before our own. Teams had ridden up to 80 miles from Yasin, Astor and Chilas, to compete with each other and the Northern Scouts. By the end of the week we know almost every player by name. Between two and three o'clock would come the first muffled drums. Then the *surnai* sang out, insistent, stirring, wild like a battle cry. Spectators begin to pour past the gates of the Rest House in a jumbled jostling tide, horses' heads nodding above the wall, sticks like lances in a great cloud of dust and behind, above and around the trotting hooves the hoarse voices and the jingle of harness, the drums beat out an urgent, hurrying rhythm.

The Gilgit polo ground lay behind the bazaar and between it and the river. Sheer from its gravelly bed rose great shoulders of boulder-strewn mountain. Enclosed on three sides by a low mud wall, an excellent grandstand had been erected on the fourth for important guests, with rows of cane-backed chairs,

small occasional tables for the cups of steaming tea that kept us
warm, our persons safeguarded by a head-high mesh of wire
netting. The afternoon's events opened with a march past by the
pipes and drums of the Gilgit Scouts in flat white Gilgiti hats
with a cockade of *chikor* feathers, tartan plaids swinging over
scarlet tunics and led by their mascot, an ibex which along with
the Northern Scouts' markhor, resplendent in scarlet and gold
coats emblazoned with the regimental crests, marched and
counter-marched with the men, proud and unled to the rousing
strains of ' Scotland the Brave ' and ' Wi' a Hundred Pipers and
A' and A' '.

First the horses are led round in circles, all stallions except
the Colonel of the Northern Scouts' beautiful mare, who perforce is paraded by herself at one end of the field, the sun glinting on blood red martingales and brilliantly embroidered
numnahs under the high peaked cruppers of the country teams.
On mounting, the player first touches his horses' ears, then his
own mouth and forehead with the tips of his fingers in a kind
of dedication, a ritual at once curious and graceful. It seemed
out of place to call these animals ' ponies ' for although trained
for the game they were several hands at least above the usual
polo pony and when not engaged in matches were used as a
form of transport – the only one readily available throughout the
Agency.

The musicians are perched on the wall opposite the grandstand at the side of the scoreboard. A bugle sounds and the ball
is thrown in to start the game – as the only lady spectator this
dubious honour only too frequently falls to my lot, never renowned for my accuracy. The white ball flies over the netting to
my great relief, and a wild mêlée of men and horses converge in
a mad struggle for possession, a kaleidoscopic jumble of flying
figures. The Mir of Hunza's son-in-law, who is also the son of
the Governor of Yasin, is pointed out to us on a splendid grey
with Arab blood, a cerulean blue and scarlet fringed numnah
over a black blanket embroidered in red. The first goal goes to
Yasin, the thunder of hooves drowned in the burst of frenzied

music from the band. The goal scored, the player takes the ball in the same hand as his stick and charges down the field like a winged Pegasus, leaning almost horizontally out of the saddle. At the half way line he throws the ball into the air and still without checking speed hits it a mighty 'Thwack!' and the crowd roars: '*Shahbashai! Shahbashai jawan!*'

'Well done, well done young man!'

A white pony with gold and blue trappings careers up the field marked by his opposite number shoulder to shoulder with a strawberry roan, knotted tails flying. Small boys perched on convenient trees shake the branches like miniature tornadoes at every goal. The sun throws long shadows, pencilling the field in streaks of moving light and shade. Number six catches the ball in his hand, plucking it out of the very air as it streaks past him, at the same time throwing away his stick. He passes it to number one who dodges the fast closing ranks brandishing the ball in his fist, shouting untranslatable taunts and insults to his pursuers, to the wild approval of the crowd, and gallops through the goal posts.

Down the field they come again, a stick thrown across a pony's withers to prevent his rider from reaching the ball. The shouts grow louder, the ranks of onlookers shudder like a field of waving corn blown this way and that with the turn of the play. Everyone in the stand rises to his feet as the field sweeps past, horses passaging at a canter, the gold shoulder of mountain behind. Captain Babur beside us claps his hands and shouts with the rest of us. Only the Governor of Yasin, who at 70 took part in the tent pegging before the match, sits calm and apparently unmoved, his flowing white beard and long white wool *chogha* embroidered with flowers, patriarchal, aloof.

Sufi has done it again! Sufi, Subadar Major of the Northern Scouts, handsome, dashing, wild, daring Sufi!

'*Shahbashai! Shahbashai* Sufi!' and a sigh like a breaking wave goes up as he tears himself away from a great giant of a man with a Yul Brynner haircut and long moustache, streaking away from his pursuers, riding like a demon, intoxicated with success. Mir Shah from Yasin suffers a glancing blow as he pulls his horse up suddenly, dust spurting from his heels.

' W'Allah ! Fiker nai Mir Shah ! Fiker nai !'

' Don't worry Mir Shah, don't worry !'

' Muktar Mukhtaa . . . ar ! Piche jao !'

' Get in behind Mukhtar !' and we are on our feet again yelling ourselves hoarse until the players vanish in a cloud of dust at the other end of the field, caught up in a great shaft of gold, left hands flicking back the whip from their wrists and Sufi's horse wheeling like a wild boar in a skid. By four o'clock and the second half, the field is a long black trough of shadow ringed with bright mountains, the peaks of Rakaposhi and Dubani riding high like great white sails behind them, and at the end of the day over a flagon of Hunza Pani, Riaz, Zulfi, Stewart and I relive the match and discuss the prospects for the next.

14

The Desert of the Peacock

This country is just beyond the Tsung Ling Mountains. The aspect of the land is still rugged; the people are very poor; the rugged road is dangerous—a traveller and his horse can scarcely pass along it, one at a time.

Sung Yun : A.D. 518

History seems to me rather like two parallel lines diminishing in perspective to a single point beyond which one cannot see. The plotting of that point depends largely upon the topography of the country's past; the more rugged, the less likely is the vista to survive even a few centuries, and so it is with the Gilgit Agency. The mountains block one's view both physically and metaphorically. Of the peoples who came and went from beyond the high Pamir and found a way down the Iskoman, Gilgit, Hunza and Indus rivers as far as the Black Mountains, almost no tangible evidence remains. Now and again a carved Buddha, a heap of stones, a crumbling Chinese fort or a blackened fire-altar stand out like slender clues in a treasure hunt, the one giving some credence to the rest.

The first Europeans to cross the Indus at Bunji and penetrate beyond Gilgit were two officers of the Bengal Army, Young and Vans Agnew, who were employed by the British Government in

1847 to report on the North West Frontier of Kashmir. It is doubtful if their findings ever saw the light of day for the report is believed to have been lost at Multan when Vans Agnew was murdered directly after his return. Twenty years passed before Dr. Leitner reached Gilgit 'under circumstances of great difficulty and after a brief stay of a few days brought back a mass of information supplemented by Mr. Drew in his valuable work on Kashmir.' In 1877 Biddulph himself was appointed to the post of Political Officer in Gilgit; Colonel Algernon Durand followed him in 1889; Younghusband passed through it several times in various capacities and little seems to have been added to their information until Colonel Schomberg travelled in these areas in the 1930s.

Since Partition in 1947 there has been a steady trickle of visitors from the outside world stopping over in Gilgit on their way to Hunza, either simply touring or engaged in some form of research; the German climbers on their way to Nanga Parbat; the Cambridge Expedition to Haramosh in whose footsteps we followed from Gilgit to Sassi, but few can have had the good fortune to wander as we did, on our own or in the company of Pakistanis who gave up so much of their time to help us on our way. If the powers-that-be tolerated our presence with barely concealed displeasure, our new friends spared no effort to counteract any misapprehension we may have had as to their hospitality. Wheels revolved within wheels, however, often most uncomfortably, and, worried lest anyone should suffer on our account, we were more than thankful when the embargo was lifted officially and we were free to journey north.

Meanwhile both Riaz and Zulfi had kindly taken us at least as far as our circumscribed four miles would allow, one of our favourite haunts the Kaghah or Kerghah Nullah, near the entrance to which is the famous rock Buddha. A few miles out of Gilgit on the road north to Yasin and Darkot, a narrow track takes off near the hamlet of Nowpoor, its ancient name Amsar and according to Biddulph once more important than Gilgit itself. Along the original trail that leads through the Kaghah valley came a small cavalcade from China led by Fah Hien when, 'in the second year of Hung Chi, the cyclical characters being *Kang tsze* (A.D. 400)', he and four companions agreed to go together to India to search for the complete copies of the Rules of the Buddhist Discipline. They journeyed across the Lung Mountains, through the province of Kansu and, 'provided with all necessities' which would make them the envy of many modern expeditions, they set off across the Gobi Desert.

'In this desert,' writes Fah Hien, 'there are a great many evil demons, there are also sirocco winds which kill all who encounter them. There are no birds or beasts to be seen; but so far as the eye can reach the route is marked out by the bleached bones of men who have perished in the attempt to cross the desert.' Indeed, 'The miseries they endured in crossing the rivers and in surmounting the natural difficulties of the road along which they had to journey exceeded all conception' wrote Samuel Beal in his translation of their travels. After being on the road a month and five days they at last arrived at Khoten. Crossing the Tsung Ling Mountains near the great Pamir plateau they proceeded in a southerly route towards Kataur or Chitral, another reference to our Kator rulers, and then down the Indus.

This is where accounts become confused. Biddulph believes that they entered the Gilgit Agency through the Darkot Pass and then went on through the Kaghah Valley to Darel where they would strike the Indus about Sazin, from whence they made their way to Ou-chang, that is modern Swat. In Beal's translation he writes that after crossing the Tsung Ling Mountains they came to a place where 'at the base there is a stream called the Sin-to (Indus). Men of old days have cut away the cliff so as to make a passage and have carved out against the rock steps for descent, amounting altogether to 700 in number. Having passed these, there is, suspended across the river, a bridge of ropes, by which travellers pass over it. From one side of the river to the other is eighty paces.'

Whatever the actual route taken, Fah Hien does speak of

having seen a rock carving of Buddha, although his estimate is of a very much larger one than that at the Kaghah Nullah, but perhaps like all of us he was subject to the very human frailty of exaggeration and I like to think of these intrepid traveller-explorers standing where we stood, silent in contemplation of the Gautama Buddha before passing on their way.

The present road to the nullah is hewn out between the boulders embedded in its edge; mountains enclose it with chutes of scree fanning out down the lower slopes while along the steep tracks running over the hillside like twisting threads totter tiny donkeys laden with wood, for all Gilgit is supplied from outside the town. We left the jeep and scrambled over rocks to where a burn tumbled over bright pebbles at our feet. There was grass and fresh green fern, watered by a wooden trough that spouted its clear stream from an old watercourse built up along the hillside with a mosaic of beautifully-cut stone, a masterpiece of engineering.

Riaz pointed upwards and there high over our heads loomed a great rock tower, battlemented like a medieval castle and on a flat slab, where the rock had split, a standing figure of the Buddha gazed down with the serene smile and heavy-lidded eyes reflecting the ideal of the suppression of all desire and total detachment that for centuries has inspired all who looked on it. At least 40 feet above us and about 10 feet high, the figure was deeply incised into the living rock and enclosed in a kind of frame or niche in the form of a pentagon, almost like a Gothic arch. Above the head the rock tilts outwards so that there is a natural canopy above the Buddha about 15 feet high.

The figure stands with the right hand held up to the breast, the hair gathered in the traditional knot on top of the head. The robustness of the sculpture, unclothed, without indication of sex, is reminiscent of the Gupta style of the fourth to fifth centuries when the garment was often rendered with a total absence of folds, giving the impression of nakedness, and yet if it was the same one seen by Fah Hien and his companions it must be of a much earlier date. Around the pentagon which frames the re-

Stewart and Lumbardars.

Chunks of meat in cooking pot
Takh Nullah.

Dancing at wedding Takh Nullah.

Man standing on edge of space – Ind

lief are 13 deep square niches cut at regular intervals, which may have been used to carry either a wooden canopy or as supports during its execution. The carving seems to have weathered little since Biddulph saw it in 1877 although the sketch in his book is a travesty of the original, revealing nothing of its beauty or strength.

Durand also found a Buddhist carving in Baltistan again at the mouth of a ravine leading up to the Deosai, but this is an altogether more elaborate and complicated frieze with a seated Buddha surrounded by a frame of Bodhisattvas and a full-length figure in preaching attitude on either side. The whole relief seems more sophisticated and delicate with a sinuous and graceful curve of draperies and may well be of a much later date.

Our necks grew stiff and tired of gazing upwards at this ancient embodiment of truth, so startling in its presence, alone in the remote and savage valley. Boulders the size of houses are strewn over the slope and the road comes to an end within the nullah itself, to be the scene a few days later of one of those incidents, which, hilariously funny in retrospect, could at the time have had serious consequences.

Stewart having ignominiously succumbed to a surfeit of buttered almonds. Zulfi suggested a drive out to explore the nullah itself. We set off, very dashing in his army Jeep, Northern Scouts crest and all, decorum being preserved, at least for the time being, by the presence of his orderly which lent a fine military air to the expedition.

To appreciate the full significance of the ensuing disaster, one had to see Captain Zulfiqar Ali's small, slender elegance, always immaculately turned out, as though ready for an immediate parade. He positively radiated charm, possessed a sybaritic taste in wine, attractive women – preferably European – sophisticated conversation and a dreamy waltz during which the combination of his personal magnetism and liquid brown eyes were used with devastating effect.

At the end of the motor road we left the Jeep in charge of

the orderly and set off on foot. Although almost old enough to be his mother, I had no illusions as to the dangers of our escapade *à deux,* but as the rocks closed in on us, the sun completely shut out of the gorge, the air refrigerator cold, it was obvious that any smouldering fires of passion were destined to be successfully frozen at birth. The Kaghah River rushed in swirls of green, glacier water at our feet, backing onto the smooth rock in miniature whirlpools and spanned by the usual slippery, single-plank bridge.

Zulfi courteously offered to carry my camera across for me, but I was born with an obstinate streak of independence which not only thwarts many willing helpers but makes it impossible for me to accept aid simply because of my sex. Not wishing to appear ungrateful, I gave him my shoulder bag and as it was always a case of ' ladies first ' with Zulfi, I stepped on ahead. One moment Zulfi was breathing down my neck, the next there was a small splash and glancing over my shoulder there was no one to be seen. Balancing with difficulty I managed to turn round. All that was visible was Zulfi's head above the water, his hands clinging to the plank, black hair plastered over his face and two brown eyes gazing up at me with the hurt surprise of a stricken deer.

Somehow our combined efforts dragged him up and back to the bank. Although his immersion had been a mere matter of minutes, he stood there, teeth chattering, water pouring from him, speechless with shock, the freezing chill of that icy water horribly evident. By great good luck I happened to be wearing over my shirt a thick, double-knit sweater, which, either due to my incompetence or to a mis-interpretation of the pattern, had turned out several sizes too large, and in spite of numberless washings perversely refused to shrink. It had become rather a joke with the family, but could be usefully worn over almost any number of garments. Whipping it off, I ordered the Captain to get out of his wet clothes at once and put it on and discreetly turning my back occupied myself with pouring the water out of my sodden handbag. Poor Zulfi, his humiliation was complete as he emerged, trailing his soaking jacket, shirt and trousers, my sweater flapping round his knees. Still blue with cold, conversation was useless and we set off at a smart trot back to the road.

His orderly who had been enjoying a quiet snooze in the back of the Jeep startled by our shouts, tumbled out and sprang to attention. I shall never forget his face, the sight of his adjutant so very improperly dressed, the muscles of his jaw contorted in an effort to control the horror, disbelief and wild amusement as he struggled to maintain a soldierly bearing. His discipline was admirable. Zulfi handed over his wet clothes and still shaking uncontrollably, ordered the chap to take them away and return with a complete change at the double. ' *Ji ha, Sahib!*' he stammered. As he clicked his heels and saluting smartly jumped into the driving seat, I yelled out . . . 'And a Thermos of hot tea!' '*Zuroor . . . bohut aachcha, memsahib!*' and the Jeep disappeared in a roar of engines and clouds of dust. We climbed up the nullah on to the high rocks above, warm and hot with the sun beating down on them, while Zulfi slowly thawed and was finally able to smile a little, sheepishly, at his ducking, and be grateful for his rescue, because, he confessed, he had never learned to swim.

After casting around for some time on the stony slope below the figure of Buddha, we walked along the shelf of the old water channel which climbed unpleasantly upwards, wondering if we could not find any other traces of the obvious past. Riaz and Zulfi soon grew tired of our amateur archaeology and producing a paper bag of sweet red apples we all sat down by the side of the stream and watched the sun climbing up the valley towards the white peaks of Dubani and Rakaposhi and thought of future travellers who might come this way within the next thousand years and of how many others the Buddha had looked upon since strong hands created him out of the unwilling stone.

The history of Buddhism in India begins with the miraculous and immaculate birth of Buddha between 563 and 483 B.C. The future Gautama had already passed through numberless existences in preparation for his ultimate transmigration, and when his hour was come he was vouchsafed to a member of the ruling family at Kapilavastu on the borders of Nepal. Queen Maya, whose name literally translated means ' illusion ', dreamed that she saw the Bodhisattva come down into her womb in the shape of a beautiful snow-white elephant. ' At that moment entire creation showed its joy in the form of miracles; musical instruments played without being touched; rivers stopped flowing . . .' trees, plants and ponds were covered with flowers. The next day four Brahmins interpreted the Queen's dream. She would give birth to a son, who would either become an emperor or a Buddha, the legend conforming strangely with the almost universally accepted mysticism surrounding the birth of god or prophet.

' When the moment of birth approached, the Queen went into the garden of Lumbini and standing there, holding the branch of a Saka tree in her right hand, she gave birth to the Bodhisattava, who emerged from her right side without causing her the slightest pain. The child was received by Brahma and other gods; but he began to walk immediately and a lotus appeared wherever his foot touched the ground. He took seven paces in the direction of each of the cardinal points thus taking possession of the world . . .'[1] And by the time of Asoka in 260 B.C. missionaries proceeding from the various centres had carried his message north and south, till from Balkh to Ceylon and from Pattala on the Indus to Temluc on the Hooghli, their teaching spread.

A few days later we found ourselves following the route – in reverse – taken by the Chinese pilgrims Fah Hien and Sung Yun and we recollected that Hiouen Tsang, perhaps the greatest of the Chinese pilgrim adventurers, ' having completed his tour of the Indian peninsula ' which sounds faintly reminiscent of Mr. Cook, save that it took Hiouen Tsang 16 years, returned across

---

[1] Larousse : *World Mythology.*

the Indus in the footsteps of Fah Hien's outward journey. Although we took with us two well-loaded jeeps, this was as nothing compared to the baggage train of Hiouen Tsang, including as it did : ' Twenty-two horses carrying 657 Buddhist works; 115 grains of relics; a gold statue of Buddha three feet three inches in height with a transparent pedestal; a second, three feet five inches high and many others of silver and sandalwood.'[1]

Stewart rode in the leading Jeep with the *khansamah,* a small boy with a tubercular hip who was being sent home from hospital to Punyal, a bearer and luggage. I followed in the second, driven by Colonel Rashid, the Agency Surgeon whose guests we were, accompanied by Riaz, more baggage and supplies. Our road, only slightly enlarged, could well have been the same one described by Sung Yun, ' rugged and dangerous '. A ledge just wide enough to contain the Jeep is cut out of the mountainside. At places the overhang is so low that we almost ducked our heads and the rocks that protrude into the road are alarming and sometimes dangerous for the passenger on the near side, if, as happens frequently, four people are squashed into the front of the vehicle.

The going was slow, for every now and then we would come to a shuddering halt, poised horribly on the edge of space to allow a small cavalcade of horsemen to sidle nervously past. Sometimes we met ponies being led and without the actual contact of rider they behaved like mad things. Fortunately this only happened on less precipitous slopes, for, wild with terror at the sight and sound of unaccustomed motor transport, the ponies reared, bucked and often, eyes rolling and manes flying, took off down the hillside, a couple of men clinging to their heads.

Inevitably there were all too frequent full stops, while our driver investigated some minor fault in one or other of the engines with a great show of knowledge and very little ultimate effect. A fine rain had begun to fall and it was bitterly cold, so

[1] Samuel Beal: *Fah Hien and Sung Yun.*

that we were glad to clamber out and stamp around and drink the hot, sweet tea that Colonel Rashid's bearer continued to produce out of an enormous Thermos flask, apparently without end, like the widow's cruse. The surgeon seemed to know everyone and in one desolate spot we were joined by two delightful old men with flowing beards, wrapped in brown *choghas* their feet in cloth *taoti*. They shared our tea and the latest gossip from Gilgit and warmly invited us to spend a night at one of their homes. We were able to give them a lift as far as Singal and they squatted happily in the back on top of all the bedding.

The sick boy's grandfather was waiting for him at Cher Kila where the Gilgit River is spanned by a rope bridge leading to Punyal. One hundred and twenty yards long, it could well have been a replica of one of those that caused Fah Hien so much agony. Although they are repaired every year the design has remained almost identical. Terrifying contraptions of slender swaying threads looping across the boiling grey torrent, they look as though the slightest breeze would carry them away. Made of twisted birch or willow-bark, three of these ropes form the bridge, the traveller walking on the bottom one, and clinging grimly to the other two which serve as hand-rails, joined by short withies to the footway. At intervals, cross-pieces of wood keep the ropes apart and some little skill is needed to negotiate these while crossing the heaving bridge.

There was a touching if unemotional reunion as the boy was lifted out of the jeep and wrapped in his grandfather's *chaddur*. Heaving the child on to his shoulder, he set off, a tiny figure high above the river, the boy holding on with one hand and in the other clutching a brown sherry bottle full of medicine, the old man like a living Saint Christopher, unperturbed and sure-footed as a markhor. 'Will he get better?' we asked. Colonel Rashid shrugged his shoulders. 'We've done all we can. It's still difficult to make them understand that we can't perform miracles. If the boy dies it will be "The Will of Allah", if he lives, *Insha'allah,* it will be because of the wonderful doctors. We need them to believe in us for their own sakes, if only they would come in time!' and we watched the pair like puppets on a string tightrope until they reached the other side.

At Singal Rest House a roaring fire awaited us, a delicious lunch of chicken *pilau* and a noble flagon of *Punyal Water,* a paler, yellowish variant of the *Hunza Pani* we had drunk in Gilgit. Colonel Rashid attended to some patients and we met Major Imtiaz whose wife accompanied us on the return journey. Imtiaz had just been officially awarded his Majority and we had a solemn little ceremony outside in the cold as Colonel Rashid fastened the crowns on his shoulders, Imtiaz standing rigidly to attention and all of us feeling that there should have been at least a band in attendance. After it was over a blushing Major was congratulated by us all, the servants rushing out to shake hands, even the cook, wiping his hands on his shirt tails, hurried up, unwilling to be left out. I photographed and filmed the event which pleased everybody and it was dark when we reached Gupis and dinner at the home of Raja Hussain Ali Khan, Governor of Gupis and Koh-i-Ghizar.

In any company the man would have stood out and he welcomed us with natural dignity that is the prerogative of kings and princes. Tall above the average, fair skinned, he wore a clipped white Edwardian beard and whiskers, all set off by a black Gilgiti hat, a sweeping *chogha* which they manage so gracefully, giving him the air of a Shakespearian actor, rich brown corduroy slacks and a long tweed jacket of local weave above a white, ribbed pullover.

After a few preliminary courtesies he invited us to dine and striding before us to the other end of his big chintz-hung living room, he threw back a striped *purdah* to reveal a long table spread with a feast that could have served ten people with ease. Steam curled up from a succulent saddle of markhor; mounds of rice gleamed silken, each grain poised separately upon the other; chicken and mutton were flanked by *dhal* and *dahi*; a sour clotted cream and not to be confused with *dhai* which means a midwife, so that being temporarily in the wilderness we saw as it were with Milton:

A table richly spread in regal mode,
With dishes piled and meats of nobler sort
And savour; beasts of the chase or fowl of game,
In pastry built, or from the spit or boiled
Gris-amber-steamed; all fish from sea or shore,
Freshet of purling brook, for which was drained
Pontus and Lucrine bay and Afric coast.

Although our fish had come only from the Gilgit river like the Lotkhuh once stocked with trout, it tasted none the less exotic and after we had struggled through as much as we could decently hold, knowing comfortably that the lesser members of the household, which would include the women, had ample left on which to sup, we sat down over cups of tea and talked far into the night.

Gupis, or Koh-i-Ghizar as it is properly named, Gupis being merely the name of the town, lies on a flat plain almost wholly enclosed by mountains. As far as the eye can see, tier upon tier of lofty peaks circle the skyline like some exaggerated theatre backcloth. Raja Hussain Ali Khan has climbed most of them, none worth calling a mountain is under 16,000 feet, the highest, Phonarashke, being 17,000 feet. A great athlete in his day the Governor of Gupis had shot over 300 markhor, a remarkable record but a sad one today when the animal has become so rare. The gorge of the Ghizar River lies one hundred feet below the plain, the whole of the surrounding country with its polished and ice-marked rocks, roches moutonnées and the remains of dead and gone glaciers, showing the result of ice action, where ' stretches of flat land of lacustrine formation meet you at every turn . . .'

The Raja of this wild and lovely land, apart from his noted athletic powers, is an accomplished *sitar* player and as we sat round a blazing fire he played for us on a five-stringed instrument with a long, delicate neck, the bowl made from a gourd and producing a strange, sweet note unlike any other of its kind. He owned in addition, of all unlikely things, a tape-recorder, and had made recordings of all the local songs. His last tape was not quite finished and he begged us to sing one of the tunes of our native land. On the spur of the moment it was difficult to think of one that we both knew that was not too obscure and short enough to fit into the space available. We finished up by singing with great embarrassment, especially on my part, for I am no singer, ' My love is like a red, red rose ', which sounded dreadful but seemed to delight the Raja, for after playing it back several times, he loaned us the tape, on condition that we sent it back to him. Nothing could quite describe the juxtaposition of these two utterly divergent types of music, but in a way it was nice to think of our voices at least remaining in that far-off corner of the Gilgit Agency.

In the morning the usual court was held outside when the Raja meets his people daily, just as Younghusband described it, settles disputes and metes out a summary but acceptable justice to all. His son was there with one of his children, who obviously took after his grandfather, for he had the fairest golden hair and bright blue eyes. His father, quite naturally and casually, carried around with him a baby's bottle with milk in it, but the child, who must have been at least one year old, was much more interested in us than in the bottle. We begged four of the lads of the village to pose for us, handsome, cheery characters wearing home-knitted, calf length hose, dazzling in squares and diamonds of coloured wool, into which their wide trousers were tucked and which are made to wear under their markhor skin boots. I told them that we knitted patterned socks like these in Scotland, which they seemed to think very funny and highly improbable.

Reluctantly we took our leave and set off for Yasin. The landscape grew wilder still with a haunting beauty, almost like a Japanese painting, the poplars like brush strokes delicately applied against the white snow, willows with hay thrust in between the bare branches. Nearing Yasin we came to the Desert of the Peacock – *Dasht-i-taus* – a rolling plain, the mountains rising sheer from its perimeter as though they had been built up without foothills; poplars like quills stood up in a long row and far in the distance was the pass to Iskoman. A small child hurried past us with a shy smile, wearing flame-coloured *shalwar,* a white chaddur over her head and a little bundle on her shoulders, her tiny figure giving scale to the dark crest of the cliffs behind.

No one seems to know why this place is called the Desert of the Peacock. There is a story current that once upon a time a local peasant fell in love with the daughter of the Raja of these parts, and she with him. Her father, in true story-book tradition, refused to give his approval to the match. Finally he agreed to set a trial for the young man. ' The girl is yours,' he is reported to have said, ' if you bring water to that piece of ground and cultivate it,' pointing to the desert. Off went the youth and like his Persian counterpart, Ferhad who had won Shireen by much the same task, he dug a long *khul* or irrigation channel and planted his sword upright in it. Calling the Raja he said : ' This is the channel that will bring water to the desert so that you can grow crops,' and pointing to his sword, ' there is the water flashing like a peacock's feather.' He convinced the father and won his bride.

The road leads on from Yasin to Darkot which we looked upon with more than usual interest, not just because it was the site of the murder of George Hayward the explorer on 18th July 1870, on his way to Badakshan, but because that day we met on the road a youth on horseback who stopped to talk with Colonel Rashid. After we had gone on a mile or so Rashid turned to me and said : ' That was the grandson of the man who murdered Hayward.' We had all heard the story of which there are several versions, and it was strange to meet this pleasant lad who carried the history of Hayward's death upon his shoulders.

The story runs that Hayward had been warned that the Ruler of Yasin meant to murder him and sat up all night writing, trying desperately to keep awake. Finally he fell asleep and was seized and bound. It seems that he was then executed but details given by a man who was present say that he was allowed to ascend a nearby mound to look once more upon the rising sun and he described Hayward as ' tall against the morning sky with the rising sun lighting up his fair hair like a glory; he was beautiful to look at . . .' then he turned and said : ' I am ready ' and was at once slain. Mir Wali, the Ruler of Yasin, met his own fate later at the hands of the Chitralis who had been sent in pursuit of him by the Mehtar Aman-ul-Mulk, whose main reason for deciding to kill him was simply that he wanted Yasin for himself and Hayward's murder provided a splendid pretext for getting rid of the ruler. Shaw and Hayward were the first Englishmen ever to reach Yarkand and it was in memory of Hayward that Sir Henry Newbolt wrote his poem, ' He Fell Among Thieves.'

' Ye have robb'd,' said he, ' ye have slaughtered and made an
    end,
Take your ill-gotten plunder, and bury the dead.'

We visited the home of the present Governor of Yasin whom we had last seen tent-pegging in Gilgit and met there again Captain Babur, of Kashmir fame, and his brother-in-law, Raja Karim Khan who is married to Babur's niece, daughter of the Mir of Hunza. While the men talked and walked beside the ruins of the old Chinese Fort I went to take tea with Raja Karim Khan's wife. She was a lovely creature, with a mass of long, nut brown hair, the elegantly-chiselled nose of the ruling family and the peach complexion for which the Hunza women are renowned. Like her mother the Rani, she keeps purdah and I wondered what she did with her days in that isolated valley so far in space and culture from gay and carefree Hunza. She had made a pet of a small cat, spotted like a snow leopard. Its antics amused her and suddenly tired of pouncing on imaginary mice it curled up in her lap and went to sleep. She stroked it with a wistful smile. Even that tiny creature was at least free to come and go as it willed.

15

Journey to Sassi

Der aayad, darust aayad
Urdu Proverb

Theoretically there is a right and a wrong season in which to journey abroad. In and around the Karakoram people constantly bemoaned our arrival in winter. 'But you should have come in the summer!' they protested, 'then you would have found our country intoxicating!' It was difficult to explain that this kind of mental inebriation was exactly what we were most desirous of avoiding. In these hidden valleys, summer brings with it a hot burgeoning of vine, a riot of apricots and wild almonds, when lack of adequate clothing against the bitter winds of winter can briefly be forgotten. If one is poor, the warm sun shines forth in a deceptive flow of well-being and even the most miserable village can appear momentarily prosperous.

Not unnaturally their pleas are shared by tourist boards, press information departments and local officials, united in a tacit conspiracy blandly to ignore or even deny the less salubrious aspects of their country's interior, such as slums, squatters, primitive drainage systems and the remote, untutored backwaters of its under-privileged citizens. Like a housewife caught in the throes of spring cleaning by an unexpected guest, the mound of dirty linen is thrust pell mell into the nearest cupboard, together with mops, brooms, pails, cast-off clothing, broken toys and the entrails of the vacuum cleaner which have obstinately refused to re-assemble, the kitchen door firmly shut on unwashed dishes and children alike and the best china deployed with ostentatious pride on a trolley in the front parlour. Provided that the visitors behave with propriety and not undue curiosity, they may well leave without the remotest idea of their hostess's problems or private life.

In order to get to know peoples and places intimately they must be seen under the worst possible conditions, devoid of the artifices of camouflage, frowsy and unwashed and newly arisen like a woman from sleep. This is a view that one can scarcely expect to be endorsed by the country's inhabitants. All manner of objections will be raised to prevent the outsider from getting access to the very places he most desires to see, to whom comfort is a secondary consideration, whose interest does not end in the main street and who cares not a jot for the modern multi-storey buildings and luxury hotels that make the skyline hideous with their ferro-concrete blocks, unidentifiable one from the other in Singapore or Suez.

Thus when we announced our desire to visit Sassi, Gilgit's current Political Agent to whom we innocently applied for permission looked at us as though we had asked to see his personal family skeleton. 'Sassi . . . Sassi . . . Why do you wish to go to Sassi?' Full of enthusiasm we told him that we understood it to be a primitive, stone-age village on the ancient route to Tibet with rock-carvings on the way which had never been deciphered. 'You have been misinformed,' he snapped, 'there is nothing to see there.' Human nature being what it is, nothing would then content us but a visit to Sassi which meant that special permits would have to be obtained to include that area. An impasse having been reached with the P.A., who could well have given us the required permission, there was nothing for it but a return to Rawalpindi.

Thanks to the kindness and understanding of our good friends

General Shahid Hamid and Lt. General Latif Khan, an interview was arranged with Lt. Colonel Yousuf, Joint Secretary of the Ministry of Kashmir Affairs. The Colonel had our permits ready waiting for us, signed and stamped and in spite of being in the midst of many pressing engagements found time to entertain us with the greatest courtesy. As with so many important and really busy people, he somehow contrived to deal with small matters as well as large ones and within a few moments of our meeting we found common ground in Scotland. By sheer coincidence one of his happiest memories was of a period of service with the Argyll and Sutherland Highlanders, to which regiment he had at one time been seconded. He knew my native town of Aberdeen, Perth and much of the Highlands, his brother married to a Scots girl. He had learned to dance our Scottish reels and one of his most prized possessions was naturally—the kilt.

We spent the night as guests of Lt. General Latif, laid in some stores which we badly needed and dined nostalgically with our friends of the Gilgit Rest House, the Crockers. Finishing the packing of clean clothes which had gone to the *dhobi* only that morning – oh shades of the most inexpensive luxury we enjoyed in Pakistan – at 2 a.m., we had to be up again at 4 a.m. in order to be at the Airport at 5 a.m., although the plane eventually only took off at 6.30. It was again a Dakota, but the pilot unfortunately was not our friend Captain Mir, so we had the salutory experience of freezing miserably along with six other passengers, too cold even to speak. Zulfi met us and having thawed out we broke the news of our return to a coldly furious P.A. and on the morning of the first of December, once again shivering with cold, we awaited the jeep in which we had booked seats; destination, Sassi.

The driver informed us sternly that he would collect us at 5.30 a.m. Groping around in the faint glimmer from a couple of candles we cursed the parsimonious custom of the Gilgit Rest House whereby 'lights out' is smugly enforced like an old-fashioned boarding school, punctually at 11 p.m., until the last streak of daylight has disappeared from the sky on the following evening. Like the total abstinence of hot water from our bath-room tap, spartan living was ensured. The last fragments of our small stock of juniper wood were used to kindle a fire in the Quetta stove, that ingenious cylinder of aluminium supported on three short legs with a tiny door through which to thrust the fuel. A sweet, aromatic smell filled the room as the bright orange wood crackled in the little stove. With icy fingers we laced up our boots over two pairs of socks and as the Jeep sputtered to a halt outside our quarters, one and a half hours late, pulled on our anoraks and set forth.

Outside Gilgit the road pencilled the mountainside like a pale grey ribbon, the great stone-cluttered valley a dark pool beneath the bright snowy heights, the sun just fingering the topmost pinnacles like a cloud's edge, then flooding a triangular, gilded ridge with pink so that the naked shoulders of Dubani and Rak-aposhi sprang suddenly from the folded hills. Somewhere high in this Gilgit Karakoram, in the second half of the millenium, a people of Iranian origin were making tools and weapons of *ayas* which must have been copper or bronze. Professor Jettmar photographed the residue of a hoard of trunnion axes and shaft-hole axes with narrow necks, and archaeologists are now reading the *Rigveda* in the light of their own evidence, the hymns pictur-ing the barbarian tribes ' with their swift horses and light chariots, with sheep, goats and cattle cultivating at first barley and wheat and later rice, their tools and weapons of copper or bronze.' Within the historic period, in such a dawn, the Chinese pilgrims Fah Hien and Sung Yun must have risen stiffly from their short sleep and wrapping their coarse robes about them watched the promised warmth steal down the valley of the Sin-to as they prepared once more to do battle with these mountain trails.

Soon we began to climb and the road dwindled to a ledge barely wide enough to hold the Jeep, the Gilgit river rushing hundreds of feet below where the rapids hung, marbled streaks of white in the green water. As we neared Parri, road gangs were trudging up from the valley, a band of scarecrow figures

175

draped in dirty, hodden-grey blankets, trailing ancient *choghas,* anything to keep out the bitter wind, feet bound up in strips of cloth or markhor skin; men from Gilgit itself, Baltis, and Kashgaris from a village about a mile and a half out of Parri, almost entirely composed of people who had fled, so we were told, because they did not like the régime in Kashgar.

We could see another Jeep approaching from the opposite direction, obviously with the same object in view, to get through at all costs before the ROAD CLOSED sign went up at eight o'clock, effectively blocking all traffic till four in the afternoon. It is one of the more alarming idiosyncracies of the drivers in this part of the world never to give way. Each Jeep advances relentlessly towards the other, bellowing like a couple of bull seals, each determined to defend to the last inch his own particular territory, until nose to nose, they are inevitably forced to halt. Honour satisfied, one of the vehicles must then back down to the nearest passing place, but how this decision is arrived at we never discovered.

This time it was our driver who, grinding into reverse, prepared to edge his way precariously backwards. At this point we excused ourselves and clambered out, ostensibly to take photographs, remembering too late that this is strictly forbidden. The labourers, delighted with the diversion, watched the manoeuvres with a kind of ghoulish pleasure, shouting directions and warnings and running back and forth to report on the distance of the rear of the Jeep from the edge of the abyss. The cries of ' *Buu . . . s! Buu . . . s!'* ' Enough! enough!' sent shivers down our spines as the wheels spun round within a hairsbreadth of eternity.

After Parri the road turns obliquely left off the Chilas road which continues south, and crossing the Alam Bridge mounts and twists in ever increasing complexity, prising its way through a maze of giant boulders that were old when Herodotus was recounting his travellers' tales from Tibet, where he had been told that the ants in the desert threw up sandheaps full of gold. The road leads the traveller onwards along the mountain ledge until he is almost paralysed from leaning unconsciously inwards, then all of a sudden the great Haramosh Plain opens out like a wild, rock-scarred battlefield, the Indus a green ribbon in a grey shale bed spread below the shelves of the plateau and straight ahead an ice-blue mountain ridge, a white snow veil flying like a pennant from the summit of Nanga Parbat. We stopped to look and gaze again on this vast panorama that stretched away into illimitable distance, while high above, like a silver beetle in the morning sunlight, droned the PIA plane on its morning sortie to Gilgit.

We have grown so accustomed to seeing wherever we go some traces at least of human habitation, be it only a field, a water channel or a haystack, that mile after mile of nothingness, with not the faintest indication that man has ever passed this way, produces a feeling of awe mixed with elation. For what seemed hours the bleak, tortured earth lay buried and useless under a river of stone, vast edifices of rock that dwarfed the Jeep, shining black and brown like a wet buffalo hide. A great silence lay like a living thing, heavy upon us. Lilliputian, we rattled and creaked through this deserted landscape, the noise of the engine a screaming anachronism against the timeless antiquity of the gaunt valleys. Below, the Sin River foamed torrentially in the rapids, choked in the narrow gorges to spill out into a deep, almond green basin, still, thick and oval. Enormous polished boulders, striated elephant grey and white, veined in broad bands outlined with thinner, delicate pencil scrawls, bore the hills, like Atlas, on their shoulders.

Not knowing where to look, we missed by some hundred yards, what we learned later to be seventh century carvings between the Bridge and the Haramosh Plain. Like the proverbial needle in the haystack, these traces of the past appear only occasionally as isolated indications, mere pinpoints of light in a vast area unexplored as outer space. Behind the mountain barrier of the central Himalayan region lies Tibet, cold, inhospitable and thinly populated. Although trade between India and Tibet has been carried on throughout the centuries, it appears that no major

M

formative influences have come into India across this frontier. From the archaeologist's point of view, which must also be the historical one, the valleys of the Hindu Khush directly connected to Central Asia, China and Persia, the western region is by far the most interesting and rewarding of the two. Only here and there do we find mention of anything of value in the present Gilgit Agency and these mainly fortuitous finds by a traveller or military historian chronicling the route march of the occasional exploratory journey.

Perhaps one day it may be possible to trace the background of this place, for there passed through it at one time Kanishka, who with his two brothers, Hushka and Jushka, ruled over Kashmir, of which the Gilgit Agency was the most northerly boundary for sixty years. By 250 B.C. Che Hwangti of China, who proclaimed himself the first universal monarch of the world, was under constant pressure from Barbarians from Tartary and built the Great Wall in the hope of preventing further aggression. The most formidable of these Tartar hordes were the Yue-chi, of whom the Guie-chang or Kushan was the leading clan. Driven from their territories by the Huns, who in their turn were defeated by the Chinese under the Han dynasty, the Great Yue-chi were finally united under the Kushan chief and proceeded to advance south to the conquest of Kashmir and Kabul. Out of this clan came Hima Kadphises, whose coins were found in the Great Stupa at Butkara in Swat State.

His successor, Kanishka, became converted to Buddhism and raised the great relic tower outside Peshawar, but before he embraced the teachings of the Gautama, his religious background was a Mazdean fire worship. Ahura Mazda, 'The Wise God', was the god of ancient Persia and the essential elements of his cult – fire. Traces of this fire-worship remain, we are told, in monuments the Kushans left in their new homes along the Indus. Like small lamps lighted along the way, we continually stumbled on Persian connections from Kafiristan to Gilgit. Unfortunately we did not see any remains of Zoroastrian rites and it is doubtful if we would have recognised these ancient fire-altars but we picked up another small clue in the Shina name for a horse which is *ashpo,* which took us all the way back to *yasp* and *ooshp* in far-off Kafiristan and Sir Olaf Caroe's link with the Avestan Persian of the pre-Christian era.

The road throughout this secret world still dips and bends and swoops like a switchback and we were startled out of our contemplation of the infinite by the gentleman behind us being violently sick, which was horrid for him and embarrassing for us as there was little we could do to help, but no one else showed the least concern, sympathetic or otherwise. Then, amazingly, like an oasis in the desert, there sprang into view the little village of Hanuchil, drowned in a mad profusion of grape-vine, apricot and walnut. The vine tendrils arched and twisted in rope-like labyrinths from house to house and tree to tree, so that the entire village seemed almost strangled by them, like the goat, which, leaping down the hillside, caught its neck in a loop of vine, described a complete somersault and as we gasped with horror righted itself, scrambled to its feet and without turning a hair scampered off again with a kick of its white tail.

Racketing across the narrow bridge spanning the stream, the Jeep squeezed its way between the houses and under the yellowing leaves, the whole place like an abandoned film set, an exotic *tour de force* somehow set down in the midst of the towering, rock-strewn landscape, and the wilderness began again. Ahead, a jagged slice of mountain soared snow-streaked to the skyline. A last six miles of road and Sassi lay before us, a wide valley steeply sloped on either side to the Sin River, and set in the centre of a ring of mountains, like a lotus sprung from the arid greyness of rock and scree, rose the twin peaks of Haramosh.

The Jeep rolled to a standstill on a flat, grassy plain, the houses climbing up the hillside, a water channel fed from distant glaciers, cold and opaque, tinkling merrily beside us. Baltis from Skardu with round skull caps and monk-like robes, wandered back and forth, on their shoulders great white stones wrapped in a piece of cloth like a shawl, for easier handling we supposed, to the site of Sassi's first dispensary. At one side a

179

couple of men chipped intermittently and unenthusiastically at a mound of what looked like solid grey granite.

The people of Baltistan are believed to be of Mongolian stock with an admixture of Aryan blood, as there has been a certain amount of intermarriage with Astoris, Gilgitis and others. In the past the poverty of their country forced them out to labour as carriers and roadmen, which many of them still do, in fact Knight says that ' Numbers here have never known what it is to have a sufficiency of food, do not even possess the clothing necessary to withstand the rigours of the climate and can be seen shivering in bitter winter weather, with bare limbs and only rags about their bodies.' At the end of the nineteenth century their existence must have been pitiable . . . ' robbed by the tax-farmers of their conquerors, hunted by Kanjuti robbers to be sold as slaves in Central Asia, dragged from their homes to do forced labour on the dreaded Gilgit road and murdered by their *Sunni* neighbours . . .' it was little wonder that when Raja Ram Singh, Commander-in-Chief of the Maharaja of Kashmir's forces, travelled through their country, he was met ' by a large, doleful crowd of ragged creatures, all wailing and carrying lit lanterns, though it was broad daylight. The Raja demanded an explanation. ' Oh Maharaja !' replied the spokesman, ' our land is so darkened with suffering that we have brought lanterns, that your Highness may see how it is with us and relieve us.' A road runs through from Sassi to Skardu closed to traffic because of snow, but men and horses still managed to get through and we found the Baltis a cheerful, sturdy people, pleased that they could keep in touch now with the outside world through the PIA service beween Rawalpindi and Skardu. The introduction of basic democracies in Baltistan and its success in promoting improvements in many angles of living on a self-help basis led to the introduction of similar tactics in the Gilgit Agency.

When the Baltis saw us climbing down from the Jeep they dropped the stones they were carrying and hurried over to have a closer look. A handful of locals materialised from nowhere, chairs were dragged forth and dusted perfunctorily with the handy *chaddur,* the uses to which it can be put as varied as the ways of wearing it. A folding table appeared upon which the crumpled, food-stained cloth was reverently spread as though it had been made of the finest Irish linen. There is no use in worrying about these trivialities, because after all it is the *thought* that counts. We were welcome, and under the eyes of all who cared to behold we sat down and made Bovril from the hot water in our flask, ate biscuits and cheese and gazed again upon the face of Haramosh, both of us silently remembering the Cambridge Expedition's ill-fated assault upon ' The Last Blue Mountain '.

A room in a small stone building nearby was made vacant and we took possession. The floor was hard-caked earth, the sole illumination coming from a tiny window high up on the wall, innocent of glass, a badly-fitting wooden shutter the only means of keeping out the cold. There were two charpoys strung with a lattice of goathair ropes, one of which had evidently been designed for a child of twelve. This Stewart nobly volunteered to occupy. A fire was lit and smoke promptly filled the room. After our luggage had been stowed, a large padlock was clamped to the door by a young man who turned out to be the driver's brother, Ijaz. His precaution amused me vastly for during all my journeys in Pakistan, over a space of 15 years, nothing has ever been stolen, surely a matter of the greatest credit in a country where the average monthly income, two years after our visit and the highest it had known, was still less than £12.

Eager to inspect our ' stone-age ' village, we decided on a preliminary sortie and set forth. Our party consisted of Ijaz, tall and good-looking, who spoke some Urdu as well as Shina, and a small, wizened old man of strongly Mongol antecedents, with thin black drooping moustache and a face like a shrivelled apple, who skipped up and down the hillside like a nimble goat and whose work, if any, must have suffered severely during our visit, for he never left our side, following us around like a small grey shadow or prancing ahead officiously clearing a path for us. His name was Sirkar and in his wake, like the Pied Piper, trotted a quiet, orderly retinue of boys and girls. Bright eyed, they had the most enchanting regular features and a great sweetness of expression, made doubly touching by the thick rough tunics of the girls above ragged trousers and bare feet and the tattered *choghas* of the boys. Nearly all of them had a sprig of white flowers stuck inconsequentially into their homespun hats, the girls with a kind of mushroom shape and the boys in the traditional rolled-back model. The effect of the fresh purity of the flowers, like a jewel, their only ornament, gave to them a kind of radiant innocence, and we were constrained to stop Sirkar from bossily shooing them off: '*Parwani . . . parwani . . .*' we pleaded, ' Let them be !'

On the rooftops, yellow squares against the slate-grey scree of the hill, women and children squatted patiently husking corn. On each roof the beehive shapes of wicker baskets plastered with white clay and holding the winter's supply of mealie cobs stuck up like chimneys. Strings of bright red chillies drying in the sun festooned the bare branches of convenient trees and on a flat, open space a man was threshing corn, the separate particles spiralling into the air from the wooden flail. The winter spinning had begun and men and children watched our passing, spindles like pendulums caught up and then released with a deft flick of the fingers, the wool magically forming itself into a ball under their arms. In the meagre rays of the mid-day sun, children huddled, in front of them little wicker baskets brimming over with goat hair like grey foam. Donkeys and goats climbed half-way up the stunted trees to strip off the bark and a flock of sheep, heavy in its winter coat, was herded along by an elderly villager with hennaed beard and carrying an open umbrella.

During our stay in Sassi, spurred on by the inescapable zeal of Sarkar, we must have visited almost every house in the village. Stone built, constructed like a dry stone dyke, most of the dwellings are sunk into the hillside so that large slabs of natural rock protrude into the single room, giving it a chill and dank air; the smoke from the fire escaping through a hole in the roof. Home-made wooden implements for raking and winnowing are stacked on the rafters, from which usually hangs a goatskin filled with milk providing a primitive churn. The resulting butter is then buried in the ground, becoming red and rancid but not mouldy and the older it is the better it is enjoyed. One man boasted that he had a store of butter 50 years old, a rare delicacy only to be brought out at weddings and funerals. Meat is mainly eaten during the first two weeks of December when goats, sheep and cattle, should the family possess any, are slaughtered, cut up and put away in a cool place for the winter, becoming hard and tough like *biltong*. Most of the cloth, other than *puttoo*, salt, oil and sugar are imported from outside by those who can afford it, the prices rising astronomically in consequence.

One of the most fascinating sights to us was the house of the *lumbardar* or headman of the village. Over 100 years old, it was an impressive, double-storey building, reinforced with wooden joists and lintels, lavishly carved shutters and boasted a built-out veranda, crammed with strings of onions, chillies and wicker baskets of maize ready to be set on the roof and covered with clay. Nearby a small wooden storehouse stood on stilts sloping slightly backwards. The cattle occupied the ground floor and rickety ladders led up to the living quarters above. Only the two end rooms had shuttered windows, so that having negotiated the climb upwards on rungs polished smooth by generations of bare feet we were led through a moving, breathing but invisible host to squat down on low stools at the central fire. Blown into life, the tiny glow picked up a pair of almond eyes, a graceful wrist thrust out from the folds of a black or dun-coloured garment, or glinted on a jingle of silver charms flashing like fishes' scales in the depths of some ocean cave.

Yuma Begum, one of the daughters-in-law of whom there were many, was nursing her youngest son, Daoud, two months old and wearing the typical little round embroidered cap with ear flaps, which must have served generations of babies judging by the faded colours dimly discernible through the grime. A tiny string of beads, a *tawiz* wrapped in a dirty bit of cloth dangled around its neck. Shahzada Khan and Shirin, her other two children, wide-eyed and solemn, were both plump and charming, accepting the sweets which fell regularly to their lot, the coloured wrappings treasured almost as greatly as the strange delicacies they contained.

The *lumbardar* Tifun Shah and his wife Rabia were a delightful and hospitable pair, in no way put out by our sudden arrival and daily seeing us off with the Shetlandic goodbye: ' Come again!' Indeed they could equally well have occupied a croft house of less than a hundred years ago in the Shetland Islands. The similarities of such remote settlements, wholly and completely isolated in time and space one from the other, only begin to impinge on the consciousness in retrospect. The exigencies of the climate, the materials at hand, the sheep and the wool, the careful husbanding of resources, continually remind one that the basic necessities by which a man can live are far fewer than we imagine. A goat hair rug was spread for us to sit on, striped in brown, black and grey, a stone cooking pot always bubbling by the fire like a French *pot au feu*.

The pots were well made and so evenly balanced that at first glance they might have been turned on a potter's wheel. Although aluminium in the form of *dekshis* or cooking pots is finding its way into the valley, Rabia assured us that she had no use for these new-fangled inventions. Stone pots preserve the flavour better, although they require a continuous and fairly strong heat and their use is restricted to those areas having plenty of fuel. We ate dried grapes, apricots and almonds out of wooden bowls and on our last day three fresh eggs were laid on top of the heap of fruit, a parting gift.

The two salient characteristics which seem to distinguish all Pakistani villagers, from the fisherfolk of the Sind coast to the tribesmen of the North West Frontier, are hospitality and cheerfulness. Wherever we went in Sassi we were offered some kind of refreshment. A woman would dart under her four foot high doorway like a black rabbit, to emerge with a platter of dried grapes, walnuts or apricot kernels, shaking it assiduously to remove the ever present grit, dust or flies. We partook happily in the spirit in which it was given and no harm ever came to us.

Poverty, sickness and disaster are accepted with Eastern fatalism and the so-called amenities of life are unknown, therefore uncoveted. It would be misleading to give the impression that the people of these hidden valleys live out their lives in a state of Utopian contentment, for hardship is implicit in every facet of their being, yet smiles are never far from the surface and a spontaneous gaiety can be triggered off by the most trivial incident.

We had stopped one day outside a courtyard where they had been husking maize. Sacking was rigged up so that the flying corn was kept within the confines of the yard and all the farmer's friends in the vicinity had come to lend a hand. Ducking under the screen, we were soon wholly occupied in photographing the men and women working patiently through the remaining heaps of yellow cobs so that not a grain should be lost. Sarkar as usual was hopping about like the compère of a show, imploring me to keep away from the family watchdog, chained up on a small shelf in the rock like a wolf in its lair just behind me and towards which I had been unwittingly backing to get the best picture.

Suddenly a small boy about three or four years old began to dance, quite of his own accord and completely unselfconscious. In short *puttoo* shirt and bare feet, he stamped out the traditional steps that we had seen the men perform on our travels from Chitral to Gilgit. Hurriedly rewinding the ciné camera we begged him to continue. With the air of an experienced trouper he removed his hat and settling it carefully on his brown curls at exactly the right angle, without the least embarrassment he took up the dance again. In a couple of seconds everyone was laughing and clapping their hands. Work was forgotten. Some of the men hummed a tune, others beat time to the rhythm and the small figure, utterly absorbed in the intricacies of the steps, whirled round and round, arms outstretched like a windmill, his small plump bare feet, heel and toe, now slow, now fast, pattering through the yellow husks, almost unaware of our presence.

' *Shahbashai buttcha!*' we all shouted as he came up to receive with shining eyes a couple of sweets which he showed off all round before peeling off the paper.

Everywhere we went we were asked for ' *gholi* ', pills, or *dwai,* medicine, to cure an endless variety of ailments, and outside our door, sternly disciplined by Sarkar a stream of patients continuously and hopefully awaited our attention. Thanks to the generosity of pharmaceutical companies in Britain we had been supplied with a fair assortment of basic drugs, which I knew from past experience, working both in and out of hospitals in remote areas, could be put to good use. Even our small efforts were quite disproportionately appreciated and it was with understandable satisfaction that we dealt successfully with such daily and accepted ailments as sore eyes, constipation, headaches and an enormous and extremely painful abscess which responded to penicillin and frequent dressings.

At the end of our visit, however, we were approached by a rather fine-looking old man who asked us to give medicine to cure his wife. Unable to find out from Ijaz's somewhat limited Urdu the nature of the complaint, we demanded to see her first and our small procession duly tramped off, much to the annoyance of Sarkar, who had ' closed ' the dispensary for the day. To our horror we discovered that five days previously she had yawned and dislocated her jaw and had in consequence been able neither to eat or drink since then. Dreadfully emaciated, her face skull-like and parchment coloured, she squatted mutely in a corner. It took a long time to try to explain to them just what had gone wrong and we finally succeeded in persuading the old man to bring her into hospital with us next day. The dislocation was of such long duration that it seemed to me to require far more expert attention than I could give and indeed I felt that it should be resolved under an anaesthetic, which in the event it was. On the other hand I argued with myself far into the night that I ought to be able to put it back into place. Theoretically and anatomically I knew exactly what should be done, but on such a fragile creature I could imagine my clumsy attempts having a shattering effect, as though her whole skull might disintegrate.

Our meal that night had been excellently cooked by our thin and weedy looking driver, both he and his brother standing by to make sure that we enjoyed it but I for one made a rather poor attempt, haunted as I was by the thought of our patient. The fire smoked incessantly. It was bitterly cold and my night was made miserable by the knowledge that I should have to take some action should the woman not be able to travel with us next day. I woke with a migraine and almost over the first cup of tea patients began arriving. We packed up our luggage in the Jeep and with Sarkar still proudly bearing the big camera, we set off on our last round of the village. This had obviously been predetermined by our guide for after climbing breathlessly up the bed of a stream we arrived at another house where there was a sick woman. Although the people of Sassi are to all intents and purposes Sunni Muslims, they kept no *purdah* within the village but the woman was too ill to come to us and although by now I was almost overcome with nervousness at what might next be awaiting us we could not refuse.

Descending a few steps we came into a well-kept room where a middle-aged woman with a distended stomach, hard as a football, complained of constant pains. She sat cross-legged, moaning gently, and a platter of raisins, nuts and dried apricots was brought for me. I carefully entered her name and all possible details of her illness along with all my other unsolved cases to report to the Agency Surgeon, who in the end nodded his head casually and said it was probably worms!

On our way down to bid farewell to Tifun Shah and Rabia, a low rumble filled the valley, swelling to a great noise like thunder echoing back and forth among the hills and a cloud of dust rose like a pillar of smoke on the opposite slopes where the track leads to the Djutial glacier. An avalanche of stones in a vast rock fall sent boulders spinning into the air and the fine particles hung in the clean air for over an hour poised like smoke from a fire.

It had taken a great deal of argument to persuade our driver to agree to carry the old couple. In fact he nearly abandoned us on the spot, convinced that the woman would expire on the journey, and several times on that nightmare trip I was almost prepared to agree with him. Neither she nor her husband would consent to sit in front, in spite of the fact that both Stewart and I would willingly have given up our seats. We tucked her up with blankets and I threatened our now sulky driver with dire penalties should he go too fast. Even at a snail's pace the woman was obviously feeling sick, which must have been agony for her. Every now and then I would call back, a catch in my throat: '*Tikh hai*, Ashraf Khan?' '*Tikh hai, memsahib!*' he would call back . . . 'All right!' his words scarcely audible above the noise of the Jeep. He was so utterly grateful to us and childishly sure of our ability to cure his wife that had she died in his arms I believe he would still have continued to give the answer he knew I wanted to hear: '*Tikh hai, memsahib!*'

Half-way from Sassi we stopped at a Rest House and I determined to telephone Gilgit and ask for a doctor to come out in the Hospital Jeep. We half-dragged, half-carried the woman into the bungalow where Stewart withered the unwilling *chaukidar* with a flow of Urdu mixed wtih Chinyanza, which so stirred him into action that he actually produced a fire and made no demur when I settled the old couple in his best chairs and ordered tea. Needless to say the telephone was out of order so there was nothing for it but to proceed.

Our driver had by now recovered his spirits and joined by another passenger we picked up at Parri, with four of us now in front, and knowing he would at least get home that night, he burst into song. At any other time we would have been fascinated by the endless repertoire of gay and haunting tunes, but with our responsibility almost breathing her last in the back of the vehicle, we were shocked by their apparent insensibility. At the end of every song I hushed them up and sticking my head out into the rushing wind called out anxiously to Ashraf. The miles crawled by and humbled by my own audacity in taking her life into my hands, I prayed as I had never prayed before, willing her to remain alive. Her death would not only have been a reflection on my own diagnosis and insistence on hospital treatment, but on the hospital itself and might well have prevented the women they were so anxious to attract from ever entering its doors. At half past seven in the evening, dusty and dishevelled and utterly worn out, I saw her safely deposited in a hospital bed which probably terrified her quite as much as the journey itself, and next day, under an anaesthetic, the operation was successfully over.

It took the best part of a week to arrange for the pair to be sent back to Sassi. They had arrived by the merest chance solely because we had wanted to visit their village and the long string of events leading up to the woman's arrival in Gilgit would stretch the imagination of any writer of detective fiction. I thought about it a lot and it seemed as though some power beyond our control had urged us on in our determination to visit this stone age village 'where there was nothing to see', and I felt justified at last in having flown back to 'Pindi and given many people a great deal of trouble so that we could travel some 60 miles out of Gilgit. But now it seemed that we still had the task of getting them home again. They had no money to hire a Jeep and there seemed to be no funds available to help them. Daily I stormed the hospital and finally, thanks to the co-operation of Colonel Rashid, it was somehow contrived and Ashraf Khan arrived at our door to say goodbye. He was quite speechless and so was I. From the folds of his *chaddur* he produced a paper bag containing four shrivelled pears, all he could afford to give me but I had my reward as he took my hands in his and bent over them with a stammered ' *Bismillah!*' And I marvelled at our casual acceptance of health facilities in Britain and wondered how many of us ever stop to think as we slip down to the surgery for a bottle of tonic, a sedative to help us sleep, a pill to pep us up, chits for an X-ray, spectacles, false teeth, elastic stockings, how pampered we are compared to hundreds of villages like Sassi.

189

The average life span of a Pakistani villager is under 30 years and over half of all deaths are among children under ten. Water pollution, malaria; tuberculosis as I found when nursing in a sanatorium in Samli; cholera; smallpox, endemic like typhoid; intestinal worms where in a single village in East Pakistan it was revealed that every single child suffered from this complaint; trachoma in West Pakistan where millions face blindness from this disease, all contribute to a fantastic death rate. With fewer than ten modern doctors per 100,000 persons, by 1963 the number of hospital beds was only 30 per 100,000 and only 2,600 nurses in the entire country, it was little wonder that a tiny village like Sassi could hope for medical treatment only at intervals.

Rural health centres are gradually being set up throughout the Gilgit Agency, but, served by a compounder, a man with some training in elementary nursing and dispensing, they leave much to be desired, especially as the great majority of women who most need skilled medical attention still hesitate to consult a male physician. The Agency Surgeon with the best will in the world can make only restricted tours in these areas, bound up as he is with the routine administration of his hospital. Much is being done to provide facilities for medical treatment and no doubt many improvements can now be seen, but with such an enormous gap in numbers between patient and doctor and without adequate well-paid and dedicated men and women there will remain for many years to come the problem of these remote and backward areas of which Sassi is only one of many.

16

The Rebellious Country

The range of which it (Nanga Parbat) is the culminating point,
forms the frontiers of the Maharajah's territories and also, it may
be said, of the known world; for beyond is the unexplored country
of the Chilas tribesmen, into which no stranger may venture.

E. F. Knight : Where Three Empires Meet : 1895

Eighty-five miles or six marches down the Indus from Gilgit,
within sight of the snows of Nanga Parbat, Chilas town sits
astride a high bluff like a hog's back, overlooking the river. The
old battlemented fort that has seen the Sikh, Kashmiri and
British invader stares out across the valley veined by the Indus
streaking bright as green jade, thick and opaque as oiled silk,
its brilliance as yet unsullied by the mud of the plains through
which its age-old passage must run until it spills out, grey and
undistinguished, into the Arabian Sea.

Into Chilas stride fierce, unkempt tribesmen from Darel,
Tangir, Babusar and Takh Nullah, sons and grandsons of the
marauding bands that descended time and again on the Astor
valley, carrying away cattle and crops, killing all the men and
making slaves of the women and children. Now they come to sell
goat hair ropes, buy salt, sugar and kerosene and finger the embroidered waistcoats, saddlecloths and rifles in the bazaar and

drink tea off plastic tablecovers in the town's one tearoom, euphemistically signposted – HOTEL. Here the Jeeps load for Astor, Bunji and Gilgit and at night the drivers crouch over small fires, smoking hookahs and exchanging the gossip of the road, a match cupped in a tented hand throwing into bold relief the black moustaches and high, swarthy cheekbones, and glinting wickedly on tall vintage muzzle-loaders.

Sandwiched in between Chilas and Gupis, or Koh-i-Ghizar, lies Yaghestan, 'the rebellious country', goal of our present journey, which appears to embrace both Darel and Tangir. No survey has yet been made of this wild tract of territory, described only 30 years before our visit as ' an extensive region consisting of a number of small republics, knowing nothing of law and order . . . the one obsession of their lives, murder . . .' Speaking a variety of languages and dialects, each small community is a separate entity with customs that seem to conform to no set pattern and it is as difficult to trace the ethnography of its inhabitants as it is to pinpoint them on the map.

We had arrived in Chilas the previous afternoon by Jeep from Gilgit and found that we were expected at the small Rest House. We had been provided with a list of introductions from Raja Karim Khan of Yasin and having long abandoned as hopeless the task of trying to unravel the mysteries of relationships in the Gilgit Agency, complex as a bloodstock stud book, allowed ourselves to be carried here and there on a tide of friendship, to discover weeks later that we were meeting brothers and cousins of our original host. We began with a courtesy visit to the Political Officer Chilas. He was enjoying his afternoon siesta and could not be disturbed. Nasir Ali, to whom we had first been commended, was nowhere to be found, so having trudged the length of Chilas we returned to the Rest House, and this time escorted by a gentleman known as the Overseer – of what we never discovered – very dashing in green crocheted beret, we set off through the bazaar to the Civil Hospital and Dr. Ahmad.

Alas, Dr. Ahmad and his wife were visiting the Forest Officer, so back we turned, making our way through a maze of narrow,

ground Garam Chashma.

Valley of Koh-i-Ghizar.

Small boy who danced for us–Sassi.

Traditional dance-mime
Thalphen.

Holding morning audience is
Raja Hussain Ali Khan, Governor
of Gupis and Hoh-i-Ghizar.

A group of young men of
Koh-i-Ghizar.

At 8,100 feet the children who
came to stare at us in Tasin.

steeply-angled lanes and finally running our first quarry to earth. Both the Doctor and his delightful and pretty young wife welcomed us warmly and at once invited us to supper. There we were feasted on delicious rice with almonds, raisins and onions; markhor steaks tasting not unlike impala, followed by a sweet topped with a fantastic bird's nest of yellow candy floss, which so intrigued us that the cook was summoned from the kitchen.

Bearing a battered frying pan in which sugar had been heated to a dark brown colour, he squatted down in a corner of the room, and with the greatest aplomb and dexterity proceeded to show us how this concoction was made. Taking a chipped enamel mug in one not overclean hand, he pressed it into the sticky mess, screwing it round and round, then drawing it high up into the air, brought with it a trail of sugar in strands of spun gold like fine hair, which he caught deftly across the other wrist.

In bright moonlight we climbed back up the treacherous slopes of the bazaar, shuttered shops on either side, to prepare for an early morning start for Thalphen, lying across the Indus in Yaghestan.

Nasir Ali turned up with many apologies for not being there to greet us on our arrival. He could well have been a Pathan from the North West Frontier, tall, lean, with an air of pride which in no sense was overbearing, a natural elegance and a keen sense of humour. He brought with him his clerk, Aman Ali and we were also accompanied by Sarfraz, the Village Aid Worker, under whose aegis lay the village of Thalphen. Although it was early morning, the women were already stooping over minute brown fields, painstakingly chiselled out of the bare rocky slopes tumbling down to the Indus. Agriculture as such is left to the weaker sex, with the exception of ploughing which demands, they tell us, more strength than they can afford.

On the outskirts of the town small boys surrounded our party, rushing to and fro brandishing the miniature sticks with which they play mock polo, the thick dust muffling the padding feet. On the plain below we stopped to watch men flaying an ox which hung suspended by one leg from a primitive wooden tripod. The skin was destined for the ferry of inflated skins at Sazin, temporarily out of use owing to the collapse of one of the hides, and the meat would be stored for the oncoming winter.

The track plunged steeply down to a *nullah* crossed by stepping stones, then climbed up a rocky path to a plateau, flat as a desert. On either side grim rock towers flanked the long, undulating stretches of seal-grey dunes, scattered with flocks of multi-coloured goats like autumn leaves, moving in a flurry of fine, wind-blown granules, and urged on by a youthful goatherd, whirling his *chaddur* round his head like a miniature dust-devil. The *sunwals*, as they are called, still optimistically wash for gold in the river in spring, although the day's takings amount only to a few shillings, all that is left of the legendary quantity of gold paid by the Indus Valley as tribute to Darius the Persian in the fifth century B.C.

Nasir Ali told us that a little gold washing takes place in the Bagrot Valley where the stream enters the Gilgit River but the yield is poor. ' Bagrotis!' giggled Aman Ali, ' *ulu qamafik!*' Apparently their stupidity is well known, but as the place where they live is well-nigh inaccessible perhaps they are just out of touch with the world around them, but many tales are told of their credulity. Once there was a Bagroti who was sent off to Gilgit by his wife with eight rupees to buy food for the household. Going through the bazaar he saw in a shop a large water melon, a thing he had never seen before. He asked what it was. ' Oh !' said the shopkeeper with a straight face, ' that's an elephant's egg. An elephant is a splendid animal and so big that all your family can ride on its back. This egg is almost ready to hatch.' So the Bagroti forgot all about the food he was supposed to be buying, parted with his eight rupees and set off in triumph carrying his egg.

As he was scrambling down the steep nullah that leads to the village of Bagrot, the melon slipped from his grasp, rolled bouncing down among the rocks and burst into a hundred fragments. As it did so, it disturbed a hare which bolted off like a flash. The

Bagroti was panic-stricken and tore away in hot pursuit. All afternoon he ran hither and thither trying to catch the animal, until darkness came and he was forced to give up the chase. His wife, furious at his late return empty-handed, demanded to know what had become of the eight rupees so he was forced to tell her the whole story of the elephant's egg. He explained that the egg had burst, the young elephant had rushed out and that he had spent the whole afternoon trying to catch it. '*Be-waquf!*' shrieked his wife, ' elephants don't lay eggs, oh foolish one!'

By the time the story had been related with frequent embellishments from Aman Ali we had reached the shore, and slipping and slithering on the steep rocks we came to a sandy beach where one of the local police force was also awaiting the arrival of the raft that would carry us across the Indus. ' Oh boatman!' shouted Jemadar Abdul Jalil in Shina, strong brown hands cupped about his lean, bearded chin. ' Eeeeee . . . *kishti wallah!*' called Nasir Ali in Urdu, not to be outdone. The voices hit the walls of rock towering above us and splintering into thin slivers of sound echoed out across the river where it ran swift and wide through the Chilas gorges. The shouting was purely a matter of form for there was nothing to be gained by this show of urgency. We all knew that the raft would not leave the opposite shore until the boatman had succeeded in loading it to its capacity and beyond, so we settled down on the warm stone to await his pleasure.

There are as yet no bridges in this area but Sarfraz assured me that a group of local *khans* had agreed to construct a ' suspension bridge ' to take the place of the ancient ferry, although I suspected that this grandiose title may only refer to one of those terrifying contraptions of plaited birch bark we had seen in Punyal, where the traveller walks on the bottom strand like a tightrope, clinging to the other two which serve as handrails. Sarfraz shook his head mournfully : ' Last year nine people were drowned on one of those . . .' nodding at the slender raft now pulling upstream. ' It capsized . . .' he added as an afterthought.

His attitude was typical. Durand relates how Dr. George Scott

Robertson on his way to Kafiristan lost nearly all his baggage and some valuable instruments which could not be replaced, by the capsizing of his raft crossing the Indus at Chakerkot, while 19 coolies were drowned. A native officer, condoling with him after the accident exclaimed with the indifference to human life characteristic of his race, 'Ah, Sahib! what a disaster! As for the coolies, we can easily find you others, but as regards the baggage, that is another matter.'

We both looked at the approaching craft with renewed suspicion but comforted ourselves with the thought that men, goods and animals had been crossing the Indus in like manner when Alexander's Phoenician oarsmen were navigating its lower reaches and the Greeks bartering the products of the Roman Empire for Indian spices, Chinese silks and gold, musk, yak tails, wool and salt from far Tibet. As we sat on the sun-warmed rock and talked with Sarfraz and Nasir Ali, the only major alteration in the country since Knight described the Chilasis as ' still very jealous of any stranger visiting their country and put to death every Shiah they come across ' was the cessation at least of outward hostilities. Altogether we felt that we were lucky to be travelling 60 years later when feelings and passions had simmered down, even though the raft at least had not changed.

Apart from Chilas itself, the peoples of this region seem to have entirely escaped any outside influences and up to the partition of the sub-continent little effort had been made to ameliorate their lot. Trade has passed them by, for there are no roads and the greater part of the Kohistan between the River Indus and the northern frontiers lies forgotten in a timeless backwater, wresting a precarious living from the unwilling soil, without schools, medical aid or help of any kind. Village Aid however, is gradually extending its field of operations and Sarfraz was responsible for 15 villages around Chilas, battling daily with prejudices and tradition, advising the farmers in new methods of agriculture, while his wife endeavoured to instil the elementary principles of hygiene and housewifery into her reluctant and apathetic pupils. The eight-bedded hospital in Chilas, most efficiently run by Dr. Ahmad, has perforce to serve an area where the bulk of the patients live far beyond its scope.

Thus poised on the edge of what might well be termed virgin soil, I tried hopelessly to convince our companions that these much-neglected tribes bore a striking resemblance in their way of life to the old Highland clansmen and that the black houses of which Sarfraz was so ashamed, were replicas of those I had known as a child in the Western Isles. Although mollified somewhat, Sarfraz obviously thought that I was making up this highly-coloured tale out of my anxiety to save his face. It is sad to think that we have imprinted on the country we ruled for so many years a picture of the British Raj, having sprung newly-formed like Aphrodite from the foam, already a finished product of civilisation, so that they cannot conceive of us ever having undergone the birthpangs of evolution.

I was spared further explanations by the arrival of the raft on which we had decided to make two separate journeys, in order to film the crossing. At first sight it almost appeared as though the miracle of walking, or at least sitting, on the waters was repeating itself before our eyes. The characters were Biblical enough and in midstream floated magically on the surface, propelled involuntarily by paddles on either side. This amazing craft was constructed from two pine logs about one and a half feet in diameter and ten or twelve feet long, across which were lashed a dozen or so poplar saplings. A few branches had been strewn sketchily over one end, topped by a piece of grey blanket.

As it happened it fell to my lot to make the first crossing, Stewart graciously insisting that I should be the one to appear on the 16mm film. Like a cat on hot bricks and supported by Abdul Jalil on one hand and Nasir Ali on the other, I gingerly made my way to what had been arranged by the addition of the blanket as first class accommodation, trusting that my foot might not slip between the branches. With the aid of those remaining on shore we were shoved off. Around and beneath us, ominously visible through the sapling trellis, the Indus swirled silken green with dapples of silver where the sun caught its polished surface. The huge, clumsy oars, made from two saplings with paddles attached, creaked in the foot-high forked rowlocks as the ferryman strained against the pull of the current, first upstream and then swiftly down, borne like a log on the rapids, to the tiny beach on the opposite shore.

The five miles of desert between Notch Ferry and Thalphen stretched out endlessly before us in a dazzle of luminous grey. Occasionally a small band of travellers shuffled past along the winding track pitted with footprints, like a tribe out of the Old Testament in their flowing blankets, the long narrow bearded faces shrouded in prophetic contemplation, or so it seemed, but no doubt the pious airs concealed all manner of mundane worries about the price of wheat, whether they could persuade the government officials of their poverty sufficiently to qualify for the cheaper prices of sugar, salt, oil and sometimes wheat, all imported from Chilas.

Thalphen itself had once played its part in the ultimate possession of Chilas by the British. In 1892 George Scott Robertson of Kafiristan fame, temporarily P.A. in Gilgit, had at the invitation of the people of Gor moved down the Indus to their border, and while there the headman of Chilas had confided to one of his men that the Chilasis were gathering and intended to fool Robertson by seizing a strategic point in the defile behind him and cut up the whole party. A march lower down the valley lay Thalphen with a small village fort, which if seized he could hold against a force twenty times his strength. He chose the boldest course and making a dash for Thalphen entrenched himself and sat down to await events. Meanwhile a raft manned by Gurkhas had been sent across the river, at the same place and in the same manner of our crossing, to bring back the Chilasi deputation. It had been treacherously fired on, three men killed and a Captain wounded. Desultory fighting went on for some days culminating in an attack on Thalpen by thousands of tribesmen which was beaten off. Robertson then turned the tables ' and with the sublime disregard for odds which characterised him, attacked in his turn with about 80 men and routed the enemy.'

The village of Thalphen, once the scene of so much bloodshed, lies in a maze of nut-brown terracing between the boulder-strewn Khinner Nullah and the silver sandbanks of the Indus beyond. Eyeless, the stone houses squat like flat cairns merging into the landscape, beside them the bare branches of the trees each bearing its load of cut maize stalks. On the flat roofs the cobs lie drying in splashes of yellow and orange. We were doubtless the first strangers to walk into Thalphen perhaps since George Robertson's fighting force, and as such caused near panic among the women. Their first reaction was to bolt into the houses, to emerge, gradually, peering suspiciously at us, heads poking out of doorways, fingers clutching the wooden framework, ready to disappear if we as much as looked in their direction.

Clothed almost entirely in black, their hands, arms and faces differed only by a shade from the dark dresses and *chaddur*. The colour of their complexions owed nothing to pigmentation but was the natural outcome of a constant exposure to soot and smoke and an almost fanatical distrust of water for any other purpose than that of irrigation, turning the mill wheels or drinking. As soap is a luxury far beyond their means, even were it obtainable, and the waters of the nullah cold enough to paralyse even the hardiest bather, it was quite understandable and not to be harshly criticised. All wore the fluted *kurta* decorated with buttons and silver ornaments, and *shalwar* tightly caught at the ankle.

Like black bats they folded their shawls around them and huddled together on the threshing floor, the sad, wild faces, eloquent of hardship and suffering, a complete reversal of the rest of the country. It was only when a baby chuckled in response to my advances that a small wave of friendliness rippled faintly through the group. A little girl, a tangle of black hair falling over the lovely oval of her face, sat staring as though hypnotised, her only clothing a ragged cotton dress and a string of beads. There is a custom in this region whereby the sexes are segregated during the summer from May till September, an old woman of the family being held responsible for enforcement of the rule. We were told too that great difficulty is experienced in rearing children, ascribed by the villagers to the vagaries of the climate, but more probably the result of lack of proper nourishment as infants, coupled with an abysmal want of even the most elementary rules of hygiene and the general tendency to intermarry, for scarcely any of these small communities marry outside their own circle. This may be partly why we saw comparatively few children and the cause also of the strange air of melancholy or passive resignation that characterised all the women of Thalphen.

It was undoubtedly a man's world, for the male inhabitants were not only distinctly cleaner than the women, but almost aggressively healthy and cheerful in comparison. We were led by a group of them to where some *charpoys* had been set on the ground covered with brightly coloured *dhurris,* overhung by the graceful branches of a huge Behd tree, small canals rippling on either side. They brought almonds, dried apricots, raisins and shelled walnuts, then pomegranates, slightly sour like gooseberries and pale yellow inside, called *Dhanu* in Shina and spoken of by Babur as ' the great Seed ' – *Dana-i-kalan.*

Sarfraz gave a talk to the gathering of farmers, answering questions on the building of water channels, ploughing, different kinds of seeds and enquiring what agricultural implements they required since his last visit. Tractors of course are useless for the tiny terraces. The people grow maize, wheat, barley and a little rice and raise two crops in the year, the first being wheat which is planted in December and harvested at the end of May. During the first week of June maize and barley are planted which will be ripe and ready to cut in mid-October. Everyone owns sheep, goats and cows. Although a family may possess only four or five of these thin cattle almost every one has a bull among them. There are three mill houses in the village where the wheels are turned by water power and they grind their own flour.

Meantime, more *dharris* had been laid out on the ground and

Aman Ali produced the first of his delectable curries which we were to remember and marvel at for months to come. We ate chicken with a sauce made with red peppers followed by a sweet and then tea. A well-matured tin of condensed milk was passed round, which was a rich, toffee brown, but we lapped it up without comment. High above us soared an aeroplane, a more familiar sight here than even a Jeep, dropping down to Chilas to pick up an engineer whom we learned later had fallen 100 feet off the newly-built road, bounced twice and came to rest with his head between two boulders. His watch and spectacles were untouched and Dr. Ahmad told us later that his only injury was a broken nose and a few scratches.

In honour of our visit a couple of men arrived and staged a traditional dance-mime which threw the audience into paroxysms of mirth. The man, clumsy and grotesque, wore a strange pumpkin mask over his face, his shirt belted with goat hair rope, and waved a great staff in his hand. His partner, alluring in orange *kurta* and shawl, coyly fended off his robustly-passionate advances. The farmers clapped and rocked about and chanted wildly; small boys threw themselves giggling on the ground, rolling about with helpless laughter and a good time was had by all.

Several of the villagers walked with us to the edge of Thalphen to say goodbye, pointing out to us what they said was a 'short cut'. Either their directions were wrong or indecipherable for we arrived eventually at a nullah too broad to cross and wandered up and down its banks for some time before Nasir and Sarfraz decided to try to pile rocks in it to make stepping stones. Feeling that much of this labour was inspired on my behalf I took a chance on it when no one was looking and hurled myself across to a fervent '*Bismillah!*' from Aman Ali who undoubtedly thought I wasn't going to make it. After this we trudged our interminable way up and down slopes of sand, one step forward and two back, our legs aching, and thankfully gave ourselves up to the coolness of the ferry crossing.

Our troubles were far from over as, with the idea of 'short

cuts' firmly implanted in their minds, the way seemed twice as long as before. We slogged up a steep, sandy slope to be faced with a wild and rocky descent to a dark nullah, the water rushing over the stones, a rider on a grey pony clattering far below us. The only means of crossing open to us consisted of two round saplings spanning the gorge, far higher than any we had attempted in Kafiristan. Due to the general unsteadiness and pliability of the bridge, we went over cautiously, one at a time. As I waited nervously for my turn, I saw Stewart's nailed boots catch in one of the logs and for one awful moment as he strove to regain his balance I thought he would plunge into the rocky bed. This slight contretemps was not calculated to inspire me with much courage, but as by now they all stood waiting impatiently on the other side of the ravine there was nothing left to do but try. My own boots, devoid of nails and now slippery and burnished with the sand through which he had tramped, gave me little confidence. Like a tightrope walker I started off determined to go slowly and steadily across. Half-way, panic seized me and I found myself going faster and faster, reaching the end at a stumbling trot, my eyes firmly shut.

After this acrobatic feat we were faced by a precipitous climb out of the *nullah,* during which I was hard put to it to cling on to the grassy shelves, not being fast enough to make enough way to carry me in one graceful movement to the top, as well as being considerably out of breath. Having finally negotiated this miniature mountain, we discovered that the effort had merely been made so that we could see the policeman, Abdul Jalil, a little further on his way. We took a polite if somewhat unenthusiastic farewell of him and proceeded back the way we had come, along the bed of the *nullah* for another couple of miles until we reached Chilas at the end of the town, two miles from the Rest House. When we finally reached home I see by my diary that the entry reads: ' Supper sent by Nasir Ali. Goat again. Wrote up notes and so to bed.'

17

Wedding at Takh Nullah

In order to see *much* one must *look away* from oneself—
every mountain climber needs this hardness.
Nietzsche; Thus Spoke Zarathustra

We had intended penetrating further into Yaghestan but
although the Assistant Political Officer, Chilas, with great kindness had wirelessed for horses to meet us at Sazin on the opposite bank of the Indus a few miles from Chilas, news came
through that not only was the ferry ' out of order ' owing to a
burst bullock skin, but the collapse of the track which had caused
the engineer's mishap, had completely cut off all communica-
tions and would take a fortnight to repair. Added to this, part
of the Gilgit road had vanished along with several tons of rock
into the river below and our retreat was cut off. Our stay in
Chilas, so fortuitously extended through powers delightfully
beyond our control, meant also that we were about to commit
the unforgivable sin of overstaying our permits, the repeated ex-
tension of which had been received with less than enthusiasm by
the Political Officer in Gilgit.

For some inexplicable reason his days were clouded by our
presence and he lived in a perpetual state of angry frustration
until the day our permits to stay in his territory should finally

expire. Our only hope now was to persuade his counterpart in Chilas, who up till now had shown us every courtesy, to intervene on our behalf and wireless a conciliatory message to the office in Gilgit. The situation was such an unusual one for Pakistan that it was only towards the end of our stay that we understood some of the petty jealousies and smouldering feuds that lay behind it. Some of our friends had either offended the Agent or his family, our own delight in their company was therefore regarded as an equal act of *lèse majesté* and we were continually assailed by the awkward feeling that in some way we were putting them in jeopardy. It was with great nervousness that we approached the Political Officer in Chilas with our request.

Khan Abdul Qadir Khan was a Pathan from Kohat, in Pakistan's North West Frontier, an area once as familiar to me as my native Aberdeenshire, and I hoped that this together with my rusty Pushto might be sufficient to break down any hostilities. As it was, Mahomet actually came to the mountain and he arrived on our doorstep to explain why we would not be able to visit Darel and Tangir. After thanking him for all his courtesy and help I explained our predicament. One can usually rely on a Pathan to lend a sympathetic ear to any proposal savouring of the illicit, for his sense of humour is such that he enjoys nothing more than stealing a march, or anything else for that matter, from a rival, and, eyes twinkling, he promised to do his best for us, invited us to dinner and suggested that Nasir Ali should take us to Babusar and Takh Nullah to make up for our disappointment.

Nasir Ali occupied some nebulous post in the Treasury. We never did discover just what he did, but before the end of our stay, two more members of that august body had defected to our service, so that we frequently wondered whether all monetary transactions in Chilas had come to a full stop during our visit. On this particular morning he was accompanied by Shahzada Khan and Aman Ali, the former quite the most picturesque of the trio, tall and handsome with a fair complexion and a gaily-embroidered *chogha*. Perhaps Aman Ali intrigued us most for he had obviously missed his vocation, turning out to be a *chef manqué*, who continued with unfailing regularity to produce a succession of mouthwatering curries in the most unlikely places, conjured up it seemed out of thin air and the contents of a large red knotted handkerchief.

We were joined by Sarfraz and together with the driver piled into an open Jeep against great hilarity and the air of a crowd of schoolboys playing truant. Three miles from Chilas we turned off the Gilgit road and headed south. The narrow track winds upwards through deep valleys buried in a winter twilight of perpetual shadow, terracing spiralling up almost to the top of the mountainside and stone houses clinging to it like eyelashes. The nullahs lay solid with ice, sculptured into shapes of bizarre beauty, shining like quicksilver in the tunnelled defiles or caught in a shaft of sunlight, blue like watered milk. Slender stalactites fringed the giant boulders and a wooden trough leading down to a millhouse spouted an arc of frozen water like a scimitar. The higher slopes were prickly with holly, laden donkeys mincing down the paths under a stack of branches, like huge hedgehogs on thin, pencil legs.

We chugged up through the villages of Dasser, Singal and Jail, the ancient engine protesting loudly, until the Jeep road came to an abrupt end at Takh Nullah where we left Aman Ali to cook lunch, turning our backs resolutely on the squawking chicken he had bought in the village and climbed up on foot to the little hamlet of Babusar drowsing in the winter sunshine in a great, boulder-strewn valley, bright with dappled snow, ringed with black pines crested with white and ten miles ahead rose the gleaming shoulders of the Babusar Pass. A couple of little girls with bare feet were down in the river bed filling water *chattis,* and at the sight of me they abandoned their pitchers and fled in terror, to peer at us from the safe shelter of a boulder.

Nearly all the children seemed to be barefoot, making me feel guilty about my stout boots and thick socks, but they padded around happily on the rooftops of houses with carved eaves, blackened lintels and doorways polished smooth as ebony over the years. Rising in layers, one above the other, like the pirates in Peter Pan, we were constantly finding a plume of smoke escaping from a hole beneath our feet, the chimney of the house below. Gradually the children became used to our presence and sidled up shyly to share in the sweets we had brought for them. I often wondered what the Scottish manufacturers would have thought if they could have seen the strange little figures that reached out for these exotic delicacies, or seen the shining eyes as, mystified, they tasted their first ' sweetie ' ! The girls were endearing wild creatures, with shining black ragged fringes under pillbox hats, round their chubby necks a blaze of cerulean beads, silver tawiz and medallions, often the only note of colour on their drab, dark tunics.

There is such a pleasant air of ' belonging ' in these out-of-the-way places where one is accepted as an equal with no thought or knowledge of the different lives we might lead. Everyone wanted us to come and visit them and I think only Sarfraz struggled between a vague suspicion that we might find his people in some way wanting or backward, and a puzzled happiness at seeing the unaccountable delight we seemed to find in each other's company. As Village Aid Officer he had been indoctrinated with certain standards of living to which somehow his pupils had to attain. It must have been an uphill task, for although he conscientiously bullied, cajoled and lectured they listened with respect and interest but still saw no valid reason for the changes he tried so hard to bring about. Like the children of Israel he was finding it an almost insuperable task to make bricks without straw.

Soon Nasir Ali came to tell us that we had been invited into a nearby house. The outer room had elaborately carved pillars supporting the roof and had been put to some use as a storehouse, but the inner room was as usual so dark that at first neither of us could see anything at all, the smoke from a tiny cooking fire stinging our eyes till they watered, the only opening a small square in the roof. Someone blew up the fire and I realised that there was a woman squatting beside it. Her husband told me that she had a baby and that it was ill. Diligently we peered all around us until he signalled to his wife to show it to us. It was almost completely covered by her *chaddur* and was finally brought to light, quite naked except for a *tawiz* round its neck, bandages covering both its little legs. These were gently unwound to reveal a couple of pieces of wood serving apparently as splints, and the father drew our attention to the baby's legs which he said were crooked.

This seemed to me a debatable point. All babies' legs curve a little and sometimes even look quite bandy. The child was plump and well nourished so I suggested that they should take him down to the Civil Hospital in Chilas where Dr. Ahmad would examine him, treat him if necessary and reassure the parents. I spoke to Sarfraz about it and he brightened up immediately at the thought of being able to be of some practical help and said that he would arrange transport. We gave them some *gholi* for headaches and rheumatic pains, cleaned and bound up a nasty cut on the husband's foot and coming out, crouching under the low lintel, we found the headman, Habit Khan, with a mallard drake he had just shot with his muzzle loader which he insisted on presenting to us, telling me we were his guests.

He accompanied us further down the village to where a second *lumbardar* had invited us to take tea on the balcony of his storehouse. We crossed from the winding track through the village by means of a plank laid across a deep *nullah,* and found chairs set out. Two were deck chairs with blue and white striped canvas; a *charpoy* with a bright red *razai* and a table with miracle of miracles a clean white cloth. We all settled down in brilliant sunshine, the gamboge of the pine storehouse staccato notes of colour in the dark brown valley ridged with snow along the terracing; yellow maize spread on some of the rooftops and stalks thrust into the forked branches of trees to be used as fodder for the cattle. Straight ahead of us was the Babusar Pass, a great kite planing down, like a piece of burnt paper against the clear blue sky. Sweet tea and hardboiled eggs were brought and there we sat in that Alpine scenery, Nasir Ali, Shahzada Khan splendid in his great chogha, Sarfraz in lilac *qamiz shalwar* and the two *lumbardars,* their guns in one corner, the mallard in his bright dead plumage at our feet.

After tea the storehouse was unlocked so that we might inspect it. Most beautifully kept with great haunches, backs and sides of beef hanging in neat rows, preserved by the intense cold like a natural deep freeze. Bins built against the wall held gold and orange maize. There were sacks of flour; butter in heavy brass pots with paper stuffed into the neck to seal them; sheep and goat's wool piled on shelves in balls of soft grey and brown and brightly coloured *razai* and *dhurries* were hanging across the beams. There were sheepskins, skin sacks for churning butter, all in perfect order. The only possible explanation for this was the fact that the storehouses were a strictly male preserve. The men alone kept the keys and when food or extra bedding was required, it was handed out, but the women might never see the inside and having no examples of cleanliness and order in front of them could scarcely be expected to make perfect housewives.

Aziz, one of the *lumbardars* who had been trying to attract our attention for some time, told us that a wedding was about to take place down at Takh Nullah and that we were all invited to come and take pictures. So off we set down the hill again, Shahzada's strong arm acting as a brake whenever my boots slipped on the icy slopes. Passing a group of houses, I spied a *kurta* spread out on a roof to air or dry and stopped to examine it. The men held it out for me while its owner smiled bashfully from a doorway. Weighing about five pounds it was made of stiff black calico, the bodice lined with scarlet, the shoulders and hem piped with the same colour and the skirt fluted from below the waist so that the hem measured eleven yards in all.

The pattern was traditional, but the embroidery, alas, had been done with a sewing machine. The whole of the bodice was covered with a tracery of cerise, purple, pale green and yellow, squiggles and lines running down and outlining the triangular insets on the skirt. It must have been made in Chilas, perhaps

The horses of the Governor of Yasin.

Children sat spinning in the meagre rays of the midday sun

The headman's house in Sassi over 100 years old.

Stewart at table, Sassi with Haramosh in backgrou

at classes run by Sarfraz's indefatigable wife, for a number sten-
cilled on a piece of tape attached to the neck read 6228. Very
strong and obviously made to last, it had a deep vee neck so that
mothers could feed their babies without undressing, a procedure
which we felt might be a rare one – occasionally I suppose they
must somehow contrive to wash; perhaps in the summer time
when the ice-cold river warmed slightly; at marriage, and may-
be death.

I could not help comparing the garment with the exquisitely
embroidered *kurtas* that used to be made in the Kaghan Valley
where a woman began sewing her daughter's wedding shirt when
she was born. It would be finished when she was 16 or 17. I
could not afford to buy the one I saw in the Craft Shop, but was
unable to resist a cushion cover made in the same way with the
most elaborate and beautiful stitching in Chinese silk of deep
dark red, overrun with gold thread. Neither are now obtainable
and the art is dying out, but my pillowcase is framed flat under
glass and is marvelled at by everyone who sees it.

As I examined the great heavy village *kurta,* the men suggested I should try it on and have my picture taken in it. This I
did amid shrieks of laughter and joy all round, everyone rushing
out to see this unusual phenomenon. So, feeling they ought to
have their money's worth, I danced a Highland Fling, which I
suppose, looking back, was a pretty scandalous thing to do in a
country where no women, or should I say only women belonging to the oldest profession, ever dance in public before men.
However there were no orthodox *mullahs* around to call down
the wrath of Allah upon me and my shamelessness was much
appreciated. They threw their arms round each others necks,
clutched at doorways and bent double, shouting and clapping
their hands. At the end I asked if they would sell me the dress
so that I could keep it always. I probably paid dearly for it, but
if the owner could send to Chilas for another two new ones, or
buy some little luxury, then it was but a small return for all the
pleasure and hospitality we received from her people, which in
this way I could honourably repay.

One has to be careful not to give offence over such transactions and I was reminded of one never-to-be-forgotten incident 1,000 miles away in the Chittagong Hill Tracts of East Pakistan which must, I think, have gone down in history. During our travels there we had made friends with a dozen or so Buddhist monks who lived near Rangamati. On one occasion we paid them a visit accompanied by two Americans who had shown us much hospitality, in fact the only people with whom we ever stayed who were not Pakistanis. Our visit to the monastery was decidedly strained as neither of the Americans would touch the dish of violently-hued cakes, specially brought from the bazaar for the occasion. They sat in patent misery, balancing cups on their knees, convinced that the water couldn't possibly have been boiled and therefore must be seething with every kind of germ and all in all Stewart and I were forced to consume a couple of cakes each and drink most of the tea to avoid giving offence, and whispering in Urdu to our puzzled friends that the Americans had not been well. The moment of departure came when Holly spied a piece of material flung over the shoulder of one of the younger monks' saffron robes.

Pouncing like a cat, she stabbed at it with her varnished finger nails, and enunciating her words slowly, carefully and loudly, as though speaking to a deaf mute, she said : ' I buy? You sell? I give you rupee?' The young man controlled himself admirably and with an impassive countenance drew himself up and explained in faultless English that this was impossible, handing her husband his card. He was a Ph.D. of Yale. Her husband gazed at it in horror. ' Aw ! . . . Holly !' he drawled.

Our own little bit of business over, Aziz was getting impatient that we should come to the wedding. Someone seized the dress and off we set at breakneck speed, skidding and sliding down the *nullah*. On the way he pointed out a single tree with a silver and tinsel ornament glittering on its topmost branch at which the guests would fire on their way to the ceremony. Weddings in these areas are generally held in the winter months, after the crops are in. Benefit of clergy is not a vital necessity in such lonely places so that the main excitement centred round the actual celebrations to which every male in the vicinity seemed to have been invited. As there were no less than six bridegrooms this was not surprising.

On a flat rooftop jutting out over the steep drop into the valley the guests were assembling, the background a long panorama of pine trees and snow, the river rushing far below and in the distance the white teeth of the mountain between Chilas and Gilgit. At one side, in a natural rock shelter, steamed two enormous blackened cauldrons, each one about two feet in diameter and suspiciously like abandoned oil drums, the smoke from the wood fires drifting upwards in a blue haze. Beside them a couple of men were energetically chopping up meat with axes, hacking it into ragged chunks which they tossed carelessly but with unerring aim into the bubbling water. Children flitted to and fro like gaudy butterflies in brilliant blues and greens, and now and then a gaily-clad girl, giggling nervously over the folds of her *dophatta*, slipped through the throng of men and darted into the house where the brides waited in lonely isolation.

Every other male carried some sort of firearm and one might have thought at first glance that they were gathering for a tribal foray. Small boys struggled with shotguns and muskets as big as themselves; there were rifles and revolvers and muzzle loaders. One bearing the date 1852 had the unmistakable letters V.R. stamped on its beautifully inlaid and brass-bound stock. There were old men, young men and children, dark and swarthy and fiercely militant with a kind of sombre swagger.

We were escorted to *charpoys* laid with brightly patterned rugs and no sooner were we seated than all hell broke loose. Men stood and kneeled on the edge of the rooftop and fired merrily in all directions. Rods were rammed home, spent cartridges flew about all over the place, the acrid smell of gunpowder vying with the contents of the boiling vats, and the whine of bullets richochetting off the enclosing hills in carefree abandon was at once ear-splitting and alarming.

Meanwhile, round the perimeter of the room, *dhurris* were

spread for the six bridegrooms who slouched over to their places looking sheepish and self-conscious in brand-new clothes, bright *chaddur,* spotless white shalwar that looked as though they had been starched, and new Gilgit hats, to a redoubled *feu de joie* from their supporters, and took their places in a row along the edge of the natural stage along with the principal guests. The local band which had been waiting with some impatience for its turn in the festivities now marched in and squatting down with flute and drums, one an empty petrol can, started up the local version of what we imagined to be the wedding march.

Immediately three young men in grey *mahzri shalwar qamiz,* bandoliers of cartridges across their shoulders, rose to their feet and began the slow, shuffling dance traditional in these areas. Arms outstretched, they moved with grace and concentration, now fast, now slow. Soon another couple of men entered the arena, one seized my newly-acquired dress and slipping it over his head, snatched a *chaddur* from someone else and turning himself into a travesty of femininity, joined his partner in a duet of love play and innuendo suitable to the occasion. She or he, allowed herself to be pursued, coquettishly twisting and turning in alluring postures, now and again repulsing with maidenly modesty the overtures of the swain; passion mounting, she drew him on, only to spurn him once again, the mime leaving little to the imagination. However, true love going unrequited and unrewarded except by the guffaws and clapping of the audience and the rather embarrassed smiles of the bridegrooms, put out a little by my presence, the couple sank exhausted to the ground and an old man, not to be outdone, leapt into the circle and with extraordinary agility executed a fast *pas seul* that sent everyone cheering and clapping once again. The first part of the wedding feast then arrived and was set before the bridegrooms, our share being brought to us in the form of a great basinful of walnuts which our nearest neighbours immediately and obligingly began to shell for us.

Greatly daring I asked if I might see the brides, and after some consultation I was told that they would be ready in five minutes, the uncle of one of them acting as messenger and reporting progress on their toilets. This completed, I was called over and escorted to the house. It was pitch dark inside and how they ever managed to dress in the gloom seemed incredible. I shuffled about nervously inside the door, wondering how I could ever get a photograph even if permission were given. Quite unprepared for such a rare occasion I had brought no flash with me.

At last one girl was dragged reluctantly from an inner room, lighting up the doorway like a slender column of stained glass, Her eyes, heavily ringed with *sur'ma*, glanced shyly up at me through looped braids of hair no thicker than a knitting needle. She was literally loaded with jewellery; a gold nose ornament about the size of a shilling, a jewel in the centre; huge silver filigree bells hung on either side of her face and her small breasts were covered with silver chains and drops that spattered across her like rain. The flame of her thin orange *dophatta* glowed over silk *qamiz* and *shalwar*. The uncle kept hauling first one and then the other forward like cattle at a market, displaying their various charms. Ignorant of Urdu, they kept trying to hide themselves and I asked him to explain to them that although I understood their customs I wanted very much to take a picture of them, feeling that even a dark one would be better than none at all. The old man dragged them up to me one by one and I wished them all happiness, prosperity and many sons. Stepping out into the bright dazzle of sunlight, humbled by the sight of so much simple happiness, I sent up a silent prayer that the mountain bulwarks of the Karakoram will withstand a little longer the inevitable march of progress, silent because I knew Sarfraz would not approve my subversive wishes.

After this it was time to go and seen off by all the men whistling and yelling, Shahzada Khan, the skirts of his *chogha* flying and under his arm my precious dress rolled up in a bundle, we set off to eat our own meal. We sat outside a house in the warm sunlight, the snow only a yard or so away, and ate once more one of Aman Ali's magnificent curries.

We had just time for a quick wash in the minute bird bath of hot water provided grudgingly by the Rest House bearer when it was time to set off for dinner with the Political Officer, Chilas. Here we were treated to yet another meal of all our favourite dishes; *kebab,* chicken, *dhal, nan,* markhor as illicit as our presence and equally unremarked, and green tea in small handleless cups, Qadir Khan nodding approvingly as, after a second cup, I turned mine upside down, an old Frontier custom, indicating politely that one has had enough.

The evening was rounded off for me by an invitation to visit his wife in the *zenana,* a rare privilege for a chance visitor. The Pathan's three material gods are *zan, zar, zamin,* women, gold and land, all three guarded with equal zeal and occasional ferocity, and only another woman or members of the immediate family are ever allowed to set eyes on the first. Protocol demanded that my host present me to the Begum Saheeba himself, and after leading me through a maze of corridors, he ushered me into a vast cavern of a room, dimly lit by two lamps in bright pink shades. On the perimeter loomed an imposing array of *almirahs,* painted trunks and high old-fashioned chests. In the centre a black stove crackled briskly, stoked by a grinning urchin of 10 or 12, still young enough to satisfy the proprieties, who staggered in and out with disconcerting frequency and armloads of wood.

The focal point, however, was undoubtedly the great divan bed covered with layers of *razai* or padded quilts and strewn with hard, oblong pillows lavishly embroidered with flowers and mirror work. There, enthroned like a Moghal Empress, sat the Begum Adbul Qadir Khan, brilliant in turquoise satin *shalwar qamiz.* A delicate gauze *dophatta* edged with gold thread modestly veiled her head and the heavy chestnut plaits that hung well below her waist. Red-gold ear-rings glowed in the lamplight, her bracelets tinkling like camel bells as she raised one hand to her forehead in the customary greeting.

All the details of her finery were only taken in gradually. At first one was drawn like a magnet by the astonishing loveliness of her eyes, so wide and almond shaped, peat-brown like a Highland trout stream and made even larger by their fringe of *sur'ma*. When I spoke to her in halting and rusty Pushtu her face lit up like a field of flowers under a sudden ray of sunshine : ' *Tashrif rahkiye!*' she smiled. ' Rest yourself !' and patted the bed beside her with a plump, ringed hand, the nails tinted with henna, my most ordinary presence evoking a welcome far greater than I deserved.

The Begum's isolation in Chilas must have been almost complete, Dr. Ahmad's wife perhaps her only close friend. *Purdah* was something to which she had become accustomed since probably about the age of 13, but here she was bereft of its companionship, of the host of sisters, aunts and cousins who normally keep the women's quarters buzzing like a hive of bees with talk of weddings, births and deaths and no doubt the inscrutable ways of their lords and masters, while all the time playing an important part in the conduct of the family.

She was eager as a child for news of home and soon we were talking of Kohat and the Frontier hills; the high watch towers of the villages and the jackal howling in the night; the metallic sound of *tonga* bells, punctuated by the driver's cry of ' *Baa . . . ttcha! Baa . . . ttcha!*'; of *loquat* like small, luscious apricots; *amroot* the size of an apple full of soft pips; cactus and camel thorn and the sweet perfume of *chambeli* flowers; the bazaars at night, the open shops, small islands of light in a necklace of naptha flares, and we were both overcome by nostalgia.

Kohat was famous even in Babur's day, the tribes from whom my hosts were descended, occupying almost the same territory as they do today, and the Bangash with whom I had lived outside Kohat on the Hungu road, ravaged in the year 1505, during Babur's first expedition, not long after he had occupied Kabul. ' Making an irruption into Hindustan ', he swept through the Khyber and hearing that Kohat was reputed to be a wealthy place gave up his idea of crossing the Indus. After plundering Kohat ' about luncheon time ' he went into action against the Bangash, describing the gorge near Hangu so minutely that it is still possible to identify it. In the following century the Moghals continued their attempts to subdue the wild Pathan tribesmen. Three hundred Orakzais were slaughtered by a subterfuge near Kohat and from that city the Moghal forces marched forth to the battle of the Sampagga Pass, described both by Khushhal Khan and by Jahangir in his memoirs.

The Begum Qadir Khan must have been a tall woman but I never saw her other than coiled up on her couch. Everything was fetched and carried by her personal maid, Zakia, a slim lovely child from her native Kohat, who in between her many errands sat perched on a *charpoy* knitting furiously at some monstrosity of a khaki cardigan. Like a piece of quicksilver she darted to and fro bringing me enormous platters of *malta*, oranges peeled deftly by her flying fingers; pears, apples and grapes, my plate continually replenished and when I called: ' *Dah kafi deh!* ' ' Enough', brought me water so that I might wash.

The warmth stole around me, a closed-in feeling like wearing the *burqa,* the age-old intimacy of the woman's world, inviolate and secret. The Begum approved of my three sons, their photographs eliciting admiring ' *Wah! Wah's* ', but not that they should be allowed to choose their own wives, while my daughter's forthcoming wedding drew forth a torrent of eager questioning, especially from Zakia. Beside the Begum's colourful and exotic beauty I shrank like a small grey mouse in my dull western clothes, naked of adornment save for my bracelet which she never tired of admiring, especially when I told her that the gold seals were my *tawiz.* Stoically fatalistic, Pathans nevertheless lay great stress on symbols and charms. Every village child will have a *tawiz* hung on a cord round its neck. Consisting of a few words from the *Holy Quran* written on a scrap of paper by a *pir* or holy man, it may be sewn up in a piece of rag or encased in a silver amulet as big as a cigarette case, and there are charms for all ills whether of the flesh or of the spirit.

Throughout the evening the word *shatraan* kept recurring like a magic spell and I understood it to be some game the Begum played with her husband. Finally, overcome by curiosity, I asked if I might see it. Zakia needed no prompting and rushed off giggling to return with a flat box which she thrust down in front of me. Watching my face intently they urged me to open it. It was a beautifully carved set of ivory chessmen. I learned much later that the game of chess probably had its origin in India and dated from the first century A.D. Originally it called for four players and the moves were decided upon by the throwing of dice. Because of its military pieces and strategy suggesting the movements of armies in battle, the game was called *caturanga* ' four corps '. From India it passed first to Persia and then to the Arab countries and was introduced to Europe before A.D. 1100 The name *chess* is believed to be derived from the old French *eschecs,* for the Persian *shah,* a king. Rook is said to come from *roka,* Sanscrit for a ship or chariot, and the word *checkmate* from *shah mat,* ' the king is dead '.

All this information was of small assistance to me during my first game of chess in a *zenana.* A small table was dragged up and nothing would do but that we should play. In vain I protested my ignorance of the game, beyond perhaps the names of the pieces. The Begum would teach me. Her eager explanations were made doubly confusing by the names given to the men, and pawns called *sepoys* and knights *ghore* (soldiers and horses) did little to unravel the mysteries of the opening moves. Bishops addressed as *topi wallahs,* ' men with hats on ' lent a bizarre air of comedy, while castles were *roz,* the splendid *Wazir* and *Waziri,* the King and Queen, imparting a fairy tale atmosphere to the whole proceeding.

The Begum proved extraordinarily patient with me and when I mistakenly tried to take her knight she screamed : ' *Yeh nai marsacta!*' literally ' You can't kill him !' At every foolish or unorthodox move on my part, which were many, she sighed, ' *Toba! toba!*' and I hoped indeed that I might be forgiven for spoiling her game. Exhausted, I was finally rescued towards midnight by Khan Abdul Qadir Khan, with whom Stewart and another couple of visitors, male of course, had been struggling with an equally trying game of bridge. Reluctantly she let me go and taking both my hands in hers as I murmured '*Pah mah khah dah khah!*' 'Goodbye!' she begged: 'You will come again?' '*Insha'allah* Begum Saheeba', 'God willing let our next game be in Kohat!' and as her husband smiled indulgently upon her with a tender show of affection rarely displayed in front of strangers, I wished that my memory had been good enough to quote them Khushhal Khan's lovely *Ghazal*:

Ta wi chih gham mah kra nur zuh sta yam tuh zma,
Zuh kho di zhwanday kram kuh darogh kre kuh rikhtia . . .

Said'st thou ' Grieve not for I am thine
    And thou are mine, my darling, mine ' –
And verily thou art as wine
    poured in the bowl of life, beloved.
Were every maid that's worshipped fair,
    and peerless beauties everywhere,
Still must I stand, still must I stare,
    at thee and only thee, beloved.

18

The End of the Road

To travel hopefully is a better thing than to arrive and the true
success to labour.

Robert Louis Stevenson : El Dorado

Of all the mute witnesses to human suffering, surely roads must
provide the most eloquent testimony, and of the millions who
travelled hopefully throughout the centuries, few arrived.
Threading a map with confident thick red lines, or labouring
tentatively in tiny dots like perforations across deserts and
through mountain passes, history is inscribed like a saga on every
milestone. Vulnerable to all kinds of attack or ambush, armies
can be halted by their possession, empires won or lost over their
building. Cultures, religions and invasions have been borne along
the tracks of ancient trade routes that existed when bronze-age
man hawked his wares across Europe, carrying his box of samples
with him and leaving stores hidden at strategic points on which
he could draw to supply his customers. Once embarked there is
no turning back, physically or metaphorically, as the sub-
continent of India and Pakistan discovered during the chaos that
followed on Partition.

On February 20, 1947, Clement Attlee, then Prime Minister,
announced that the British would leave India in June 1948 and

despatched Lord Louis Mountbatten to India as Viceroy to direct the operation. Four months later, Mountbatten was back in London and on June 4, 1947, he announced suddenly that independence would be given to both India and Pakistan on August 15, almost a year in advance of the expected date. Mass panic ensued.

No other population movement in history involved so many people in so short a time and the roads became choked with the tens of thousands fleeing from their homes, killing and being killed. The Grand Trunk Road of the Moghals was scattered with dead and dying and within a few months at least 500,000 people had died, either violently or from disease and starvation.

The Gilgit road too has known its Golgotha. Once a mere footpath running for 240 miles from Gilgit to Srinagar over some of the worst country in the world, it was called only 60 years ago, ' The Siberia of Kashmir' and has been one of the most bloody in its toll of human lives. As the northernmost outpost of the old Indian Empire, Gilgit covered all the passes over the Hindu Khush from Shimsal in the east to those of the Yasin River on the west. The valley route was vital to Kashmir in order to hold in check the raiding tribes from Yasin and Hunza-Nagar on the north and those of Chilas on the north-west. An enormous transport service was needed to supply the garrisons on these frontiers with grain, and thousands of Kashmiri Muslims were driven off every year to toil as carriers on the Gilgit road. Dragged from their homes and families, hundreds perished of cold, hunger or thirst.

' When a man is seized for this form of *begar*, his wives and children hang upon him weeping taking it almost for granted that they will never see him more. A gang of these poor creatures, heavily laden with grain, toiling along the desert crags between Astor and Gilgit on a burning summer's day, urged on by a sepoy guard, is perhaps as pitiable a spectacle as any to be seen on the roads of Siberia. But these are not convicts and criminals but Mussulman farmers, harmless subjects of the Maharajah . . .

all Hindoos being exempt from this form of forced labour.'[1] With the construction of a mountain road, ten feet in breadth throughout, a properly organised coolie corps with mules as pack animals began to take the place of the miserable bands of impressed Kashmiri Muslims. The engineering difficulties involved in the building of the road were described by Knight as ' almost insuperable . . . To construct a road that would not be repeatedly swept away by falling rocks, while the loose mountainside, ever ready as it is to slide away, affords the least secure of foundations.'

The same problems obtain today with the added hazard of the new Indus Valley Road being built some hundred feet above the present one and it was with mixed feelings that we received the news that the road was once again ' open to traffic '. Nasir Ali came hurrying round to help us find seats in a jeep leaving the following morning, for we dare not postpone our return a day longer than we could help. The bazaar had suddenly flared into life and drivers who had spent two or three pleasant days idling in the tea-shop, smoking endless *chelums* and playing games of chance, were roused into frantic if belated activity, loading, haggling over prices and and tinkering ineffectively with last minute repairs, so that it was some time before we found one with two places, or rather a driver who was prepared to squash us into his already overloaded vehicle.

Early in the morning our friends came to say goodbye bearing farewell gifts; a leopard's claw for luck – a commodity we felt might well be in short supply on the crowded road – a basket of fruit, and from Nasir Ali a magnificent *Murgha Zerin*. It was long after we had returned to Scotland that I discovered that this ' Precious Fowl ' was indeed an Impeyan Pheasant, *Lophophorous Impejanus,* described as the most iridescent and brilliantly coloured of all the pheasants, those ' birds of Phasis' brought to Greece by the Argonauts from the river of that name in the ancient province of Colchis.

[1] E. F. Knight: *Where Three Empires Meet.*

The heavy-bodied, short-tailed pheasant, known as impeyan or monal, live in the high Himalayas, usually near the snow line and in the adjacent mountains of India and China. Just over 29 inches from beak to tail, the bird has a wingspread of about 28 inches. The tiny feathers on its elegant head are bright, iridescent emerald, the most distinguishing feature its graceful crest of 16 or so delicate plumes waving on slender stalks like fine wire, tipped with flat, blue-green feathers with a central vein like a leaf. The crest is much prized and worn by men like a cockade at the side of their grey homespun hats. The neck passes from burnished red into greenish bronze, and the entire back and wings are a blaze of brilliant green and prussian blue, save for an almost triangular white patch above the square, brown-gold tail feathers. It seemed little short of desecration to shoot or capture these birds and one must be glad that they live in such inaccessible places. Like the snow leopard, the ibex and markhor, their numbers must have dwindled sadly with the advent of the rifle.

Our farewells were cut short by impatient hooting from our driver, Shakoor Beg, a Hunza man, and therefore to my wishful thinking surely an experienced and capable one, but we had barely time to stow our luggage and clamber in when he set off. The big camera case lay at our feet, our knees huddled up to our chins, shins pressing against the dashboard and in the small space remaining rested the canvas bag of provisions. On my lap were the small cameras and the *Murgha Zerin*, swathed in a plastic bag, its crest waving proudly in the air. The jeep was open, without doors and already heavily loaded. A couple of hens clung to the sacks of maize behind us with remarkable tenacity.

We had no sooner cleared Chilas when the exhaust began to give vent to frequent and alarming reports every time Shakoor Beg lifted his foot off the accelerator. Clean shaven, a peaked cap pulled low over his eyes, his mouth and nose muffled in a large scarf wound several times round his neck, a glove on his left hand and the sleeves of his *chogha* folded back to the elbows, he drove with the speed and dash of a rally competitor and the air of an American gangster. Below us the Indus coiled grey green like silk, broken here and there by pebbled backwaters and the ripples of the narrows between tall banks of smooth rock like giant sandcastles, turreted and divided and thrusting upwards against clouds windswept like fine hair.

Slowly we slithered and scraped round the first bad bit of road in a constant and seemingly unending state of repair, the new road several hundred feet above, supported like the Great Wall of China by a neat compact mosaic of rock pieces. Every so often showers of gravel cascade in high pillars of dust; boulders bounce off from rock to rock; men stand nonchalantly leaning on a spade like eagles perched on an outcrop of stone, or flatten themselves against the overhang as we crawl past. A young boy, instead of keeping to the inside will deliberately dash across in front of the Jeep, lower his bundle behind him and lean calmly against the fragile bulwark airily disposed along the perimeter, a few boulders all that stand between him, or us for that matter, and eternity.

The journey is never dull. Sometimes we come to a complete impasse as blasting has been in progress and the narrow track is strewn with enormous chunks of grey rock spewed from the hillside above. Men with mallets, steel bars and other useful implements split them still further until either they are of manageable proportions or of a suitable size and shape to build up the bastion below. Those not actually wanted are lightheartedly tossed off into space. More often than not there are no stones to mark the edge, the actual value of a parapet being more psychological than physical for nothing would stop our overloaded Jeep were Shakoor Beg to relax for a second or make one ill-timed judgment.

The Indus Valley road that occasioned so many problems must follow in part the strange journeys once made to Swat by Tibetan Buddhists in the eighth century A.D. The floods that caused the decay of Buddhist centres and monuments in Swat in the sixth and seventh centuries, left Buddhism open to the incursion of aboriginal cults, and the tendency towards magic for which Uddiyana had been celebrated, increased markedly. The last form of Buddhism, The Diamond Vehicle (Vajrayana) acquired a great vogue, its leading exponent Padma Sambhava, a great Tantric miracle worker. His fame spread by word of mouth, carried by pilgrims and traders along this self-same route all the way from Swat to Tibet and in A.D. 747 King Thri-srong-det-san of Tibet invited him to assist in the foundation of the great temple of Samye.

Armed with his ritual sceptre the sage set out, nothing daunted by the rigours of the way, on his marathon journey, to embark on an all-out campaign against the evil spirits implicit in Tibetan theosophy. He must have been as discerning and broad-minded as he was hardy, for once arrived in Tibet he realised that it was a hopeless task to wean the Tibetans from their taste for the supernatural, and evolved the compromise of Lamaism. This was the result of a fusion of Tantric Buddhism with Shamanism, the worship of good and bad spirits which have to be honoured and propitiated. Prayers were no longer offered to a divinity distinct from mankind, for mankind itself is part of the absolute; hence the practice during meditation of visualising a divinity in order to identify oneself with it, accounting in this way for the multiplicity of Tibetan gods.

Tantraism, like Brahmanism, has always attributed a magical significance to mystical patterns or formulas and in the end the rites no longer need even to be spoken and the written word printed on the prayer wheel can be released as powerfully as the spoken formula. Padma Sambhava from Swat was regarded as the founder of this Lamaism and Swat became a kind of holy land for Tibetans eager to go on a pilgrimage to the country where this most revered master was born. And so perhaps our paths had crossed; the route to Sassi may well have been that taken by those dogged pilgrims of over 1,000 years ago and the Indus heard their mumbled chant of *Om ma-ni pad-me hum*; the roads we thought too dangerous would have been small miracles to Padma Sambhava carrying his message hopefully from the paradise of Swat over mountain ranges to the barren uplands of Tibet.

The sun shone faintly and intermittently through the cloud cover, the wind piercing our layers of sweaters. One foot was completely numb and a curious lump had developed in the springs of my seat which grew in size and sharpness as the miles went by. We drew up for a brief stop at Gonderfarm almost frozen into position. Stewart climbed out while I endeavoured to stretch my cramped legs, and Shakoor Beg kindly sent us tea from the bazaar in small straight cups, hot, thick and sweet, which we clutched gratefully in our stiff, cold hands. A blink of sun as though in answer to a prayer suddenly switched on like an electric fire and we gradually thawed. Things had to be done to the engine as usual and the driver and his mate fitted on the exhaust pipe with a piece of wire. Half a mile out of the village it fell off with a great clatter whereupon it was permanently abandoned and we cracked our way merrily onwards.

Coming round a blind corner in one of the deep gullies on the road we came across a small group, possibly Gujars, the woman wearing a short *kurta* or tunic tied at the waist and *shalwar* tight to her ankles; a little girl with medallions of silver shining on the bodice of what might once have been a shirt of gay colours, now worn with age and dirt to a dull, reddish black. A donkey in a panic at our approach tripped over three hens, their legs tied together, and Shakoor Beg and its owner exchanged a few well-chosen words. On one of the few straight pieces of road we over-took a man riding a beautiful bay with white stockings. Reining in, the horse reared splendidly and then, the bit between its teeth, took off, galloping madly ahead, the rider grinning at us over his shoulder, his flat hat clapped well on, his black *chogha* streaming in the wind.

Shortly after this there was a sudden jerk, a screeching of brakes and we shuddered to a stop. At first sight it appeared that we had come to a dead end. There was nothing to be seen but an immense vista of tumbled rocks severed from the slabs above as though a gigantic landslide had filled our immediate

P

world with the turmoil of creation. In the midst of this mountain of rock, half-way up the hillside, tiny figures were building a supporting wall, almost lost to view behind the slate-grey boulders. Like ants they toiled away, grey-bearded men and young boys, no bulldozers or grabs to help move the tons of boulders, not a spear of green or even a patch of earth, only the hot rock baking in the sun. The men smiled at us over the cloths and scarves covering their mouths against the fine powdery dust that floated upwards with every movement of stone below, and after a consultation with Shakoor Beg we understood that the road would be closed till four o'clock.

It was then just past noon so we settled ourselves in the shelter of a piece of rock about the size of a young elephant and much the same colour, and drank Bovril and ate bully beef which we shared with a cheerful group of splendid-looking ruffians who appeared suddenly, as people do in these parts, as though irresistibly attracted out of thin air by our presence. Armed to the teeth with rifles and muzzle-loaders, imposing bandoliers of cartridges and bullets across their chests and round their waists, they were off to shoot markhor, the binoculars slung casually round their necks looking oddly out of place as though they had decided to take in a race meeting *en route*. We knew and they knew that markhor is on the list of proscribed game, but might was right and no one was liable to argue with such a battery of firearms. A shout interrupted our conversation – the road was clear and we could get through, so off we chugged and bumped over a surface like a miniature quarry and under fire from an intermittent hail of small stones and dust from above. We were glad to escape with nothing more than a few near misses.

Rattling our way through Jenepur we crossed the river by the Rakhiot Bridge, one of the many suspension bridges built by the British Army in 1915 and bearing on its southern pier a brass tablet inscribed to the memory of all the Sherpas and Sahibs of the 1937 German Expedition under Dr. Karl Wien to Nanga Parbat. It was during the night of the 13-14th June that all members but one of this expedition were assembled in Camp IV at an altitude of 20,200 feet on the highest terrace of the Rakhiot Glacier. At midnight a comparatively small cornice from the west flank of the Rakhiot ridge broke loose and buried the entire team, together with their Sherpa porters, under its masses of ice.

At Talichi which had been the base camp for supplies for the victorious German Expedition of 1953, I leapt out to photograph Nanga Parbat. From Gor, not so very far away, Karl Herrligkoffer, whose half brother Willy Merkl had met his death on the mountain in 1934, and who took part in the successful 1953 expedition, described the view : ' Its outline partly obscured by the foothills, but to the left we could see the East Arête rising from that spot where in 1934 Camp VII had stood on the Whipped Cream Roll, up towards the Silver Saddle, which in turn was flanked by the mighty cones of Silver Crag and the South East Summit. Between Silver Crag and the North Summit a depression in the rock formation of the north east flank, completely filled with snow and ice, makes an almost horizontal plane which then in drops of several hundred feet at a time, plunges into the north east wall of Nanga Parbat. From this icefield, the Silver Plateau, situated at a height of 25,000 feet, masses of ice in the form of snow-dust avalanches hurtle through the couloir in the north east face down to the Rakhiot Glacier . . .'

The Astor River joins the Indus at Ramghat or *Shaitan Nullah,* ' the devil's nullah ' as it was called before the Maharaja of Kashmir piously renamed it. Ramghat was once a place of the utmost importance as the only line of communication between Gilgit, Astor and Kashmir crossed the Astor River at this point. ' It is a weird spot ' says Durand : ' the river about a hundred to a hundred and fifty feet wide dashes through a gorge, making two turns at almost complete right angles, so that, standing on the bridge, you cannot see more than a couple of hundred yards in all. The force of the water is terrific, the noise deafening and the heat in summer awful . . .' We could not remark on the summer's heat but we found the road devilish enough. Plunging downwards to the bridge in a series of loops, the upward angles so acute that Shakoor Beg was forced to back several times to negotiate the first one, his mate leaping smartly out and thrusting boulders behind the rear wheels, our way curved on over a paving like a causeway and we could feel the tyres spinning round desperately trying to get a grip.

The road to Bunji, about eight miles from the river, runs over a vast plain on which the town stands, about 250 feet above it. We had dropped off two of our passengers at the bridge but we ourselves came to an unexpected halt when the engine petered out 50 yards or so short of the village. As soon as we had stopped, a chap with a horrid swelling practically closing one eye dashed up and asked if we wanted tea. One could scarcely imagine that he was employed as a tout for the local teashop, there being only one, so we put down his solicitude to the normal anxiety for the comfort of travellers which is still extant all over Pakistan. We were a trifle reluctant to leave all our luggage, cameras and films, but he assured us with a fearful grin that it would be perfectly safe and off we set at his side up the main street.

He led us confidently and with some pride to the Bunji tea house, about as far removed from the Corner Café as one could possibly imagine. It was a great bare comfortless place adorned with no less than three mirrors which simply prolonged the barren vista of its interior; long wooden tables, their only covering the pattern of tea-stains and grease spots that spattered their surface, and hard wooden chairs. Strictly for the male sex, no woman would be seen within its doors, although *Angrezi memsahibs*, especially when trousered and ' of a good age ', as a Sikh engineer once admiringly described me after I had dragged his young and sweating assistants all over a half-built hydro-electric scheme, are equally welcome to eat with the men and also visit in the *zenana*.

A calendar hung crookedly on one wall, its ends curling despondently, featuring the leaders of Pakistan, and next to it two coloured charts showing Children of the World, like those we had remarked with ill-concealed horror in Sarfraz's home in Chilas, and we wondered again just what the children in this remote area made of their counterparts as depicted on the wall. An American child was pictured in the uniform of a cowboy with a bucking bronco in the background beside some outdated Red Indians in full war paint; an African child stood in immodest nakedness brandishing a spear; France was represented by two children who appeared at first glance to be hitting each other very hard; on closer inspection we decided that they were either playing badminton or battledore and shuttlecock, probably the latter considering the antiquity of the general conception. An English child, smug and sedate in sailor suit was riding a bicycle, while German children were gazing abstractedly at what seemed to be a Christmas tree which must have been quite inexplicable to Muslim children. And there, like Strabo's universe, the world came to an abrupt end.

A small boy brought us hot, steaming tea in a battered red, gold and pink Russian teapot, its lid attached by a silver chain, its cracks mended over the years with wire staples. Meanwhile the crowd of loungers outside derived much innocent enjoyment from our presence. We on our part, from the dim recesses of our cave-like sanctuary were able to watch unseen the bargaining in the shops across the road and were intrigued to see a man sitting happily astride a chair admiring himself in a small hand-mirror, grimacing this way and that and twirling his moustache.

Bunji signifies the number 50 in Shina, and is believed to have been given to the place because at one time there were 50 villages in its environs and considerable cultivation in the now near-desert vale of the Indus between the mouths of the Astor and Gilgit Rivers. Its prosperity began to decline at the beginning of the nineteenth century under the battery of a spate of incursions by the rulers of Yasin and Chitral which finally led to the Sikh occupation of Gilgit. A great flood finally completed its devastation in 1840. A whole mountain near the Hattu Pir, the 6,000 foot spur along which the road once ran, looking down on the Shaitan Nullah, suddenly fell into the Indus. This gigantic landslip probably followed an earthquake and the entire hillside facing the Indus, just above the Lechur Nullah, was flung into the valley below from a height of about 4,000 feet above the river, and impinging on the opposite bank brought down on that side a secondary hill fall.

The course of the Indus was completely arrested by a huge dam thousands of feet thick and some hundreds high; ' the water must have risen at the dam,' estimated Durand, ' to fully 1,000 feet above the present level.' The Bunji plain became a vast lake and the Gilgit River which runs into the Indus six miles above Bunji, was dammed up for 30 miles to just below the present fort of Gilgit. Apparently the dam held for several months, but finally the rising lake reached the top and, forcing a breach, overflowed it and then with irresistible power the immense wall of water from the 30-mile-long lake swept down carrying all before it.

All down the Indus Valley to the plains the people were prepared for the rush of the great tidal wave and though miles of cultivated land were ruined there was remarkably little loss of life. But where the river begins to open out into the plains near Attock, a portion of the Sikh army was encamped practically in the river bed and was completely obliterated by the wall of water that suddenly engulfed them, and ' As an old woman with a wet cloth sweeps away an army of ants, so the river swept away the army of the Maharaja.'

Finally we understood the Jeep to be ready and crossed the street to find it almost invisible under its new load. Around it clamoured the passengers, who we felt must surely have mistaken it for a small omnibus. A *lumbardar,* obviously of some note, nice-looking, youngish and wearing a white sheepskin *poshteen,* carried a two-year-old *Ram chikor,* the Himalayan Snow Cock, a beautiful bird, its legs tied together with black wool, which he was taking to an officer in Gilgit. He told us later that it would be used as a lure for the catching of goshawks. The bird is put into a box on the ground, a piece of string attached to its leg and a man concealed nearby. The goshawk swoops down on its prey and the man pulling the string makes the hawk think it is losing its quarry and thus it takes a stronger hold and is easily captured.

We felt that this treatment couldn't be very pleasant for the *Ram chikor* but our friend assured us that little harm came to it. He fed it on maize, grain and onions chopped up among ordinary grass or vegetables and it certainly looked in splendid condition. With longish, flat tail feathers, it was a soft, light beige flecked with brown and grey and half as big again as the ordinary partridge or *chikor* described by Babur who gave such delightfully detailed accounts of everything he came across. Its metallic cry caught his fancy and he wrote that the Astarabad partridges are said to call : ' *Bat mini tutilar!*' ' Quick ! they have caught me !' while the partridges of Arabia are understood to cry : ' *B'il shakar tadawm al ni'am!*' ' With sugar pleasure endures.'

The *lumbardar* was joined by a handsome fellow with rust wool cap, *mahzri* shirt and *shalwar* and a magnificent belt to hold bullets and cartridges, in red leather with separate lidded pockets, and carried a rifle, the barrel adorned with a small beaded and fringed ornament which dangled just below the sights, probably a *tawiz* for luck. Another of the group had his rifle in a khaki carrying case and sported a black *chaddur* bordered with dark red. The chap with the bad eye, plus Shakoor Beg's assistant, now made nine of us in the Jeep, and we picked up the two men we had dropped off at the bridge, making eleven in all, four in the front and the rest clinging on to the luggage behind.

At Parri everything was off-loaded once again and the bottom of the Jeep lined with petrol tins, then sacks of maize, rock salt and *razai* until the whole thing was once again well beyond the Plimsoll line. Three women who had been fetching water suddenly caught sight of us and dashed round the corner of the local shop, giggling like mad and slopping water down their backs to roars of laughter from the men, only to creep back seconds later, *chaddur* pulled up to their eyes, to peer at us from the safety of a wall.

It was not long before we were held up once again by a mass of rocks strewn on the roadway. Everyone jumped down, the owner of the *Ram chikor* giving directions as to how the stones should be moved. A few hundred yards further on we parked beside a small crescent cut into the mountainside, while the man with the swollen eye was despatched ahead to look out for any Jeeps coming the other way as it was by now 4.30 p.m. We found the road gang being lined up beside a primitive weighing machine, waiting for their allowance of maize which was being weighed out on the flat scoop balanced on a wooden tripod. Our precautions had been well advised for no less than nine Jeeps crawled past going in the opposite direction, each one more laden than the last.

Worried about the *Ram chikor*, now half sitting on my shoulder due to the pressure of passengers behind it, I offered to hold it and it travelled the rest of the way in the crook of my arm, puffing itself out to the size of a football and lovely and warm. Nine miles from Gilgit we again ran into trouble. A tractor and trailer had stuck, naturally in the middle of the road, one wheel off the trailer. Here we were held up for the best part of an hour. A man came along and peering at my unlikely armful of bird looked at the *Murgha Zerin* in its plastic bag and asked if it was alive: ' *Zinda hai?*' he enquired, his eyes goggling. ' No,' I replied, ' but this one is!' showing him the *Ram chikor* snuggled into my arms.

Darkness had now fallen and by the light of flaming sticks and twigs about 15 men endeavoured to fix the wheel. Every now and then someone would climb into the tractor and rummage hopefully in the tool box. There were all kinds of mysterious bits and pieces strewn all over the ground and men groped about for missing nuts and bolts. From time to time someone would stroll along and announce cheerfully : ' Five minutes, *memsahib* !' By now a long line of Jeeps stretched out behind us, giving vent to impatient hoots and somewhere a wireless was blaring forth Urdu songs.

At last the tractor limped on its way and we started off on the last lap. By now our headlights had almost given up and only came on intermittently. For half an hour we would tear madly onwards and then the lights would go out and we would screech to a halt. At last we drove into Gilgit and up to the Rest House exactly 12 hours after we had set out.

We had only succeeded in lighting a fire and tidying up a little after our marathon trip when Zulfi and Riaz arrived with a great flagon of *Hunza Pani* to celebrate our last evening. As it happened Stewart contracted a bad cold, which was scarcely surprising, and Dr. Rashid who came down to see him forbade his travelling by air until he was better as the Dakotas are not pressurised. This was almost the last straw as far as the P.A. was concerned, but we had at least established a record for our stay – six weeks – and we wished it could have been six months.

So much of the past had come alive for us, each road, river and rock carved indelibly upon our memory; and we carried within us as in a mirror the fleeting images of Greek, Iranian, Mongol and Turk. Beside us had walked Darius, Alexander of the Two Horns, Kanishka and the Buddhist pilgrims, carrying his faith like a small lamp across the mountain passes; Chinghis Khan from Karakoram, Tamerlane, Babur and the Moghal Emperors, ' whose distant footsteps echoed through the corridors of time.' We could not but marvel at our extraordinary good fortune in having been able to slip about the country so quietly in their wake, welcomed so unaffectedly by their descendants. Yet looking back, there was so much left undone, so much to be learned before it is too late. We felt as though we had been loaned a book that we must read too quickly and longed desperately to be able to linger on each page. As we sat over our small fire, tired but happy, we could say with Mr. Valiant-for-Truth : ' Yet now I do not repent me of all the trouble I have been at to arrive where I am.'

Bibliography

Babur-Nama: A.D. 1526. Tr. by E. Beveridge
Larousse: *World Mythology*
Samuel Beal: *Fah Hien and Sung Yun*
E. F. Knight: *Where Three Empires Meet* 1895
Sir Algernon Durand: *The Making of a Frontier*
Francis Younghusband: *Heart of a Continent*
R. C. F. Schomberg: *Between the Oxus and the Indus*
Domenico Facienna: *A Guide to the Excavations in Swat*
    1956-1962
George Seaver: *Francis Younghusband*
Sir Olaf Caroe: *The Pathans*
The Memoirs of the Agha Khan
Travels of Marco Polo: Tr. by Ronald Latham
Stanislas Julien: *Historie de la vie de Hiouien Thsang*
Joseph Kessel: *The Horsemen*
Jacquetta Hawkes: *Dawn of the Gods*
Churchill: *My Early Life*
Strabo: *Book XV*

Glossary

Chapter	Urdu or Pakhtu	English
	Urdu is really the lingua franca of Pakistan and is spoken and understood by most men all over West Pakistan in addition to their own native tongue of Sindhi, Punjabi, etc.	
	Pakhtu is spoken by the North Eastern tribes of Pathans and Pashtu by those to the south west, the main difference being the use of the hard *kh* as opposed to the soft *sh*.	
I	tindal	boatman or bosun's mate
	lunghi	a piece of cloth used as a wrap.
	burqa	long, tent-like garment either made of white cotton and pleated on to a headpiece with a latticed strip across the eyes, wholly concealing the person, or made of coloured silk like a coat with a separate headpiece
	mali	gardener

235

Chapter	Urdu or Pakhtu	English
	chappatti	rounds of unleavened bread
	paratha	like chappatti but with butter added to the mixture of flour and water
	pan	edible leaves but used to describe the little bundles of spices and nuts wrapped in pan leaves as a kind of sweetmeat
	nimbu pani	a sweet drink usually made of limes, sugar and water
	serai	(Persian sarae, an inn), resting or halting place
	shalwar qamiz	baggy trousers and long shirt or tunic worn over them
	dak	post
	hujras	men's common rooms in the North West Frontier villages
2	burif	spelled *barf* – ice
	chador	used to describe a burqa in villages, or blanket used as a wrap
	purdah	a curtain or screen but used to describe women " in purdah " behind the veil or burqa and unseen by men except near relatives
	sur'ma	antimony used to outline the eyes
	ghazal	form of poetry often set to music or a folk song
	atchghan	long coat worn by men with high neck and buttoning down the front – usually worn on formal occasions
	char yeh feasible be hai, practical be hai	if it is feasible it ought to be practical
	apko sanction dedi-yeh?	will you sanction it or give sanction?
	khulla	tight fitting stiff cap round which the Pathan winds a long strip of material to complete his head-dress

Chapter	*Urdu or Pakhtu*	*English*
	Haj	pilgrimage (usually referring to Mecca)
	'Id	festival
	kaisora	pouch for tobacco usually embroidered in the shape of a bag with drawstrings
	battera	fighting quail (pl)
	jawan	young man
	sabaz chae	green tea
3	stare mah sheh!	may you never feel fatigue
	khwar mah sheh!	may you never encounter adversity
	jor yeh?	are you well,
	khushhal yeh?	are you happy?
	tazah yeh, takrah yeh?	are you fresh and strong?
	(Pakhtu greetings)	
	wah! wah!	well, well!
	pilau	mixture of meat or chicken and rice
	kebab	pieces of meat and vegetables cooked on skewers
	dhal	split peas
	nan	thick unleavened bread
	pari	fairy
	Bismillah!	God be praised!
	pani	water
	sherab	alcohol
		saddlecloth
4	mahzri	
	numnah	grey homespun
	chappals	sandals
	chikor	partridge
5	dophatta	long piece of material worn like a shawl over the head
	tana	station usually used by police
	malish	massage
	tehsildar	sergeant (of police)
	chogha	long woollen garment like a dressing gown

Chapter	Urdu or Pakhtu	English
	tubla	drums
6	bhang	drugs like opium
	charras	
	hakim	doctor or herbalist
7	hookah	water pipe for smoking
	charpoy	string bed
	razai	padded quilt
8	chatti	earthenware water jar
10	halela zurd	yellow laburnum
11	nullah	ravine
	jezail	muzzle loader
12	tika	ornament worn hanging down over the forehead
	dekshis	aluminium cooking pots
13	lukri	wood
	wallah	the doer of anything
	djinn	genie
	topi	hat, cap or top
14	ji hah	yes indeed, very good!
	zuroor	important, urgent, certainly
	bohut aachha	very good!
	khansamah	cook
	Insha'allah	God willing
15	der aayad, darust ayyad	what comes late comes in the right form
	dhobi	laundry man
	chaukidar	watchman
16	ulu qamafik	like an owl, term of opprobrium
	be-waquf	stupid
	kurta	tunic
	dhurris	rugs